Blue Plastic Cow

One woman's search for
her birth mother

Barbara Attwood

First published in Great Britain by Gadfly Press in 2021

Copyright © Barbara Attwood 2021

The right of Barbara Attwood to be identified as the author of this work has been asserted by him in accordance with the Copyright, Designs and Patents Act 1988. All rights reserved

No part of this book may be reproduced, stored in a retrieval system or transmitted in any form or by any means (electronic, mechanical, photocopying, recording or otherwise) without the prior written permission of the author, except in cases of brief quotations embodied in reviews or articles. It may not be edited, amended, lent, resold, hired out, distributed or otherwise circulated without the publisher's written permission

Permission can be obtained from gadflypress@outlook.com

This book is a work of non-fiction based on research by the author

A catalogue record of this book is available from the British Library

Typeset and cover design by Jane Dixon-Smith

Spelling Differences: UK v USA

This book was written in British English, hence USA readers may notice some spelling differences with American English: e.g. color = colour, meter = metre and = jewelry = jewellery

For my family

Contents

PART 1: ADOPTION	1
Chapter 1 The New Baby	3
Chapter 2 West Bank	6
Chapter 3 Celebrations	21
Chapter 4 Psychiatrist	27
Chapter 5 Rita	41
Chapter 6 First Love	49
Chapter 7 Growing up in the Sixties	55
Chapter 8 The Cavern	66
Chapter 9 Hitching a Ride	78
Chapter 10 The Wings Club	87
Chapter 11 Back to Work	102
PART 2: THE SEARCH	111
Chapter 12 Awakening	113
Chapter 13 Social Worker	124
Chapter 14 The Search Begins	146
Chapter 15 Surprise Caller	160
Chapter 16 St Catherine's House	168
Chapter 17 Margaret	173

Chapter 18 Desperate Measures	182
Chapter 19 Meeting	191
Chapter 20 Greater Manchester County Record Office	201
Chapter 21 Mam	207
Chapter 22 Dorothy	215
Chapter 23 Hypnotherapy	221
Chapter 24 Private Detective	227
Chapter 25 Meditation	233
Chapter 26 Conceived in Love	238
Chapter 27 Thomas	245
Chapter 28 Diane & Judith	256
Chapter 29 Media Frenzy	267
Chapter 30 Birth	273
Chapter 31 Constable Country	278
Chapter 32 Ariel Bruce	290
Chapter 33 Cloe	303
Chapter 34 Sisters	317
Get A Free Book	325
Other Books by Gadfly Press	327
Acknowledgements	328
About the Author	329

PART 1: ADOPTION

Chapter 1

The New Baby

Florrie

Pale winter sunlight revealed the bareness of the room. Florrie wrapped the baby in an enormous shawl, and walked with her husband Jim out of the red-bricked orphanage and down slippery steps, through ice and snow to the bus stop. Huddled in a wooden shelter, surrounded by freezing fog, they waited for an hour until the bus arrived.

Black icy patches covered the roads, and through the mist, the weary driver, guided only by a faint headlight, carefully manoeuvred the bus. Snowflakes settled on the windows, obscuring their view.

Seated in the back of the chilly bus, Florrie touched the baby's face. Jim looked down and smiled. 'She's ours now.'

'Not until *she* signs.' Florrie frowned. She didn't use the words *her mother* because she was the baby's mother now. Bending to kiss the baby's forehead, she whispered, 'But I'll keep the name she gave you ... Barbara ... it suits you.'

It was two hours before the driver shouted, 'Widnes bus station!' The exhausted couple stepped down from the bus in time to catch a connection to West Bank.

The fog had lifted from Parsonage Road, where their seven-year-old daughter, Lily, was jumping up and down with her friends in the crisp, crunchy snow. As they got closer, Lily ran towards them, her cheeks glowing red. 'My Christmas present's arrived. It's a baby sister!' she shouted.

As soon as they entered the warmth of the house, Lily sat on the sofa, her arms outstretched. 'I want to feed her, please, Mam!'

Florrie placed the baby carefully into Lily's arms. Lily grinned as Barbara grasped the bottle in her tiny hands and sucked hungrily at the teat.

The front door burst open and banged shut. Joseph, a dark, handsome lad of fourteen, bounced in. 'The Scouts Christmas party was great.' Abruptly, he stopped in front of the sofa and stared. 'Oh, she's here, is she?' he said, wrinkling his nose as he watched Lily holding the baby.

'It's Barbara and she's mine!' Lily shielded the baby from his gaze.

'It's your new sister,' Jim told him sternly. 'She's a gift from God.'

'OK.' He shrugged. 'I'm off snowballing.'

That evening, Jimmy, their eldest child, returned from national service on Christmas leave from the Air Force. 'It's Barbara, your new sister. She's six months old,' Florrie told him, pointing to the cradle in the corner of the living room.

Jimmy raised his eyebrows and elbowed his father in the ribs. 'You randy old sod! Is this the seven-year itch?' Jim didn't smile.

'Shush!' Florrie shook her head and raised her finger to her mouth. 'We're going to adopt her. I'll explain later.'

Jimmy's eyes darted from Florrie to Jim. 'Oh! ... All right! But you could have warned me.' He smiled down at the baby and held her chubby hand. 'Hello, little sister.'

***

During Mass in St Patrick's Church on Christmas morning, Florrie heard Jim whisper, 'If the adoption goes ahead, I'll provide for her and I'll love her like she's my own.'

Sat on the hard wooden bench, with Barbara on her knee, she stared at Jim as he kneeled in prayer. *What a kind, unselfish man I married*, she thought. She'd longed for another child, and there was no objection from Jim when she told him that she wanted to adopt.

As the eldest girl in a family of eight, Florrie's mother had relied on her to keep order. When *her* father got drunk, he'd hit her mother and she had to protect the younger children from his anger, hiding them wherever she could. She'd resolved to make a better life for herself and her own children.

Turning her head towards the nativity scene on the side altar beneath a Gothic stone arch, she offered up a grateful prayer, 'Thank you, Jesus, for making my family complete.' She looked down at Barbara, who opened her eyes and let out a cry, struggling to sit up. 'There, there,' Florrie said soothingly, and as she held the baby close, and kissed her smooth pink cheeks, she couldn't remember the last time she'd felt so content.

Walking home through the crisp snow, they exchanged greetings with all of the passers-by near or far. 'Merry Christmas!'

'All the best!'

'The same to you!'

Florrie beamed with pride whenever a neighbour stopped to peep inside the pram and congratulate the family on their new arrival.

Jimmy lit a cigarette and trailed behind with Joseph, laughing loudly at each other's jokes, their breath a cloud of mist in the cold air.

Holding onto the pram, Lily slid over patches of ice. 'This is the best Christmas we've ever had,' Florrie said aloud to herself.

Chapter 2

West Bank

In West Bank, an area of Widnes facing the River Mersey, the breeze from the Estuary cooled Florrie's flushed cheeks. 'Go to sleep, my darling, close your pretty eyes,' she sang, as she pushed the pram along the side of the house that was shaded from the hot August sunshine. Stopping beneath the parlour window, she rocked the pram in an effort to lull her to sleep, but Barbara pushed herself up into a seated position, holding out her chubby arms. 'Mama! Mama!' Barbara cried, until she was lifted from the pram.

'That baby's getting spoiled!' Mrs Sykes shouted from her front door.

'She's only one,' Florrie said, 'I want to spoil her.' *The darling child is no trouble. Why can't people just mind their own business?* 'She's been through enough already.'

'I suppose so.' Mrs Sykes came closer. Straining her neck, she glanced sideways down the street and asked quietly, 'Has the mother signed the papers yet?'

'Last week, thank God!' Florrie sighed, holding Barbara close and letting the child's sleepy head rest on her chest. 'We thought she'd changed her mind at one point, but she can't have her back now.'

'She put you through it, though, didn't she, that girl?'

'Yes, but it's over now,' Florrie said with determination.

'I hope so.' Mrs Sykes glanced slyly at the baby. 'They soon grow up, kids.'

'I don't want her to grow up.' Florrie patted Barbara's back.

'No. You enjoy her while she's a baby.' Mrs Sykes crossed her arms and pursed her lips. 'The McNamaras adopted a baby boy and I *hate* to say it but …' She looked at Florrie with hard eyes. 'He turned out to be a bad one. Got into all kinds of trouble – stole money from them. You adopt that lovely baby …' She nodded towards Barbara. '… But you never know how it'll grow up.'

'I'm going inside.' Without a smile, Florrie turned her back.

In spite of the August heat, the parlour was cool and shady as she sank into her rocking chair, cradling Barbara until she fell asleep. Gently rocking in a half sleep, she thought about the day she chose Barbara, and whispered, 'There were so many babies left in orphanages after the war that I could take my pick, even though I'm forty-five years old and have three children, but I chose you, my little love. I stopped by your cot, and the doctor warned me that you'd be a lot of trouble, something about your ears. That settled it for me. I told him you were the child I wanted and you smiled up at me as if you knew. Something just clicked between us. You chose me.' The door banged shut, startling Florrie and waking Barbara, who let out a cry.

'Is tea ready?' Lily burst into the room shouting. 'I'm starving!'

***

Every week, Florrie scrubbed the front doorstep, swilling it with a bucket of hot soapy water, making rivulets across the pavement. She swept the suds into the gutter with a yard brush, and stared down Parsonage Road, breathing in the salty air.

She was proud of their large double-fronted, three-bedroom house overlooking the river. It was the house closest to the railway bridge, but she'd got used to the noise from the trains that rattled the windows, and it never disturbed her sleep.

Their house was right under the railway bridge and she remembered a man committing suicide by jumping off the bridge. He'd landed on top of the street lamp right outside their house and she'd found him hanging from it the next morning when she was getting the milk in. The story was his wife had run off with a Yankee soldier.

She'd always lived in West Bank. It was a community that had a hustle and bustle separate from the rest of Widnes. Neighbours combined resources to make everything, from costumes for maypole dancing, to hotpot for bonfire night. Front doors were never locked and everyone knew everyone else's business.

She knew that the neighbours gossiped about her and Jim adopting a baby. She'd warned them not to tell their children, afraid that Barbara might find out from an innocent remark, or a spiteful child telling her deliberately. It was Florrie's worst fear. She'd tell Barbara someday, when she was ready, but she didn't want to think about that now.

People who visited West Bank complained of the smell and said they could taste the pollution being spewed into the Mersey from the chemical factories lining its banks. She didn't notice. Being so close to the river had its advantages: in the summer, it was like being at the seaside.

***

Florrie sat on a stool – a wooden chair Jim had chopped the back off – while Lily spread a checked cloth on the sand, ready for their picnic. Florrie couldn't swim and she didn't like water, but she enjoyed the warmth of the July sun on her face. She laughed and gossiped with the neighbouring women, and shouted warnings to the youngsters if they went too close to the water's edge.

Sandwiches and home-made cakes were grabbed by small, sand-covered hands and stuffed into eager mouths. Lily made sandcastles for Barbara, who squeezed the wet sand, grinning with excitement. Florrie looked at Barbara. She was three years old and more secure these days. She'd become so much part of the family that Florrie sometimes forgot she'd adopted her.

Jim was far out in the river, swimming with the men. If she stretched her neck, she could see heads bobbing like seals swimming in the glistening waves.

Watching the Transporter Bridge slowly inching its way across the horizon, carrying passengers and cars over the river to Runcorn, she spotted her sons, Jimmy and Joseph, amongst a group of lads. They had climbed up the Transporter's spindly ladders and were holding onto the iron girders beneath the moving parts of the bridge. 'I wish they wouldn't do that.' Florrie tutted. 'The ticket inspector gets really mad.'

'It scares me when they jump off onto the canal wall,' Mrs Byrne said.

'Go on, lads!' someone shouted. 'You can do it, Joe!

Florrie held her breath, waiting to see if the dangling, silhouetted forms, with legs kicking in all directions like giant spiders, would fall off. Lily stood on a rock to get a better view. Barbara sat on Florrie's knee and covered her eyes with her hands, peeping through her fingers. Shouts from the shocked crowd made Barbara jump, and Florrie held her close. 'One of the lads has lost his grip!' someone yelled. 'He's plunged into the water!'

'Oh no!' Florrie said. 'The currents are treacherous!' *Don't let it be one of mine, God, please.*

Tears formed in Barbara's eyes. 'Don't let my brothers drown, Mam.'

Florrie wiped her eyes. 'Don't worry, love, Jimmy and Joseph are still holding on.' But she wasn't sure. Knowing they were all good swimmers, Florrie hid her fears with a smile. 'Your dad taught all the lads round here to swim, so whoever it is in the water, he won't drown.'

'Jim'd take them down to the promenade when the tide was in and throw them in where it wasn't too deep,' Mrs Evans said.

'They'd sink or swim.' Florrie nudged the woman, and for a moment they laughed.

'There's a strong current today! I think he's struggling,' a male voice echoed on the breeze. A gust of cool air made Florrie shiver.

Neighbours shifted closer to the water's edge or scrambled up the promenade to get a better view. Florrie felt Barbara's small hand touch her cheek. 'What's happening, Mam?' Barbara asked.

Shouts came from the direction of the embankment. 'He's made it!'

'He's climbing up!'

'He's on the wall!'

Florrie sighed and lifted Barbara up, but the lad standing on the canal wall waving both arms at the cheering crowd was too far away to identify.

'It's Jimmy O'Brien!' voices echoed through the crowd.

'Your brothers are safe.' She hugged Barbara and smiled at Lily.

'Let's finish the sandcastle,' Lily said, grabbing the spade.

Barbara

In the alleyway that ran along the back of their house, Barbara played with Billy and Eddie Jones, brothers a couple of years older than her. 'Let's play doctors and nurses.' Billy looked sideways at Eddie, who dug his hands in his pockets and stared down at his shoes.

Smiling, Barbara pointed to the dolls scattered across a red woollen blanket spread on the dusty cobbled floor. 'My dolls can be the patients.'

'No. I'm the doctor and I have to examine you two.' Billy shook the dolls from the blanket. 'Lie down. The blanket is the hospital bed.'

Barbara lay down while Billy prodded her chest. 'Lie next to her.' He tugged Eddie's arm.

'You can examine me standing up,' Eddie said, pushing him away.

'OK!' Billy said. 'But the doctor has to check your bum and hers.'

A tingle in Barbara's stomach told her it was wrong, but she bent her knees and wriggled her knickers down to her ankles. Eddie giggled and his face turned red as he unbuttoned his short pants and pulled them to his knees. When he pulled down his underpants, Barbara gasped. 'Oh! That's rude! I don't like boys.'

Billy started to laugh and pointed at Eddie's privates. 'Haven't you seen one of them before?'

'No! And I don't like this game.' Barbara rolled over and sat up, but her knickers had got twisted.

A gate creaked. Footsteps approached. her mother appeared round the corner. 'What's going on here?' Her eyes narrowed, her face flushed. 'Get up, you naughty girl! And clear off, you beggars!' The boys dodged her mother's fists and Eddie yanked up his pants as they ran off.

Barbara cried and fumbled with her knickers, desperate to pull them up. 'Oh, Mam, I didn't mean to. Eddie told me to.' She held out her arms. Her mother pushed her away.

'I don't know where I got you from,' her mother said, hard and angry.

Barbara helped her mother pick up her dolls and take them into the house. Pulling the blanket tightly round her shoulders, she sat on the bottom stair in the hallway, sucking on the frayed edges of the wool. 'I don't know where I got that child from,' Barbara heard her mother muttering to herself, before she turned to her and said, 'You're nearly five! You can't behave like this when you start school in September.'

***

At St Patrick's school gate, Barbara clung to her mother's coat. She'd been at school for three months but she hated it because she had to leave her mother.

'Why do you come to school in a pram?' Johnny and Thomas made nasty faces at her.

'It's a pushchair, not a pram.'

'You're a baby. You can't walk.' They ran off laughing.

Sat in class, her cheeks were hot and her eyes stung. She wanted her mother. At break time, she crept past the teacher on yard duty and slipped through a gap in the railings. Her legs ached and her heart pounded as she ran down Viaduct Street to her house.

Pushing the back door open, she stepped into the kitchen, where her mother was kneading pastry on a large wooden board. 'Oh!' Her mother raised hands sticky with flour and lard. 'What are you doing home?' Barbara buried her face in her mother's apron, the smell of sugar and apples so strong she could taste it.

She clung to her mother's legs. 'Please let me stay with you, Mam. I don't like school. The boys made fun of me for going in my pram.'

'Cheeky beggars, what's it to do with them? It's quicker if we take the pushchair.'

'They're nasty to me.'

'If it was up to me, I'd keep you here with me all day.' Her mother washed her hands. 'But I can't and you have to go to school.'

'Can I walk to school tomorrow?'

'Course you can.' Her mother looked sad. 'But we'll have to walk up to school now and tell Miss Roberts where you are. They'll be looking for you.'

'Can I come back home with you?' Barbara rubbed her tummy, making circular movements with her small hands. 'Please, Mam. I feel sick.'

'I suppose so. You're so clingy. Not like your brothers and sister.'

'Didn't they like school?'

'Not particularly, but they didn't run away.'

There was a knock on the back door. 'Is Barbara there?' Mr Simms, the school caretaker shouted.

Barbara hid behind her mother.

'Yes, she's here.'

He wagged his finger at Barbara. 'You had everyone at school worried, young lady.' Barbara lowered her head and sucked her thumb. He looked at her mother. 'But as long as we know she's safe, she might as well stay home for today.'

Barbara smiled and thought about the apple pie she'd have for pudding.

Florrie

After tea, Barbara watched as Florrie unrolled her hair. Freed, the wavy hair fell loosely round Florrie's shoulders, and down to her waist. 'It feels so soft,' Barbara said, stroking the strands. 'But why is it so grey?'

'Your hair *goes* grey when you get older.'

Barbara frowned. 'The boys said you're my granny, not my mam, because you're too old to be my mam. Johnny said I haven't got a mam. He said someone left me with you when I was a baby.'

'Oh, they did, did they!' *What have those little beggars overheard? No wonder she doesn't want to go to school.* 'They're teasing you and telling lies, and Mr Simms told me he's going to keep an eye on them.'

Florrie stared at herself in the parlour mirror and thought about the mums at the school gate still in their twenties or thirties. She was fifty and hadn't changed her hairstyle or clothes much since she had been a girl. She was comfortable in her cosy knitted cardigans and huge, floral-print wraparound pinafores, that tied at the back over her corseted and flattened figure. *Not like these young women today with their tight trousers, short skirts and bleached hair. They've got no modesty, no shame.*

Barbara pulled on a strand of her hair and Florrie turned from the parlour mirror and stared at her anxious face. 'Teresa's granny died. You won't die and go to heaven without me, will you, Mam?' Barbara started to cry. Florrie lifted her onto her knee and wrapped her in her arms.

'Shush now! I'm not a granny, and I'll never leave you.'

Barbara

'Dad's taking us to the pictures on Saturday to see a cowboy film.' Lily grinned.

Barbara imagined her father slicking back his thick dark hair; dressing up in his best cap, tie and jacket, and holding her hand as they walked to the nearby Cenny picture house. She loved her father. He shouted a lot, mostly at her mother, because she nagged him, but he didn't mean it, and he never shouted at Barbara. 'You're my little girl,' he'd say to her.

He was a foreman at the Brom, a local corrugated iron factory. When he came home on Thursdays, her father would dig in his pocket, pull out a crumpled packet and hand it over to her mother, who gave him back pocket money for bacca and comics. Barbara waited. He winked and gave her two pence pocket money, stuffing the rest inside his jacket.

After he ate his dinner, he sank into his armchair by the fire. Kneeling on the floor next to him, Barbara helped him prepare his smoke. He tapped his pipe on the iron fire grate to loosen the stale tobacco, tossing what he called scum into the flames, turning them blue and making the fire hiss. Barbara passed him the pipe cleaners, and he shoved them down the barrel, removing every last bit of stale bacca. 'I've got the tin. *Ogden's St Bruno Cherry Ready Rubbed*,' she read aloud, running her fingers over the red and gold letters, before she handed it to him. He opened it and let her sniff the moist, earthy tobacco inside. Carefully, he pinched the brown flakes with his fingertips, filling the bowl of the pipe and kindling it with his lighter until it caught fire. As he sucked in and puffed out, wisps of smoke filled the room, spreading the sweet smell of dried hay and cherries.

Her mother came in from the kitchen, waving her hands. 'The house smells like a sweaty sock.' But that didn't stop him and he leaned forward and spat into the open fire, the moisture sizzling on the coals. He winked at Barbara and his eyes creased into a smile. Laying his head back, he closed his eyes and took another long deep puff. She was thinking how he always looked after her, when his head lolled to one side and he started to snore. She took the pipe from his hand and put it in the ashtray.

***

Barbara's tummy rushed as she ran down the brew to the promenade following Lily. From the concrete walkway, they jumped onto the alley rocks: large slabs of sandstone eroded into various shapes by the tides. They rested on a bed of mud, dried and cracked in the sun, and curled into large pats that Barbara broke and shaped in her hands.

Lily lifted Barbara onto the highest rock, the one they called the Queen Mary. She looked across at the enormous sandbanks floating in the waves, the sun glistening on the horizon. She heard shouts.

A mud pat flew past and landed on top of Lily's head: the dry crumbling mud spattered dust on her face and dress. 'You little devils!' she shouted, jumping from the rock. 'It's Harry and Tom from White Street.'

Barbara bit her lip as Lily chased the boys along the water's edge. When she caught them, she smacked them hard on the back of their heads but they broke loose and pulled faces at Lily, sticking out their tongues and shouting, 'We know a secret! We know a secret!' They pointed at Barbara. 'Your sister's adopted!'

Lily grabbed Harry and held him tightly by his collar, while Tom ran off. 'Who told you that?'

'I heard Mam tell Aunty May.' He looked scared.

'Do you know what it means?'

'No!' He wriggled and kicked his legs. 'Let me go!'

'Keep still.' Lily pinched his neck and he squealed. She glanced at Barbara, before telling Harry, 'Don't you ever say that again or I'll tell our Joe and he'll grab you, put you in a sack and drown you in the Cut.'

Harry's dirty face turned white. 'Please don't tell Joe.'

Lily let him go and he scarpered off with his brother, who was hiding behind a rock.

Tired and dusty, Barbara held Lily's hand and they walked home.

'Been rollin' in the mud, have you?' her mother said, when they arrived. Barbara stood next to Lily, looking down at the dried mud clinging to their shoes. 'Jim! Jim! Get the bath!'

Her father fetched the large tin bath from the outhouse and shovelled more coal on the fire while her mother boiled a pan of water on the hob and slowly filled the bath. The heat of the fire was hot on Barbara's face as she soaked in the warmth of the water, while her mother scrubbed her back with strong-smelling soap, and her father topped up the water as it cooled.

'What's adopted, Mam?' Barbara asked, swishing the bath water with her hands.

'Stop that splashing!' Her mother looked angry. 'What you talking about?'

Lily told her mother what the boys had said.

'They're cheeky lads. Take no notice.'

Barbara wondered why they'd said *she* was adopted and not Lily when it was Lily who hit them.

'I'll take you up on the railway bridge tomorrow, if you like,' Lily said, drying her back with a towel. Barbara remembered the deafening sound of the trains as they passed by the walkway, and the dizzy feeling she'd had staring down through gaps in the wall – like castle windows – at the river far below; waves lashing against the rocks.

'It's scary up there,' Barbara said. 'Besides, it's Sunday and Dad's taking me to the boat. He's going to fix the engine.'

***

Barbara held her father's hand as they crossed the bridge over the Sankey Canal. Afraid of the rushing water below, she squeezed it tighter. Pale skinny lads shouted from the embankment and waved as they jumped into the canal they called the Cut. 'You'll drown in there,' her father called out to them. 'It's dangerous. Too many weeds and rubbish.' But they took no notice.

Away from their shouts, seagulls squawked and circled in the clear blue sky. The breeze blew her hair, and her wellies sank in the mud as they crossed the marsh known as Spike Island. Her dad and brothers moored their boat alongside converted gunboats and yachts. Barbara was fascinated by the static boats stranded on the muddy marsh which the tide changed into sailing ships.

Today the boat was still. Her father lifted her onto the deck and climbed up behind her. In the distance, sailing ships bobbed like toys on a pond. Laying her dolls on bunks smelling of oil, mud and salt, she dreamed of sailing to a magical island with no school where she could play all day long.

'We won't shoot birds with guns like Dad and my brothers,' she told her dolls.

The engine started, juddered, then stopped. 'Damn!' her father shouted.

The last time before her father had gone away, she'd sat on the tiled kitchen floor in Parsonage Road, watching as they'd cleaned the bores and rubbed down their shotguns with solvent that stung her eyes. They'd planned their voyage, talking and laughing loudly about the changing tides and weather forecasts, not noticing she was there.

She sighed thinking about the lifeless birds with their bloodstained necks hanging limply over the white stone sink in the kitchen, eyes dull, beaks silent.

A smooth humming sound made the cabin tremble, and her dolls rolled from the bunks onto the dusty floor. 'It's going!' her father shouted. She picked up the dolls, rubbed off the dirt and climbed onto the deck.

'Can we sail to Rhyl instead of going on the bus?' Barbara looked up at her father as they walked back across the marsh. 'It takes ages on the bus.'

'You won't get your mother on a boat.'

'Mam said we might get a car.'
'Cars cost a lot of pennies.'
'You can keep my pocket money.'
Laughing, her father patted her head.

Florrie

Rents were cheap, and Florrie had been thrifty with the family's money. Compared with their neighbours, they were well off, and she'd saved enough to buy a caravan in Rhyl as well as a car to take them there.

'Jim! Watch out! He's coming round the corner too fast!' In the passenger seat of the new black Ford Standard, Florrie gripped the leather arms. Jim was a good driver; he'd driven a St John's ambulance during the war, but Florrie was relieved to get home and put the kettle on. While Jim tinkered with the car, she sipped her tea and thought about all the places they could go to in their new motor.

Jim may have read somewhere that Widnes was a 'poisonous hell-town' but conditions in the factories had improved – thanks to the likes of Jim, who was a shop steward with the union. Sure, bad smells came from the factories, some worse than others, but you got used to it. They were fortunate living in Widnes, with forty-five chemical factories employing the men. Florrie and Jim had got married in 1926 during the General Strike, and she knew how the poor suffered from unemployment.

Life was better than it had ever been. Florrie smiled to herself, then her thoughts turned to Barbara, who was a nervy, shy child, difficult to understand. She didn't want to treat her differently but a feeling that she couldn't describe was always there. To distract herself, she turned her thoughts to planning their Easter holiday in their caravan in Wales.

Barbara

They travelled slowly along the coast road to Towyn. 'First one to spot the sea gets a sweet,' her mother said. It was the Easter holidays and the first time they'd been to the caravan at Rhyl in the car.

'I can see it!' Barbara knelt up and banged on the window. 'There it is!' In the fading sunlight, blue waves edged with white foam rolled over pebbles and sand. Her mother gave her a pear drop. 'Are we nearly there?' Her tummy ached with excitement.

'By the time you've sucked that sweet, we'll be at Winkups camp, unpacking,' her mother said.

The next day, after breakfast, her father shouted, 'Get your bucket and spade.' He led Barbara and Lily along a winding path, over a railway bridge to the seafront. He swam in the sea, while Lily paddled with Barbara near the shore, their knitted swimsuits drooping with the weight of the water. After his swim, her father took them crabbing in the rock pools, unearthing small creatures hiding in the crevices. Barbara shrieked, afraid the tiny crabs might nip her feet.

'Lily, bring the bucket for the periwinkles,' her father said. Barbara helped him and Lily wrench the winkles from the rocks.

She stared into the bucket where the winkles, afraid to peep out, hid in their shells.

Their squeals as they hit the pot of boiling water that her mother had steaming on the stove startled Barbara, and she put her hands to her ears. She watched with horror as her father hooked the tiny curly bodies with a pin, and yanked them from their shells. She refused to eat them.

When it went dark, her mother drew the flowered curtains and took a box of dominoes and a pack of cards from a shelf above the cooker. Cosy and warm, they played for halfpennies in the dim, gas-lit front section of the van, on a table that doubled up for a bed when everyone got tired.

She woke to the smell of fried bacon and Calor gas which

filled the small van in the morning, as her mother cooked breakfast before they started the journey home.

'I want a wee, Mam,' Barbara said, as they pulled up outside their house.

The outside toilet was next to a garage, used as a chicken shed at the rear end of the yard. Barbara moved her legs about uncomfortably on the spot. Her mother unlocked the back door and Barbara peeped into the yard. 'Sammy's out!'

Her mother picked up the yard brush leaning against the back door. 'Follow me.'

At the sound of their footsteps, Sammy, the cockerel, raised his hackles and crowed loudly, strutting up the yard towards them. Her mother ran at him with the brush, gesturing to Barbara to get in the toilet. Sammy squawked and backed off.

'Don't leave me,' Barbara pleaded.

Her mother stood guard while Sammy waited in readiness for the flush of the chain. When Barbara opened the door, he attacked again with greater ferocity. Flapping his wings, he pecked at the brush as her mother shielded Barbara and they fought their way to the back door.

'That bird's making her constipated. She's afraid to go to the toilet,' her mother told her father. 'Those chickens will have to go! We need the place tidying up a bit for Jimmy's wedding and the street party.'

'What street party?' Barbara asked.

'For the Queen's Coronation in June.'

Chapter 3

Celebrations

Florrie

Shouts from the street brought Florrie and her two daughters out of the house. Like the Pied Piper, Joseph swaggered along, followed by an assortment of kids running after him expectantly.

'Joe's home!'

'Hiya, Jo!' echoed down the street and through the railway arches.

Full of pride, Florrie looked up at her son, strikingly handsome in khaki, the brass buttons on his uniform reflecting the sun. Everything about him glistened, from the darkness of his shiny crew-cut, to his highly polished black boots.

Lily looked at Joe with adoring eyes and he hugged her.

Joe swept Barbara off her feet and swung her in the air. 'Hiya, baby sis.' She rubbed the stubble on his chin and patted his face as he held her on his arm.

'I've a special surprise for you,' he told her, and she snuggled close.

Joe kissed Florrie on the cheek: she got a whiff of aftershave, cigarette smoke and beer, and wrinkled her nose. He could do no wrong in her eyes and she didn't begrudge him his pleasures, but it was early in the day for drinking.

Still holding Barbara on one arm, he waved to the neighbours who'd come to their doors to see what the fuss was about. He felt in his pockets with his free hand, shouting 'Catch!' as he threw packets of sweets and chewing gum to the kids hanging round.

In the house, Joe lit a cigarette, smiled his broad, white-toothed grin and sat back on the sofa. 'It's great to be home, Mam.' He sniffed the air. 'Mm! I've been dreaming of your onion gravy all the way home.'

Florrie was pleased to have him back safely, if only for a few weeks. He drove a tank and her worst nightmare was another war breaking out and Joe being called up and trapped inside the vehicle, his handsome face burned and scarred for life, or worse.

Climbing onto Joseph's knee, Barbara cupped her hand and whispered in his ear.

'You want your surprise, do you?' Joe rummaged in his kitbag, and handed Lily a blue patterned vanity case.

'Aw, thanks!' Lily dug into the case, and smeared blood-red lipstick on her lips. 'I'm going to show Astrid, Mam. See you later, Joe.'

'She's too young for that muck,' Florrie said, when she heard the door shut.

'Oh, leave her alone, Mam! She has to grow up sometime.'

Barbara stared at the kitbag, and her face brightened when Joe pulled out a doll wearing a traditional costume, with long blonde plaits twisted round its ears in coils. 'She's called Inge.'

'I'll teach her English.' Barbara disappeared under the stairs and dragged her box of dolls into the hall.

'She plays school for hours, lining those dolls up on the stairs. You can hear her telling them what to do.'

Joe looked at Florrie and frowned. 'Have you heard from her mother since?'

'No, thank God.'

'She's a great kid.' He lit up a cigarette. 'You've no regrets, have you?'

'None.'

'We're lucky to have her.' He took a long drag. 'Now, where's this liver and onions?'

Across the square wooden table, she watched him mop up the gravy with a thick slice of crusty white bread.

'How are the wedding plans going?' Joe asked.

'Fine,' she said flatly. Florrie felt a pang of regret at the thought of losing Jimmy's wages.

'You know Jean's not a Catholic. She goes to St Mary's on the other side of the tracks, but she's been to classes and she's made a better Catholic than Jimmy.'

'That's not hard,' Joe said with a snigger. 'So, they'll be married in St Patrick's then.'

Barbara

On the day of the wedding, Lily fastened the headdress of lace and pearls onto Barbara's soft brown hair. Her mother had tortured her with a Toni home perm, resulting in a lot of frizz; now it had calmed down. She climbed onto a chair and looked at herself in the parlour mirror, admiring her blue silk dress overlaid with net and decorated with satin ribbons.

At the wedding reception, Barbara stood next to the other small bridesmaid, Madeleine, but she felt the guests stare longer at her. They whispered and said she was tall for her age and asked questions about her as though she wasn't there.

'Is she a good girl?'

'Do you have any problems with her?'

It was always like this; it made her feel uncomfortable, different somehow, and she wanted to hide away.

A year later, Jimmy's wife, Jean, glowed with pride, showing off her new-born son to the guests at the baby's christening. 'We've called him James, after his dad and granddad.'

'James the third,' Jimmy said. Everyone laughed.

In the front parlour, her mother handed out sherry in her best glasses and gave the men beer. As the guests drank and ate sandwiches, Barbara heard someone talk about godparents. Her mother was busy chatting, but Barbara tapped her on the arm. 'What do you want, love?' Her mother looked down at her.

'You said baby James has godparents.' Barbara pointed to Jean's cousin who was holding the baby. 'What's godparents?'

'Your godparents make a promise to God that they'll make sure you grow up to be a good Catholic and go to church every Sunday.'

'Who are *my* godparents?'

Mrs Wilson stared at her, and her aunts looked at each other. One of them laughed and then coughed into her serviette, covering her mouth. They all stared at her mother and her face turned red. 'Mickey Rooney and Judy Garland,' she said, laughing.

'What's wrong?' Barbara demanded, hands on hips, head to one side. 'What's funny?'

'They're film stars,' Madeleine said, grinning oddly.

Barbara didn't know who they were, but she could tell from the laughter and the sly looks that it was a lie. 'Where are they now then, Judy and what's his name? Why don't they come and take me to church?' she asked her mother.

'They're too busy making films in Hollywood,' Jimmy said. Everyone laughed louder.

Why is everyone laughing at me? She wanted to cry but was determined not to.

'It's not true, is it, Mam?'

'Here.' Her mother, still grinning, handed her a piece of christening cake. 'Never mind about that now, love.' Barbara sat in a corner nibbling the icing on the rich fruit cake, thinking they all knew a secret that they hadn't told her.

Florrie

Florrie had been up at dawn making sandwiches, raspberry jelly and pink blancmange for the Coronation celebrations. Lily helped her decorate the trestle tables, while Barbara played with her best friend Trisha, crumpling the red, white and blue crepe paper, thinking she was helping. Florrie wrung her hands. *I'll never get finished on time.*

'The lads have done a good job.' Florrie looked up at the bunting hanging from the lampposts that lined the street and the huge Union Jack that Jim had hung from their front bedroom window, fluttering in the breeze from the river.

Lily had been chosen as the Coronation Queen for the neighbouring streets, and Barbara and Trisha were to be her maids of honour. Florrie smiled with pride at her thirteen-year-old daughter. Barbara, who was six that day, watched as Florrie fixed a cardboard crown – which she'd sprayed with silver paint – onto Lily's dark wavy hair. 'Is the party for my birthday?' Barbara asked.

'Of course it is.' Florrie winked at Lily. 'But it's for the Queen as well. She gets crowned today.'

In time for the Coronation, Florrie had ordered a television. It showed black and white pictures on a fourteen-inch screen, and was housed in a shiny mahogany box. Florrie was thrilled that they were the first on their street to have one, and she invited the neighbours to crowd into their living room to watch Queen Elizabeth crowned live on the BBC. When Elizabeth appeared, everyone gasped.

'Doesn't she look beautiful!' a neighbour said.

'And Philip's so handsome in his uniform.'

'Lizzy's dress was made by Norman Hartnell.'

'So was mine!' Mrs Knowles stood, held out the skirt of her cotton frock, and curtsied. 'Can't you tell?' The neighbours giggled.

Transported into a world of pageantry, Florrie imagined what Elizabeth's life would be like. Very different from her own, but that was what she'd been born into and nothing could change it.

'Is *Andy Pandy* coming on?' Barbara stood up and waved her flag in Florrie's face.

'No, not today. If you don't like watching the Queen, go out and play.'

Mrs O'Brien hung around after the other neighbours had left the house. 'Barbara's grown into a lovely kid. Let's hope she stays a good girl.'

'What do you mean?' Florrie snapped.

'Fred's sister adopted a girl. When she was barely sixteen, she ran off with the window cleaner, a married man. It caused a terrible scandal. Rumour was she was pregnant. They disowned her. Told her never to come back and she never did. They've never got over it.'

'Barbara's no trouble.' Florrie stiffened. 'Not since I stopped her playing in the alleyway with those lads from Church Street. And she'll turn out fine.' *Some people take pleasure in reminding me that Barbara could have come from bad blood. Does bad blood always come out?*

'I'm sure she will!' Mrs O'Brien said, smirking.

Chapter 4

Psychiatrist

Barbara

'We're moving house,' her mother said. 'They're going to build a new bridge over the river and our house will be right underneath the approach road, so they'll have to pull it down.'

'Oh no!' Barbara imagined the bricks falling around them. 'Where will we go?

'Remember that house in Pine Avenue that we looked at, on the estate near where your Aunty Maggie lives? I got a letter from the council today and we've got it. It's right near Victoria Park. You'll be seven by then, so you'll be able to go up there with your cousin Jean in the summer holidays.'

***

Pine Avenue faced the sun: the front bedroom, which Barbara shared with Lily, was filled with warmth and light. Her father built a swing for her on the lawn, surrounded by beds of marigolds, dahlias and sweet-scented peas.

'The swings at the park go higher,' Jean said, her pale skin flushing.

'Let's go then.' Barbara said. They ran in to tell her mother.

In the park, they climbed onto the bandstand. Shouts from boys playing football echoed across the grassy playing fields.

'I want to see who's playing tennis first,' Barbara said.

'I want to go to the swings now!' Jean dug her hands into her pockets.

'It's up to me what we do!' Barbara pointed at herself. 'I'm the oldest!'

'No it isn't!' Jean looked mean. 'You're a bossy boots!'

Annoyed, Barbara paused and wondered how she could upset Jean. 'Bernadette MacMullen is my best friend now, not you, so there!'

'I don't care anyway.' Jean's pale blue eyes narrowed. 'You're not my *real* cousin.'

Barbara froze. 'What?' Anger rose from her toes: her face became hot. 'You're lying. I *am* your cousin, you little fibber.'

'No! It's true. My dad told me. You're not my *real* cousin.'

'Liar! Liar!'

Jean continued to taunt her in a sing-songy voice until Barbara slapped her in the face as hard as she could.

Jean's hand shot up to her reddened cheek. 'I hate you! I'm glad you're not my real cousin!' She jumped off the bandstand, crying. 'It *is* true and I'm going to tell my dad on you!' she shouted, as she hurried towards the gate.

Barbara stood silently on the bandstand, sucking her fingers. *Why did Jean say that?* She made her way past the bowling green and through the gate, walking slowly down the length of Sycamore Avenue to the two houses at the bottom that were on Pine Avenue. *What could Jean have meant?* 'Ouch!' She tripped on the back doorstep.

'Watch out!' Her mother was chopping vegetables on a wooden board by the kitchen sink. Her mouth hardened to a thin line when Barbara told her what Jean had said. 'Who told her that nonsense?' she asked.

'Uncle Tom.' Her mother stopped chopping and her face wrinkled into a frown. *Something's wrong.* 'Why did he say that?'

'Jean's being silly.' Her mother stared at her. 'She's just teasing you. I know you're two years older, but you shouldn't boss her. We asked to be moved up here so I'd be near to Maggie and you could play with Jean. You should be kinder to her.'

'But *am I* her *real* cousin?' Barbara pleaded.

'Of course you are, love.' Her mother handed her a slice of raw carrot and continued chopping. 'She's made it up just to annoy you. She is your *real* cousin.'

Barbara felt a sense of unease, as she gnawed at the carrot. *If it's not true, why did Mam get so angry when I told her and why does she look so sad now?*

The next day, in the back garden, Jean followed Barbara as they crept along a narrow gap between the privet hedge and the garage wall, to a triangular piece of land where they hid from adults and collected ladybirds in matchboxes: the ladybird club. Barbara stared intently at Jean. 'My mam said you *are* my real cousin.'

'I know.' Jean's eyes fell to the ground. 'My mam shouted at me. My dad got mixed up. You are my real cousin.'

Relieved, Barbara smiled at Jean. 'You can be my best friend again.' Her eye caught sight of a ladybird climbing on a clump of wild Irises. 'Look, there's a big one!' She pointed. 'Catch it before it flies off!'

Florrie

Florrie sat in the consultant's waiting room watching Jim pace back and forth, his hands clasped behind his back. 'Barbara banged her head against the wall today, screaming with pain,' he said, the lines on his face deepening. 'She's had her eyes tested and every other test, so what could be wrong with a twelve-year-old child?'

'We're going to find out.' Florrie joined her hands together, as if in prayer. *One minute could change our lives.*

'Mr Simpson will see you now,' a nurse invited them into the room.

Sat opposite the doctor, Florrie was alarmed by his grave expression. *God help us!*

He pushed back his thick grey hair and adjusted his spectacles. 'I'm very sorry to tell you this, Mr and Mrs Tiernan …'

Florrie sat up straight and gripped the arms of her chair. 'What?' she said.

'Barbara has a brain tumour.'

'Oh no!' She slumped back and Jim took hold of her hand.

Jim's eyes searched the doctor's face. 'Can anything be done for her?'

'Yes, we can operate. But …' He paused and looked directly at them. '… If she survives the operation, there's a high possibility that she'll be severely brain-damaged. The tumour is in an awkward position.'

'Is there an alternative?' Jim asked.

'If it's left, she'll be in constant pain as the tumour grows, followed by an early death.'

'Oh God! No!' *We've got no choice.* 'We'll sign for the operation,' Florrie said. 'I'll take care of her no matter what.' Jim nodded his agreement.

'You know we adopted her,' Florrie said.

'Yes, it's all in her file.'

'Excuse me, doctor, but I've just remembered something,' Florrie said. 'The doctor at the orphanage warned us not to take her because she'd be trouble? I wonder if he knew something about her mother that they didn't tell us?'

'No, I shouldn't think so. Brain tumours aren't hereditary.' The doctor smiled a practised smile and handed them the consent forms.

At visiting time, the bell rang and a nurse swung open the doors. 'Barbara's watched the clock all day,' she said. Florrie gave her a weak smile. *Why does my child have to go through this?*

Barbara's face lit up as they approached her bed and kissed her.

'How are you doing?' Lily sat close to her on the bed.

Barbara frowned. 'They've shaved my hair. It looks terrible.' She turned her face and rubbed her hands across the back of her head.

'It'll grow back in a few weeks and you can't tell from the front,' Lily said.

'See that girl over there.' Barbara nodded towards a teenage girl with a bandaged head. 'She was kicked in the head by a horse. She's weird. She started whispering stuff that I couldn't understand, and pulling faces at me.'

'She's just trying to be friendly.' Florrie gave a deep sigh. The half-hour visiting passed quickly, and she hated leaving Barbara in a ward with adults and mentally ill people.

Florrie held Lily's hand and leant against Jim as they walked down the corridor. Walton was an old hospital in need of a lick of paint. The walls were a nasty green colour and completely bare. It was autumn and cold outside, but the heat was suffocating and the radiators made a clanking noise. She wanted to run back to the ward, gather Barbara up in her arms and take her home no matter what the consequences. But her daughter was ill – seriously ill. *Please God don't let her die.*

***

On the day of Barbara's operation, Florrie had the school, the church and everyone she knew praying. She wasn't as deeply religious as Jim, but she entered St Bede's Church and knelt in front of the side altar.

The church was empty: the smell of incense lingered from the morning service. Gripping the altar rail, she gazed up at a statue of the Virgin Mary. 'You're a mother. You understand a mother's love for her child. Please ask Our Father in heaven to help Barbara. I'll make sure she goes to Sunday School and Mass, Communion and Confession every week. I'll say the Rosary every day. Please grant my prayers.' She took her Rosary from her bag and sat back on the hard wooden pew. For two hours, her fingers moved slowly from one glossy black bead to the next, and with closed eyes she recited the prayers. 'Our Father, who art in heaven …'

The following day, Florrie clasped and unclasped her hands around the handle of her handbag as they sat waiting to find out if the operation had been successful. 'We can't lose her.' Florrie glanced at Jim's tired and worn face.

'Our Lady will see she's all right,' Jim said. 'I've prayed to her all night.'

Let's hope she's listening.

'Mr Simpson will see you now,' the nurse said.

His smile gave Florrie hope. 'These are the test results,' he said, tapping a pile of papers on his desk, 'and I've got good news.' Florrie gasped and held her breath. 'The tumour was more accessible than we originally thought, and I removed it successfully.'

Florrie let go of her breath, closed her eyes and whispered, 'Thank you, Holy Virgin Mother of God and thank you, Jesus.'

Jim crossed himself and moved his lips silently.

Mr Simpson paused, raised his eyebrows and looked from one to the other before he spoke. 'It's early days yet, but we're expecting Barbara to make a good recovery. We'll need a psychiatric report, of course, but it's much better than the original prognosis, I'm happy to tell you.'

'Thank you, doctor, thank you.' Florrie shook his hand, hardly believing what he'd just told them.

'It's a miracle,' Jim said. He put his arm round Florrie's shoulders and they walked along the corridor towards the ward.

Florrie and Jim sat by Barbara's bedside. 'Before you come home,' Florrie said, 'you have to see a special doctor called a psychiatrist.'

'Do they expect me to be crazy after my operation?' Barbara rolled her eyes.

'No, don't be silly,' Jim said. 'They're supposed to help people.'

'I don't need any help.'

Barbara

The following day, Barbara turned towards Mrs Briggs in the next bed, a grey-haired lady with a funny accent who made her laugh. 'I'll be going home soon.' She ran her fingers along the stubble on the back of her head. 'I'm not going to school till it's grown back.'

Nurse Jones came to her bed and told her to put on her dressing gown: she was going to see another doctor. *Oh no! It's the psychiatrist!*

'Good luck,' Mrs Briggs said with a smile. 'There's nothing to be afraid of.'

The nurse led her along a dark corridor and up in a creaky lift, to a door with a gold plaque: *Dr Clegg* was written in black letters.

'Don't be afraid.' Nurse Jones knocked on the door. 'He just wants to ask you a few questions.'

What questions? Reluctantly, she entered his office.

'Hello.' Dr Clegg smiled and gestured to the seat opposite him. Barbara eased herself onto the chair. He was young, dark-haired and good-looking. Blushing deeply, eyes cast down, she pulled the belt on her gown more tightly around her. 'You're just here for a chat. Nothing to be concerned about. But first, I'd like you to do these.' He slid three puzzles across his desk towards her. 'They're IQ tests.'

'What tests?' Barbara panicked.

'Don't worry, just try them.' He came round the desk and bent over her. 'Let me show you how they work.' His closeness made her uncomfortable.

For twenty minutes, she concentrated, connecting corresponding shapes, squares and triangles. She sighed with relief when she'd finished.

'You've done well,' he said, smiling.

Her body relaxed and she scanned the wooden bookshelves that lined the walls. The muffled sound of hospital traffic hummed through the window and her eyes rested on a model of a sliced human brain sitting on the windowsill. The outer shell looked like the fat maggots that her brothers used for fishing bait.

Dr Clegg coughed, got her attention and questioned her about school. More at ease, she smiled as they chatted about her relationship with her mother, father and family.

'You do know that you're adopted, don't you?' he asked.

Everything stopped. The room went silent, the air still. Her mouth fell open, her face drained and her throat constricted. All the strange things that people had said – the way she'd always felt different. *I don't know where I got you from. Isn't she tall? Your godparents are film stars. You're not my real cousin.* Now she understood.

'You *do* know you're adopted,' a voice somewhere in the distance repeated.

You're adopted. You're adopted. The words echoed. She blinked hard, as if to wake herself up from a dream, but it wasn't a dream: she was adopted. Unsure of how to react, she stayed silent, her thoughts in turmoil. Gulping hard, she refused to cry.

He tapped the fingers of his manicured right hand on his lips. 'You didn't know, did you?' He took a deep breath, releasing it slowly through his nostrils.

'No … I didn't know … I really didn't know. Mam didn't tell me. Why didn't she tell me?' She sunk in her chair and cried without restraint, her body heaving with each long deep sob. He pushed a box of tissues in her direction and rang for the nurse, shuffling papers on his desk until she arrived.

'Calm down, come along now.' Nurse Jones took hold of Barbara's hand and they walked back to the ward.

In between sobs, Barbara confessed, 'My mam's not my *real* mam … he said I'm adopted.'

Nurse Jones raised her eyebrows. 'My God! And you didn't know?'

'No!'

She hugged Barbara tightly and wiped her damp cheeks. 'I'm sure your mother loves you just the same.'

'How can she? I'm not her *real* daughter.'

Back in her bed, Barbara stopped crying. Anger at being told something so intimate by a cold, indifferent stranger made her head ache. A terrible resentment grew towards her mother. *Why didn't Mam tell me herself?* She buried her head in a pillow and lay in agony, confused, hating the psychiatrist, her parents and herself.

Mrs Briggs tried to comfort her. 'It's shocking, him telling you like that. But your mam loves you. She's always here on time to see you. Always the first in when they open the doors. Never misses a visit.'

'But she's not my mam. Don't you understand?'

'Yes, I understand, of course I do. Come over here, love.' Mrs Briggs held out her arms. Barbara lay on the bed next to her and sobbed as Mrs Briggs caressed her in a way her mother hadn't done since she was a little girl.

'You're going home soon.' Mrs Briggs stroked her hair.

'I don't want to go home.' Barbara pushed her hand away and sat up.

'Your mam seems like a very nice person to me; you're being silly behaving like this.'

'She's nice to other people, such as tramps!'

'What do you mean, tramps?'

'Months ago, a dirty old tramp came and sat in the gardens in front of our house. It's sort of a triangle with grass, and it has two wooden benches for pensioners to sit on and look at the flowers. Sometimes Dad sits out there to get away from Mam and smoke his pipe. I saw the tramp out the window and I told Mam about him. She was cooking our Sunday dinner. When she'd finished cooking the chicken, she put it in a dish and told Lily to take it to him. I followed Lily.'

'Oh my goodness!' Mrs Briggs's eyes widened. 'What did he do?'

'His hands were filthy, and he snatched the chicken and bit into the leg with rotten teeth. Ugh! When we went back into the house, I joked about him, but Mam got angry. "Don't make fun of people less fortunate than you," she said. "You've never been hungry." And all we had for dinner was potatoes, gravy and veg.'

Mrs Briggs laughed. 'Well, she's a very kind woman. Very Christian. In fact, I know a lot of Christians who wouldn't have such a good heart as to give up their Sunday dinner for a tramp.'

Barbara smiled at Mrs Briggs, then she remembered. 'I don't care. She's not my real mam. She lied to me and I hate her.'

Florrie

'The welfare lady wants to have a word with you.' The matron looked concerned as she ushered Florrie into an anteroom at the hospital.

'What's wrong?'

'Mrs Forster will explain.'

Florrie had arrived at the hospital feeling optimistic. *What were they troubling her about now?* The operation had been a success: her daughter was coming home tomorrow.

If Dr Clegg had been in the room when Mrs Forster told Florrie of his blunder, she would have physically attacked him, the rage within her was so strong.

'I didn't want her to know!' she shouted. 'I've had her since she was a baby. She's mine. There was no need for him to tell her like that without my permission.'

Mrs Foster nodded. 'Dr Clegg must have assumed she already knew, with her being twelve years old, I suppose.'

'Well, he shouldn't have assumed anything.'

'It's a shame *you* hadn't already told her.'

What a cheek! How dare she hint at it being my fault. 'I was going to tell her when I thought she was ready for it.'

Unable to offer a satisfactory explanation, Mrs Forster let Florrie continue to rant.

'Psychiatrists! What do they know about anything? He should be struck off! It was none of his business.' Florrie broke down. 'I bet she's really upset, isn't she?'

'Well, yes, she has been getting upset.'

'No wonder!' *Oh God!* 'What am I going to tell her?'

'Tell her the truth.'

Seething with anger and filled with dread, Florrie made her way to the ward. *I can't tell her the whole truth.*

'Hello, love. How are you?' She sat at Barbara's bedside and leaned across the bed to touch her daughter's arm. Barbara withdrew her arm as though it had been scalded, holding it close to her body. She turned away, her face puffy from crying, and refused to speak.

Florrie's hands shook as she placed sweets on the locker. She started to talk about Dr Clegg.

'Shut up!' Barbara scowled. 'You're not my *real* mam!'

'But you're coming home tomorrow. I'll explain it then.'

Unmoved by Florrie's concern, Barbara stared down and picked at the frayed edges of the bedspread. 'I'd rather stay here with my friends. *They* don't tell me lies. I don't want to go home with you.'

'You don't mean that.' Florrie felt tears forming but she swallowed and forced them back.

'Yes, I do! You're a liar. Go home. You're not my *real* mam.'

'I *am* your mam and I'm coming with your dad to pick you up tomorrow.' Florrie left, dabbing her eyes with her handkerchief, and cursing Dr Clegg for ruining their lives.

On the bus journey home, she composed herself and planned what she would tell Barbara when she got her home. *She'll run away and try to find Carole. I can't let that happen.* Somehow, she'd make Barbara realise how much she loved her; that she was her real mam; that the girl who'd had her didn't want her. Panic. Sickness. The motion of the bus made it worse. 'Stop! I'm going to throw up!' In a quiet country lane, the driver waited while Florrie vomited behind a hedge, the glaring passengers rubbernecking.

'Are you OK, love?'

'Yes, thanks.' The conductor held her arm as she got back on the bus. 'I can't lose Barbara,' she whispered, staring out of the window. 'What can I say that will stop her hating me?'

Barbara

When her mother left, Barbara looked around the ward as if searching for something she'd lost. The chatter and the movement of nurses and patients across the ward didn't stop her feeling alone. Children who she'd made friends with sat at tables in the middle of the room doing puzzles or reading magazines, but she didn't want to be near them. She wanted to hide from everyone and she buried her head beneath the sheets.

'I think she's asleep,' Mrs Briggs told the nurse, when they brought round the warm milky bedtime drinks. 'Leave it on her locker. It's best not to disturb her. She's been upset since all that business with the stupid psychiatrist. Let her sleep.'

But Barbara wasn't asleep, she was listening. The hatred she felt for her mam had left her body worn out, but her brain wouldn't stop, and thoughts about the woman who'd left her in an orphanage wouldn't go away. She was her *real* mother, but why should she want Barbara now? Her stomach ached. She pulled her knees up and hugged them with her arms, burying her head further beneath the bedclothes.

Her mother had given her no instruction in the facts of life, but she'd heard whispers at school about girls who'd got pregnant and given their babies away to someone else to bring up. She was one of those babies. Illegitimate. A bastard. Someone who'd been taken in.

Mrs Briggs had told her that she could have been left in that home forever if her mother hadn't taken her. But she felt no gratitude towards her mother, only resentment. All the family knew she was adopted, but she didn't feel their betrayal in the same way. It was her mother she couldn't forgive.

The day after she returned from hospital, Barbara sat on the sofa reading a comic. Her mother came in from the kitchen and sat next to her. Her mother smelt of onions and Barbara shifted to the far end of the sofa; hugging the armrest, she pretended to read.

'Put that down,' her mother said. The comic slipped through Barbara's fingers and she bent forward to pick it up. 'Leave it!' her mother said. 'Listen! I want to explain about the girl who gave birth to you.'

'Oh!' Panic! Barbara's hand covered her mouth. She sat up, every nerve in her body alert.

Her mother folded her arms. 'A boy got her into trouble. Do you understand?'

'Yes.' Barbara stayed rigid, unable to move.

'He wouldn't marry her, so when you were born, she put you in an orphanage.'

Barbara stared, helpless, chewing her fingers. Her mother looked at her as if trying to judge her reactions: her voice got louder.

'She didn't want you. She left you there so she could go off and live her life without you tying her down.'

Barbara's hands trembled. She swallowed hard. Her head ached. *How can Mam tell me such awful things?*

Her mother's voice softened and the corners of her mouth turned up into a sort of smile. 'If I hadn't seen you and fallen for you, you'd still be there. The doctor at the orphanage told me you had runny ears and no one else would take you. It made me determined to adopt you. I couldn't bear the thought of you being left there.'

Barbara gulped and bit her bottom lip, sucking it into her mouth to stop herself from crying. *Why won't Mam stop?* She felt trapped, like a wild animal facing assault on a grassland.

'But I'm glad she gave you away ...'

The room started to move and Barbara gripped the edge of her chair to stop herself from falling. 'Stop!' she shouted. 'Stop! Don't tell me any more!' Tears stung her eyes. 'I don't want to hear it!'

Her mother stood up and her face became angry. 'She'll be married to someone else now, and she'll have her own kids to think about. She left you. She won't want you now, so it's no use going off looking for her. She'll be far away. You'd never find her.'

Barbara's heart thumped wildly. 'Shut up! Stop talking!' She sprung to her feet. *Why would I want to find someone who'd abandoned me?* 'I don't want to find her. I hate her and I hate you!' she screamed, running up the stairs. At the top she stumbled, lurched forward and landed on her knees. Sobbing, she crawled to her bedroom and locked the door behind her.

'Barbara! Barbara!' Her mother's voice became louder as she crossed the landing. 'Come on, love. Open the door.'

'Leave me alone! You're not my mam! Go away!'

'Won't you give me a chance?' her mother asked, tapping on the door.

'No!'

Cries were muffled; footsteps faded; the door closed; everything went quiet.

Barbara sat on her bed, hugging her body, swaying back and forth. She wanted her mother to be her *real* mother and for everything to be back like it was. Thinking about that other woman made her feel sick. Her mother was right, that woman would have more children to love now and she wouldn't want *her*. Why did her mother think she'd want to find the person who had abandoned her? Barbara felt ashamed of being illegitimate, dirty and inferior to everyone else, and somehow it felt like it was her fault. Exhausted, she lay down and fell asleep.

Chapter 5

Rita

'You have to visit your nan with me,' her mother said. 'You've not seen her for ages.'

'She's not my nan and I don't want to go anywhere with you.' Barbara stood in the hallway, defiant. 'I'm going to the park with Rita.' She stared at the statue of the Sacred Heart standing on the windowsill: the edges of his robe glowed in the sun beaming around him, like a spirit from heaven. *Was* He *listening?* she wondered.

'I don't know what that one who left you in the orphanage was like.' her mother frowned. 'A bad one, I'll bet.'

Barbara's stomach clenched. 'Why do you say that all the time?' she screamed. *Why do you make me feel so worthless?*

'Because it must be true.' Her mother's mouth became a straight line. 'Now get your coat on.'

'No! I'm meeting Rita.' Barbara was taller than her mother now. She grabbed her coat from the hanger, pushed past her mother and left the house, slamming the door behind her.

Barbara and Rita were similar in height, with the same shoulder-length chestnut brown hair. People often thought they were sisters, but Rita's eyes were blue, Barbara's brown. Sitting next to each other on the swings in Victoria Park, they swayed their legs gently back and forth in the cool autumn breeze. Suddenly, Rita dug her heels into the powdery earth, bringing the swing to a halt. 'I've got a secret.'

Barbara stopped, just as abruptly. 'What?'

'I'm adopted. I overheard Mam and Dad talking about it.'

'Oh wow! So am I.' Leaping from her swing, she put her arms around Rita and they hugged. 'Do you know who your real parents are?'

'No, they wouldn't tell me.'

'Just like mine, liars.'

Muttering hatred for their parents, they walked along the crazy paving, past the scented rose garden to a shelter in Lovers Lane.

'Let's run away!' Barbara's tummy tensed, hoping Rita would agree.

'OK.' Rita looked scared. 'But where should we go?'

'What about Liverpool? Mam takes me sometimes. There's lots of shops and stuff to do.'

'Where will we sleep?'

'We'll find somewhere,' Barbara said. 'There's hostels where young people can stay. I've got some pocket money and I know where Mam keeps the milk money.'

'My mam'll be upset when she knows I've gone.'

'She's *not* your mam.'

'I know, but she'll …'

'Are you coming or not?' Rita's hesitation was annoying.

'Yes! But when should we go?'

'Next Saturday.'

***

Rita's face turned white as the huge steam train pulled away from Widnes North Station. 'We've done it now.'

'They'll never find us in Liverpool.' Barbara stared out of the window, excitement bubbling in her stomach.

She held Rita's hand as she dragged her off the train and fought her way through the crowds in Central Station. The buildings in Church Street were taller than she remembered, the traffic noisier and the people more aggressive, elbowing the girls out of the way as they hurried past.

It was early afternoon on a dull October day and a fresh breeze blew up from the river. Barbara shivered. 'There's Lewis's! Let's go to the café.'

Wandering through the store, they stopped at the make-up counter and sprayed themselves with perfume testers. Sales girls with perfectly made-up faces watched them suspiciously, as they fingered the lipsticks and rouge. In the clothing department, they rummaged through rails of outfits too old for them, and tried on high-heeled shoes they couldn't walk in, laughing as they tottered up the aisles. The café smelt warm and they ordered cake and hot tea, and read comics they'd bought from a kiosk.

'We're closing now. You'll have to go,' a woman in overalls told them. Outside, Barbara trembled, shocked to see how dark it was: street lights and shop windows lit up the inky blue sky.

'What'll we do now?' Rita looked worried.

'We'll go down to the river and see the boats.' Barbara hoped to cheer Rita up but she was afraid. *What have I done?*

The shops got fewer and the street lights dimmer as they walked down Lord Street. They stopped to sit on the steps of the monument to Queen Victoria in Derby Square.

'On this site ... formerly stood ... the Castle of Liverpool,' Barbara read slowly from a plaque on the wall that showed a model of the castle.

'I didn't know there was a castle in Liverpool. Do you think they had a king in the olden days?'

'Probably.'

The breeze from the river swirled around the statue, scattering leftover chip papers and tin cans: Barbara shivered.

'Are we *still* going to the river?' Rita crossed her arms and hugged her body.

'Yes! Come on! You can get a ferry to New Brighton.'

'Not at this time of night. It's dark down there.'

'We'll be OK.' Barbara wanted to turn around and run back to the station, but she couldn't admit her fear to Rita. 'There might be something open. I can see a light further down, a red light.'

'*Surely* you know what *that* means?'

'Yes, I'm not stupid.' Barbara thought of the woman who'd had her. *Was she a prostitute?*

In an alley, at the top of James Street, a middle-aged man wearing a cap and leaning against a brick wall shouted across to them, 'Where're you two little birds flying off to?'

Alarmed, Barbara glanced in his direction. 'None of your business.'

'Flighty little pieces, aren't you? It's dangerous down there, you know. Sailors and dockers. They'll have you!' He grinned, baring brown stained teeth. Barbara watched as if hypnotised. 'Come with me somewhere nice and warm and I'll buy you a drink. I've got something to show you first. Something that you'll like. Come back down here with me and I'll show you what I've got and then we'll go and get you a drink. What do you like, gin or vodka?'

'No, thanks!' Barbara gulped.

'We don't want a drink!' Rita shouted. 'My mam told me not to speak to strange men.'

'Well, you know me now, don't you?' He spat out his cigarette, stubbed it into the ground with his boot and walked quickly towards them.

'Oh God no!' Barbara looked at Rita.

His hand gripped Barbara's shoulder. She flinched, ducked and jumped as if stung. 'Come on! Run! Run!' she said, grabbing Rita's hand.

The man laughed hoarsely. 'Silly little tarts! Go home to your mummies before the bogeyman gets you!'

They darted across the road, ran past the monument and up Lord Street like two Olympic sprinters.

When the station was in view, they stopped running and looked back, panting. There was no sign of the man. Sat on a bench in the station, her face hot, her heart still racing, Barbara turned to Rita. 'It hurts where he grabbed me,' she said, rubbing her shoulder. 'Don't tell anyone.'

'I won't. It was the scariest thing that's ever happened to me!' Rita started to cry. 'I want to go home. I love my mam.'

'You said you hated her.'

Rita stopped crying. 'I lied.' She looked down at her hands and twiddled her thumbs. 'It was all a lie. I'm not adopted.'

'What!' Barbara took hold of Rita's arm, pinching it and glaring at her. 'Why did you lie to me?'

'Leave me alone,' Rita said, wriggling free. 'I'm your best friend and I was really miffed that you couldn't even tell me you were adopted. So, I made it up.'

'That's crazy! Why did you run away with me, if you're not adopted?'

'I thought it'd be an adventure. I didn't think we'd get chased by a horrible man.'

Barbara stared at Rita, puzzled. 'When did your mam tell you *I* was adopted?'

'Your mam came to our house. She was crying and really upset because of all the trouble you were causing and because you wouldn't talk to her. She said she was afraid you'd run off, like we have done today. I bet she thinks it's my fault and that we've gone looking for your real mother. She asked my mam if I'd talk to you. She thought it might make you feel better.'

Barbara pictured her mother's tearful face. Knots tightened in her stomach. For a moment, she felt guilty for making her mother cry, but then she thought about her lies. 'I don't want to talk about it anymore. I don't care if she cried. She's not my mam.'

A station guard approached. 'Are you girls OK?'

Rita looked up at him, her eyes tearful. 'I want to go home. I want my mam.'

'OK, love, don't cry.' He patted Rita's shoulder. 'Tell me your names and where you live.'

Upon them doing so, he replied, 'There's a search party out for you two. Come on, let's get you on the last train to Widnes. Your parents must be worried sick!'

For an instant, Barbara dreaded seeing her mother's angry face, but in the warmth of the carriage she relaxed, secretly relieved they were travelling home.

'Don't you *want* to find your *real* mother?' Rita leaned forward. 'If I was adopted, I'd want to know who *my* real mother was.'

'Well, you're not adopted, are you!' Barbara leaned back in her seat. 'Why should I want to find someone who left me in a home.' She stared at the darkness outside, aware of the beating of her own heart.

Rita gave Barbara a cautious glance. 'What about your *real* father?'

'He didn't want either of us.'

Rita touched Barbara's arm. 'That's a shame.'

'It doesn't matter.' Barbara shrugged Rita's hand away. 'Will you *please* stop talking about them.'

'I'm sorry.' Rita looked sad.

'I won't fall out with you because you tricked me. We're still best friends.'

Rita smiled. 'I'm glad, but they'll kill us when they get hold of us.'

Barbara wiped the steamy windows with her hand as they approached the station, searching for her mother's face on the platform, but she couldn't make it out. A guard appeared through the carriage door. 'Come on, you two runaways.' The other passengers stared and Barbara's face burned, as he helped them off the train and handed them over to her mother and father, who were stood on the dimly lit platform. Rita ran to her own mother and was smothered in hugs and gentle reproaches.

With her head down, Barbara walked slowly to her mother, who put her arms around her shoulders. 'What were you thinking going off like that? We've been frantic. Your dad and brothers have been searching for you all over Widnes. The police came knocking on our door to tell us you were in Liverpool, of all places.'

'I'm sorry.' Barbara cried, relieved to be back with her mother, and determined to be a good girl from now on.

***

A few days later, they argued again. 'I'll run away on my own this time and I'll never come back!' Barbara shouted to her mother and stormed out of the room, her face hot with anger.

Joseph, who had married and left home, was visiting and witnessed the argument. 'So, she's still misbehaving? You shouldn't have to put up with this, Mam.' Barbara stood in the hall, listening to their conversation before climbing the stairs.

Joe caught up with her on the landing and grabbed her arm, squeezing it tightly. 'Why're you behaving like this? Threatening to run away again! Worrying everyone! Don't you know Mam thinks the world of you?' Joseph had never touched her in this way before. She was stunned and struggled free from his grip, unable to reply. 'Mam cried and cried when you were in hospital with that tumour and she thought she might lose you, and now you treat her like dirt.'

Barbara hung her head and said nothing. Turning her back on him, she gently shut the door of her room and sat on her bed. His words triggered a memory of her lying in the hospital bed, crying for her mother. It had been visiting time. She'd been told the fog was too thick for her mother and father to travel in.

'You've been spoiled by us all, and you think you can do what you like!' Joseph shouted through the door. 'Mam doesn't deserve it. She loves you. We all love you, but you can't go on like this!'

Her stomach churned, and she knew he was right. She sat in her room loathing Joe for stirring up uncomfortable thoughts, determined not to go down until he'd gone home. She knew they all loved her, but she'd always felt different. It was as though a part of her was missing: there was an empty place, deep within her.

***

'Now that Lily's gone, why don't you sort your stuff out?' her mother asked.

'Lily's left an underskirt in the dresser.' Barbara felt the soft silk, lace-edged material, held it close to her cheek and thought about Lily. Barbara had been chief bridesmaid at Lily's wedding to Trevor at St Bede's. She missed Lily's comforting presence in the house. They'd shared a bed and Lily had kept her warm on nights when the frost made patterns on the inside of their bedroom window.

Rummaging through a chest of broken jewellery and old toys, she saw her baby toy: the blue plastic cow; its legs were broken and its body was scratched. *What's that doing here?* She couldn't remember bringing it when they'd moved house or even when she'd last seen it, but she picked it up and shook it, amused by its rattle. She felt its significance and it triggered thoughts that disturbed her.

She'd be fourteen in June and the anger she felt towards her mother was confused. She hated her mother saying she didn't know where she'd got Barbara from. But even if her mother wasn't her *real* mother, she had always been there for her, and sometimes they laughed and had fun.

She reasoned that the woman who'd left her was probably not as bad as her mother made out. She might even feel sorry for leaving Barbara. But thinking about her made Barbara sad, and she buried those thoughts deep inside her.

There were so many questions, but her mother would only repeat those awful things if she asked her. She was afraid to ask any other member of her family: it was never mentioned.

Hardly aware of what she was doing, she wrapped the cow carefully in a lace handkerchief and hid it amongst her woollens in the bottom drawer of her dressing table.

Chapter 6

First Love

'I'm calling at the Regal to see your Aunt Lucy,' her mother said. 'Do you want to come with me?'

'Yes!' Barbara's stomach flipped thinking of Conor, the handsome eighteen-year-old who worked on the projection team. He looked like Billy Fury and everyone at school thought he was gorgeous.

Searching through her wardrobe, she scattered clothes across the floor until she found a soft red jumper and brown knee-length skirt. *Will he notice me in this?*

She'd developed breasts early but her mother had refused to buy her a bra. When Lily bought her a pretty lace-edged bra, her mother had said she was too young and argued with Lily, but then changed her mind and said she could wear it. In front of her bedroom mirror, she stuck out her chest and ran her fingertips gently over her breasts, admiring the womanly shape the bra gave her.

'What are you doing up there? Are you ready?' her mother shouted.

'Don't go without me!'

Lucy, who worked in the ticket office, met them at the cinema door. She looked pleased with herself and whispered to her mother as Barbara followed them upstairs passed the projection box to a back room. A bare lightbulb hung from the ceiling and a radio crackled in the background. Lucy pointed to a table. 'Sit down.' A mixture of cigarette ash and tea formed puddles on the bare Formica. 'Fancy a brew?' Lucy removed an ashtray overflowing with stumps and wiped the table with a dirty dishcloth, sweeping over the ingrained tea stains.

Barbara's eyes darted back and forth towards the door, while she sipped the hot mug of tea. *Please God let him come up here.* Quick footsteps on the stairs. The door burst open. There he stood. As soon as Barbara saw him, feelings she'd never experienced before stirred and she shifted on her chair. While he chatted to her mother and Lucy, she watched his softly quiffed blond hair fall forward every time he moved his head. *He doesn't even know I'm here.*

He turned to her and smiled with perfect white teeth. 'Hello.'

Her body stiffened. ''Ello,' she managed to say in a hoarse whisper.

'Lucy, you told me about your niece, but you didn't say how pretty she was.'

Oh God! Barbara blushed.

'It runs in the family,' Lucy said, laughing loudly.

A few weeks later, Lucy invited her workmates to her son's twenty-first party at a local club. Barbara stared beyond the plastic flowers decorating the party tables, at Moira, an older girl who was an usherette at the cinema. Her mother said she was Conor's ex-girlfriend.

It was late summer and the room was warm. Fans, hung from the ceiling, spun in vain, making only a mild draught. A group belted out Elvis's 'Hound Dog' while couples jived, girls flashing bare legs as they twirled around their partners. The smell of sausage rolls drifted in from the kitchen, but Barbara wasn't hungry.

Moira laughed and flirted with Conor. Aching with envy, Barbara eyed Moira's tight-fitting black dress, with its low-cut sweetheart neckline and pencil-slim skirt. Her auburn hair shone and waved around her shoulders, falling over her left eye. Full lips and painted fingernails gleamed bright red against her white skin.

Barbara sighed and looked down at the pleated skirt of her best party frock. *Moira's beautiful. He'll never look at me.*

'Hello again!' Barbara looked up, startled. Conor's deep blue eyes stared down at her.

'Hello.' *What does he want?*

'I've asked your mother, and she said it's OK, so can I take you to see Elvis's new film *Blue Hawaii* next Saturday at the Plaza? Lucy said you're an Elvis fan.'

She felt her heart frantically pumping blood and her face getting hotter. *What should I do?* 'Yes!' she said too loudly, forcing herself to answer before he changed his mind. 'I love Elvis.'

***

Six months later, Barbara paced back and to from the window, expecting to see Conor walk up the path in his checked shirt and jeans with a bundle of LPs under his arm, but he didn't come. She looked through the records he'd bought her, touching each one. They played them on the Dansette she'd got for her fourteenth birthday, filling the living room with the music of Buddy Holly and Elvis, forcing her father to sit in the garden and her mother to stay in the kitchen. She remembered the cool autumn evening when they sat on a bench in the park, leaves scattering in the breeze around their feet, and Conor telling her that he loved her and that when she was sixteen they'd get married.

Conor didn't take advantage of her youth: he made her feel secure. She never thought about her adoption while she was with him. If he knew she was adopted, he never mentioned it. Her mother had said she'd been better behaved since she'd met him. He was all she could think about. *Where are you, Conor?*

She forced herself to sit down and pretended to watch TV, her eyes blank, the screen a blur. They didn't have a phone, so there was no way of contacting him.

When he didn't arrive the next night, Barbara panicked. So did her mother. 'I'll go and see our Lucy. Find out what's gone on,' she said.

Barbara agonised about what had happened. *Had he gone back to Moira?* Rita had said that Moira was an old tart with crooked teeth and that he'd never go back to her. *But how did she know?*

When her mother returned, she hung up her hat, scarf and coat and sank into her armchair by the fire. Barbara stood over her waiting for an explanation. Her mother frowned. 'I'm sorry, love.'

'Why?' Barbara demanded. 'Is Conor all right? Has he gone back to Moira?'

'No. It's you he likes, there's no question about that.'

'Where is he then?'

Her mother took a deep breath. 'I met Lucy in the café and she told me that Conor's family are Protestants. He'd never told his mother that he was courting a Catholic, because she hates Catholics and that's what it's all about.'

'Oh! So, that's why he never took me to his house or introduced me to his parents.' She thought of the gangs of lads who hung around the playing fields after school, throwing stones and calling each other 'prodidogs' or 'catlics'. Her mother and father had never taught her to hate and she found it hard to understand.

Her mother's eyes were heavy. 'She locked up his trousers, so he couldn't come out that night, and then the next day she told him that if he ever saw you again, she wouldn't let him back in the house.'

'Poor Conor.' Barbara's legs gave way and she flopped down in a chair opposite her mother, Conor's handsome face, no longer smiling, set in her mind.

'He'd have a hard time going against his mother. She's a big bully of a woman,' Barbara's mother said, staring into the fire. 'She went to the Regal shouting abuse and blaming Lucy because she brought you and Conor together. She threatened Lucy with all kinds.'

Enflamed by the heat of the fire, Barbara's face burned. 'Our Jimmy married a non-Catholic. But you didn't lock up his clothes, did you?'

'No.' Her mother slowly shook her head. 'But Jean turned Catholic so she could marry Jimmy, and she's kept the faith.'

'Does Conor's mam want me to become a Protestant? Well, I'm not!'

'She hates all Catholics, and she doesn't want Conor marrying a Catholic because he'd have to promise to bring his children up in the Catholic faith.'

'Why does she hate Catholics so much anyway?'

'You'll be too young to remember the Orangemen, but there were always fights between them and us Catholics. They used to march every year down West Bank, wearing orange sashes, waving their banners and provoking our lads. Conor's family's from Northern Ireland, where all the Troubles began. It's murder over there. They kill each other, and if the IRA …'

'Who're the IRA?'

'The Irish Republican Army – the Catholic fighters.'

'Why are they fighting?'

'For the rights of the Catholics who are treated badly by the Protestants. They can't get houses or jobs. The two sides hate each other. If the IRA find out that a Catholic woman's gone out with a Protestant man or collaborated with them in any way, they shave her hair, and then pour hot tar down her back and stick feathers in it, so everyone knows she's a traitor.'

Barbara shivered, imagining hot tar burning her skin. 'God should stop it! He can do anything! Jesus said to love thy neighbour and to forgive people.'

'They're bitter. They don't think like that.'

'If that's what religion makes people do, I don't want to be religious.' She broke down, unable to stop the tears. 'I want to see Conor.'

'Don't get upset,' her mother said, touching her arm. 'You'll find someone else, one of your own kind. You've got plenty of time, you're only young.'

Barbara didn't want anyone else and she blamed God for her misery. Before the break-up with Conor, she'd attended Mass, Holy Communion and Confession every week. A true believer, she felt special being a Catholic: one of God's chosen people. Now, it all seemed pointless. No use praying to a God who allows people to hate and kill each other in His name. She began to doubt His existence.

Without the distraction of Conor, the emptiness returned and the antagonism she felt towards her parents resurfaced. She resented them and their religion. On Sunday mornings, she'd refuse to go to church and lay in bed shouting, 'There is no God!' Her mother and father never preached hell, fire and damnation, but she knew she was damned by the expression in her father's eyes.

Chapter 7

Growing up in the Sixties

Florrie

'I'm *not going* to work in a shop!' Barbara stood glaring at Florrie, who was sewing a button on Jim's shirt. 'I got distinctions in Art, History and Maths, and I've been accepted on a secretarial course at the Tech, so that's what I'm going to do.'

'That means another year at school,' Florrie said, without looking up. 'You'll get fed up with it.'

'No, I won't! You're not making me go out to work like you did with the others. I know it was you who stopped Jimmy and Lily from going to the grammar, and Joseph from art school when his headmaster said he was a gifted artist.'

Florrie gave Barbara a hard stare. '*They* would never have spoken to me in that way. I don't know where *you* came from!'

Barbara bounced out of the room and ran upstairs. Florrie stopped sewing, and remembered opening the brown envelope with Lily's exam results: she'd passed the 11+.

'Girls don't need an education,' she'd said to Jim. 'They have to give up work when they have kids. I gave up work as soon as I married you, so I could have your dinner ready and on the table when you came home, and you were glad that I did. It's what you expected.'

Jim nodded. 'Does she want to go?'

'She won't want to go. As long as she can read, write and add up, she'll get by. Grammar schools! They're not for the likes of us. They're for rich kids whose parents can afford to pay for uniforms and satchels.'

Thud, thud on the stairs. Barbara banged the door open, disturbing Florrie's thoughts.

'No matter what you say, I'm going to the Tech. I'll leave home. I'll go and live with Lily. She'll let me go.'

'Lily knew her place,' Florrie muttered to herself. *You're a hard, determined little beggar.* 'Who do you think you are? Secretarial courses indeed!'

'I'm me, and I'm starting college in September no matter what you say.'

Barbara

In the typing room, Barbara stared at a replica of a keyboard hung on the wall, and tapped away at the blank keys on her typewriter. Miss Fitzgerald pulled her knitted cardigan tight round her ample back, adjusted her horn-rimmed glasses and stared round the room, an uneasy look in her eyes. Barbara took her eyes away from the wall and her hand from the keyboard to yawn. Bang! Miss Fitzgerald struck her desk with the board duster. 'Tired, are we?' Barbara flinched.

A loud giggle came from a girl sat behind Barbara. The board duster whizzed past Barbara's ear, hit the girl on the shoulder and landed on the floor. 'That hurt!' the girl screamed, and held her arm. Miss Fitzgerald ignored her and walked slowly down the aisle to pick up her duster: the girls sat rigid, clicking at their keyboards.

Later that day, Barbara sat in Miss Fitzgerald's office, staring at the shocking pink nail polish she'd applied at break time.

Miss Fitzgerald coughed and forced a smile. Barbara looked up. 'You've passed your 120 words per minute shorthand test.' She handed Barbara the results slip.

'Oh, thanks.' Barbara examined the slip, smiling to herself. 'I like shorthand. It's like learning another language.' The mysterious squiggles that she scrawled across her notebook were like a secret code only she could translate. It gave her a buzz.

'But ...' Miss Fitzgerald frowned and fiddled with her

pince-nez. '… I wish I could say the same about your typing. You need to get your speed up to forty words per minute before the end of term or you'll not get a job.'

'I know.' Barbara pursed her lips and stared again at her nails. 'I'll get it next time.'

Barbara met Sheila in the corridor after class. 'It's all boring, especially Commerce, and I die in the Bookkeeping class.'

'But we're going to be secretaries. Don't you like any of it?'

'I like the Art class.'

'That's not going to get you a job.'

'No.' She'd got the school prize for Art and dreamed of being an artist, but after she'd argued so hard to get on the Commercial course, she couldn't admit her disappointment to her mother.

Outside, Sheila pointed to a figure standing at the gate. 'Look, there's Ella. I wonder if she's got them?'

'Hope so,' Barbara said. On the way to town, they stopped to pick Rita up from Nancy's hairdressers, where she was apprenticed.

'Have you got them?' Rita asked Ella, pulling on her coat.

'Course I have,' Ella replied, rummaging in her vanity case and pulling out a packet of Senior Service.

Barbara stared at the white packet with a sailing ship circled in a blue wreath, much more glamorous than the Woodbine packets her brothers left lying around. She was fifteen and underage, but everyone at college smoked.

'I know where you've been,' her mother said, when Barbara came home, 'for a smoking session in the park.'

'No, I haven't.'

She grabbed Barbara's right hand and waved it in her face. 'Do you think I'm blind? I can see your fingertips stained yellow and I can smell the smoke on your clothes. It's disgusting. College! Ha! All you're interested in is boys and smoking!'

Barbara pulled her hand away and buried it in her coat pocket. *How dare she grab my hand.* Her mother never usually touched her, in anger or affection.

'Lily never started smoking. It's just what I'd expect from you! Where do you get the money from?'

'Pocket money.'

'Well, I'll tell your dad and you won't be getting any more.'

'I'm going to my room.' *Why is Mam so mean? I hate her!*

'Give me the cigarettes you have in your bag.'

'No! You let Jimmy and Joseph smoke all the time when they were at home.' Barbara stared at her mother, defiant.

'They're men. Only common women smoke. I don't know what that one who had you was like! Common as muck, I'll bet!'

Here we go again! How do you know whether she was common or not? Just because she had a baby before she was married. Hot with anger, Barbara shouted, 'I'm not common! Don't say that! Everyone smokes and you can't stop me!' Barbara pushed past her mother and ran upstairs. *Perhaps I am bad, like my real mother.*

***

Sitting next to Barbara on the bus, Sheila combed the fringe of her short brown hair down to rest on her thick dark eyelashes. 'We were lucky to get tickets.'

They'd seen a poster at college advertising the three dances: two in September, one in October. It was the first time Barbara had been to a dance and she sat erect, fingering the tickets they'd queued for hours to get. 'I heard "Love Me Do" on the radio yesterday. It's out next month. It's fab.'

As the bus pulled up outside the Queen's Hall, Sheila wiped a circle with her palm in the steam dripping down the window. She nudged Barbara. 'Look at the crowds!'

'Wow!'

They stood in the queue that wound down Lacey Street and listened to the excited chatter of teenagers eager to get inside.

Outside the cloakroom, Barbara spotted a photo stuck on the wall by the door.

John, Paul, George and Ringo was written in biro. She stared at the grinning faces. 'I like John.'

'Paul's the best-looking. He's my favourite,' Sheila said.

'Come on! Let's go in.'

They made their way along the corridor, past the refreshment stand, hardly speaking to each other. The air hummed with the sound of girls laughing and talking.

At the ballroom door, Barbara stopped, blinked her eyes and looked around the enormous dance floor, startled at the number of people standing in groups, mostly girls. 'Love Me Do' blasted from speakers on the walls at the side of the stage. She looked at Sheila, grabbed her hand and they walked across the polished wooden floor, glad to take refuge on chairs that leaned against the wall, where the lights were low.

Lily had said the Queen's Hall lacked atmosphere because the ceiling was too high and the lights too bright. It didn't matter that night: raised voices and eager young bodies filled every inch of space. Bright lights shone on expectant faces, and eyes darted to and from the stage. The lights dimmed and Barbara put her hand to her mouth. *What's going to happen?*

'Let's give a warm welcome to our supporting group Rory Storm and the Hurricanes,' the compère announced. Loud cheers and claps came from the crowd. Someone close by said Ringo used to be their drummer.

'Should we jive?' Barbara asked Sheila, hoping she'd say no.

'If you *really* want to.' Sheila looked terrified.

'Yes, come on.' Barbara took a deep breath. *I want to feel part of this.* She smoothed down the flared skirt of her rayon dress, took Sheila's hand and they edged towards the dance floor. Caught up in the music, she forgot about the boys they were there to impress and danced wildly, her heart beating in harmony with the throbbing music, until the group stopped playing.

The microphone crackled. 'The Beatles will be appearing in ten minutes.' Noise and tension increased, spreading through the crowd on a wave. Boys leaning casually against the back wall stirred; others hurried from the refreshment room onto the dance floor. Everyone moved towards the stage, leaving the back of the hall empty. Barbara and Sheila squeezed in and wriggled their way to the centre, through tightly packed bodies. Barbara, taller than Sheila, could just about see the stage. Infected with the thrill and anticipation all around her, she grinned at Sheila, who was standing on her tiptoes. 'We made it!'

The curtains opened and Barbara saw George hurriedly stubbing a cigarette out before John shouted '1-2-3-4,' and started the mournful harmonica introduction to 'Love Me Do'. Screams! Shouts! Cheers! Claps! Handsome in long-sleeved white shirts, thin black ties and waistcoats, the Beatles shook their mop heads as they sang. Dark hair, soft and floppy, moved with the rhythm.

'Oh God!' Barbara yelled. 'This is amazing! They're fab!'

No one danced. All around them, girls screamed and jumped up and down, waving their hands and shouting.

'Paul!'

'George!'

'Ringo!'

Barbara and Sheila joined in, screaming until their voices became hoarse. When John sang 'Money (That's What I Want)', the screams and shouts of the crowd reached the ceiling. Every beat of the amplified music sent vibrations through Barbara's body and she wanted it to last forever. Every time the Beatles said it was their last song, the crowd shouted for more: the intoxicating sound lingered long after they left the stage.

Pushing her way out through the crowded door, red-faced and sweating, the cool night air made Barbara shiver and she quickly put on her coat. Frenzied fans overflowed onto the pavement singing Beatles songs, their voices echoing down Lacey Street. Barbara and Sheila queued at the bus stop, watching tearful girls pull at their hair and moan, 'I love you, John.'

'I want to marry George.'

'Ringo's so cute.'

'Can't wait to see them next Monday,' Sheila said.

'And the week after.'

***

'There's a dance at the Columba Hall on Saturday night, and we're all going to go.'

'What should I wear?' Barbara asked Lily.

'You can't go to the Columba in any of these clothes,' Lily said, thumbing through Barbara's wardrobe. 'They're all too childish. But I've got a really nice pattern. I'll get some material from the market and make you a dress.'

'Aw, thanks!' *What a great sister.* 'What's the Columba like?'

'Different from the Queen's Hall.' Lily laughed. 'You won't see the Beatles there. It's mostly local groups. It's a bit of a dive but you'll be OK.'

Before the dance, Barbara pranced round the living room, glancing in the mirror, thinking how cool she looked in the dark blue wool dress with its tight-fitting bodice and pencil slim skirt.

'Now for the hair!' Lily set Barbara's hair in large rollers. When it was dry, she tried to backcomb it into a beehive, but the virgin hair – soft and floppy – would only stay up with the help of a can of glue-like lacquer.

Barbara stared into the mirror, amazed at the three-inch bump on the top of her head. 'Thanks. It looks fab!' Her eyes, dark with mascara, stood out against her face and lips, pale with pan stick foundation. 'Wow!' she said. 'I look so much older.' She heard her mother on the landing. *She won't like it.*

Her mother looked her up and down, and frowned at Lily. 'This is your fault.'

'She's *sixteen* in June.'

'You're not going out looking like that,' her mother said.

'Yes, I am,' Barbara said, grinning.

Unlike the Queen's Hall, the Columba was dark, muggy with sweat, cheap scent and cigarette smoke; and so packed with bodies that Barbara had to feel her way around, beneath the low ceiling. The boys were older and some of them smelt of beer. She watched the black shadowy figures jiving on the dance floor to Sonny Kaye and the Reds, longing to join them.

'Wish we could go to the pub,' Ella said, as they searched for somewhere to sit. 'We're too young. They won't serve us.' Sheila pointed to four empty seats

along the wall by the toilet, where the girls lit up.

'Guess what I've got?' Rita slowly unzipped her bag and uncovered a Vimto bottle surrounded by tissues and make-up.

'Is it gin?' Barbara asked, remembering sneaking Pop's gin on sleepovers at Rita's.

'No, it's Pop's Elderberry wine.'

They squeezed into a cubicle in the ladies' toilets and Rita passed the bottle to Barbara, who took a long swig before she handed it to Sheila.

'Ugh! It's bitter.' Sheila screwed up her nose.

'That doesn't matter!' Ella grabbed the bottle. 'It makes you happy!'

Flushed and giddy, Barbara took to the dance floor, where the girls danced round their handbags. A tall boy with slicked-back hair tapped her on the shoulder and asked her to dance. She owned the dance floor and couldn't stop smiling, wiggling her hips beneath the tight-fitting skirt, making it ride up above her knees nearly to her stocking tops. The boy came back at the end of the evening, when the tempo slowed down and they shuffled round the room. He pulled her close and she could feel his body stiffen as he pressed against her. 'Can I take you home?'

At the back door of her house, he kissed her hard on the lips, unbuttoned her coat and slipped his hand onto her breast. *This is what Lily warned me about*, she thought, excited and alarmed by the power she suddenly had over men. 'Get lost!' She pushed his hand away and he sloped off down the path.

'See you around.'

***

'There's a letter for you!' her mother shouted.

Still in her dressing gown, Barbara rushed downstairs and

grabbed the letter, tearing it open. 'I've got an interview for a job as office junior at a wine merchant in Liverpool.'

'Your brothers and sister were happy enough working in Widnes. Why do *you* want to work in Liverpool?'

'The music scene! The Cavern! The Beatles! Ever heard of them? *How can she be so stupid?* 'It's only twelve miles from Widnes and it's the *only* place on earth that I want to work.'

Her mother frowned and scratched her head. 'You'll have to pay train fares.'

'They might offer to pay something towards them.'

'You'll get into trouble down there with all those scousers.'

Barbara sighed. *Why does Mam have to make me feel bad about everything I do?* 'They speak differently to us, but they're the same as anyone else, except they live in the incredible city of Liverpool. I'm going for the interview. It's next week.'

Barbara boarded the steam train at Widnes North, squeezed into an empty seat and re-read the letter. Dizzy with excitement, she got off at Central Station.

She walked up Bold Street, and stopped to stare at the outfits in Jaeger and the posh boutiques, wishing she could afford to buy the collarless suits with box jackets and pencil slim skirts or the elegant shift dresses. The smell of coffee from the Kardomah coffee shop drifted down the street. Her interview was at 2 p.m. She checked her watch – it was 12.30 p.m. – and went inside.

Sat in a corner, she sipped her coffee and watched two businessmen chatting to a young waitress who lingered too long at their table. University students with rucksacks read books while they drank their coffee. She sighed. *I've got to get this job. I've got to be part of this scene, so different from boring old Widnes. Even the coffee tastes better.*

She hesitated outside the huge Victorian red-brick building in Dale Street, breathing deeply to stop herself from shaking, before she rang the bell.

A woman with ash blonde hair and a perfect smile invited her in and shook her hand. 'I'm Valerie, Mr Sanderson's secretary.

If you get the job, you'll share my office.' She pointed to a small desk at the far end of the room. 'And you'll report to me. Come through here and I'll give you a shorthand and typing test.'

Barbara managed to smile, in spite of Valerie's abruptness. Her hands shook as she fed the paper into the typewriter and her eyes blurred as she tried to decipher the squiggles she'd written on the notepad. *Please God don't let me fluff it!*

She'd just finished the test when Mr Sanderson put his head around the door. 'How's it going?'

'All done.' Valerie gave him a wide smile and handed him the typed letter.

'Come through to my office, Barbara, sit down.' He scanned the page. 'Looks good. Just one error, and we'll put that down to nerves.'

Thank God! Barbara smiled.

Tall, broad, with dark hair greying at the temples and a smile that lifted his blue eyes, Mr Sanderson made her relax. 'You're the last one we've seen, and I'm giving *you* the job.'

His stare bore into her. 'Thank you.' Barbara grinned, and thought how blue his eyes were.

'I'll show you the cellars and introduce you to the staff who clean, sort and label the wine.' She followed him down the stone steps and stopped, startled at the dark cavernous cellars, crammed with huge oak barrels, shelves of bottled wine, crates of empty wine bottles, labels and machinery. It smelt damp and musty, and the cold made her shiver. Mr Sanderson put his arm around her shoulder and gave it a rub. She felt uncomfortable and moved away as soon as she could, but afraid of upsetting him, she continued to smile.

'Patrick! Agnes!' he shouted loudly, making her jump. To her relief, a boy and girl wearing plastic aprons appeared beneath the stone arches like trolls from under a bridge. Patrick was tall, with thick black hair and dingy teeth, Agnes short and plain, with mousy, lank hair tied back off her face. They were friendly, especially the boy, who eyed her up and down.

They're all a bit strange, especially their accents. So what! I've got my first job in Liverpool!

A few weeks after she'd started work, Barbara was walking down Dale Street when she heard footsteps close behind her. Someone tapped her on the shoulder and she turned abruptly. 'Idiot!'

'Hello, tatty head!' Like his hero, John Lennon, Patrick called everyone tatty head. 'Sorry! Fancy coming to a lunchtime session at the Cavern on Friday?'

Barbara hesitated. 'With you?'

'No.' Patrick glanced down at his black Beatle boots. 'Me and Agnes.'

'OK.' Barbara was desperate to go to the Cavern but she didn't fancy Patrick and would have felt guilty rejecting him.

'Faron's Flamingos are on.'

'Fab!'

When she got home, in her excitement she told her mother, who frowned. 'Lunchtime sessions indeed! I've never heard of such a thing. You'll lose your job!'

Why doesn't Mam understand?

Chapter 8

The Cavern

At the top of Church Street, they hopped on a bus to Mathew Street. Barbara stared out of the window at the bustling city traffic. *How lucky am I!*

Agnes sat next to her. 'You'll love it!'

'It's fab!' Patrick held onto the strap and grinned down at them, swaying with the motion of the bus.

As they hurried down the steep stone steps to the Cavern, the noise of the group rose up to greet Barbara. 'What's that smell?' she asked.

'It's the rotting fruit from the warehouses,' Patrick said, rolling his eyes at the ceiling.

'And the disinfectant they use to clean the place with,' Agnes said. 'You don't notice it after a while.'

At the bottom of the stairs, she struggled to hear the cloakroom attendant ask for the 1s/3d entrance fee. Yelling over the sound of the guitars and maracas, she handed over the coins.

She scanned the room. It looked just like the cellars at work, but the heat hit her in the face and she started to sweat. Cigarette smoke hung in the air, creating a grey cloud. Moisture from body heat glistened in the dim light and trickled down the walls. Barbara looked down at the hard stone floor where puddles had formed, dampening the white slingback shoes she'd bought from C&A with her first week's wages.

'Damn! Mam will go mad if I ruin these shoes.' She wrinkled her damp toes.

Rows of what looked like dining-room chairs were placed in

front of the stage. 'You two sit down and I'll get some cokes!' Patrick yelled. 'They sell burgers in the café at the back. Do you want one?'

'No! I'm too excited to eat,' Barbara said.

'Get me one, la.' Agnes gave him coins. 'The chairs are all taken. Let's dance,' she said. 'Do you know the Cavern Stomp?' Barbara shook her head. 'You just stand in one place, swinging your arms and legs like this.' Agnes took Barbara's right hand in hers and flung her free left arm out to the side, at the same time her legs kicked out to the left and the right. Barbara copied, her eyes shining, hair damp with sweat, stomping until Patrick returned with the cokes.

'The queue was so long, I ate my burger.' He handed Barbara a coke and Agnes a soggy bun, oozing tomato ketchup. He looked at his watch. 'Our lunch break's nearly over, even with the extra half-hour Mr Sanderson *kindly* said we could take. We'll cop it if we don't leave now.' When they got their coats, Agnes dragged Barbara by the arm and they fought their way up the stone steps.

'Come on, tatty head!' Patrick shouted from the top stair. Outside the air was cool on Barbara's flushed face, and they hurried to get the bus back to work.

'Valerie'll tell on us if we're late,' Agnes said. 'She thinks she's somebody, but she's dead antwacky.' Agnes called anyone or anything she thought was outdated antwacky.

'And she's having it off with the old man,' Patrick said.

'Yes! Mind you, don't catch them at it!'

Barbara had seen the way the boss looked at Valerie, and sometimes he looked at her like that, too. 'Last week, I put my hair up and Mr Sanderson stared at me and said it made me look older. Valerie was extra mean to me when he'd gone, and made me wash the cups twice cos she said they weren't clean.'

'Miserable cow!' Patrick said. 'You wanna watch him. He might be getting fed up with old Val.'

'He's too old for me!'

They ran up Dale Street as though they were being chased.

Patrick and Agnes disappeared down the cellars, like rats through a trapdoor. 'Good luck with tatty head,' Patrick said under his breath.

Barbara pushed the heavy wooden door open as quietly as she could. It creaked.

A chair moved. Valerie jumped up. 'You're late!' Her brow wrinkled into a deep crevice.

Barbara wanted to say *What about the two-and three-hour lunches you have with Mr Sanderson?* but she didn't want to lose her job. She stared at the floor. 'Sorry, we missed the bus.'

Valerie made her stand at the far end of the office filing invoices, a job she hated. She peeped across at Valerie. *She is ant-wacky with her bouffant hairstyle. I'd hate to be twenty-one. You're welcome to old Mr Sanderson.*

On the train home, Barbara picked up an *Echo* someone had left on her seat and thumbed through the pages reading bits of news. The Beatles had made Liverpool famous. People were coming from all over the world to listen to the groups, and while they were in Liverpool they shopped in the boutiques, and ate and drank in the restaurants and pubs. That was the Liverpool she felt part of.

Most lunchtimes, she wandered round the city, feeling the buzz, the energy and the optimism that seemed to flow through the air on the fresh breeze that came up from the river. Boys in the city copied the Beatles 'moptop' hairstyle: girls had stopped backcombing and wore their hair in a natural style. Herbert's was the place to have your hair done, but Barbara couldn't afford it. Lily cut her dark shoulder-length hair into a sort of bobbed style that was fashionable, smooth but not very even.

***

Barbara first met Monica on the platform while waiting for the early morning train to Liverpool. Monica's hair, jet black and styled in a perfect bob, shone in the morning sun through the clouds of steam belching from the train engine. They boarded the hissing train and sidled along the corridors until they found an empty carriage, where they lit up Embassy No 6 cigarettes and prattled on undisturbed.

Tall and slim, Monica worked on the make-up counter at George Henry Lees down Church Street. Being a shy person, Barbara was attracted to Monica's self-assurance and they became best friends. She was two years older than Barbara, and she'd introduced her to all the trendy clubs in Liverpool and Manchester. 'Mam's moaning about me going out too much. I think she hates me,' Barbara said.

'No she doesn't,' Monica said. 'She's probably just worried about you.'

'You don't know the nasty things she says.' Barbara stared out of the train window. She'd never told Monica that she was adopted.

'This'll cheer you up,' Monica said, grinning. 'It's the Beatles' last gig at the Cavern. They've got so big now, the Cavern can't hold the fans. I'm a member! I can get tickets! They're going on sale on 21 July, so we'll have to be quick. Do you want to go?'

'Are you kidding? Of course I want to go.'

'It's 9s/6d, a lot of cash. Can you afford it?'

'No, I can't! I only earn three pounds and ten shillings a week, and I have to pay my train fares out of that.'

'Can't you borrow it?'

'Maybe my dad will lend it to me,' Barbara said, 'I'll ask him tonight.'

***

Good old Dad! Barbara thought. He'd muttered and grumbled about Liverpool, but he'd given her the entrance fee and he didn't even say she had to pay it back.

They pushed through the crowd in the Grapes, a pub close to the Cavern. Monica, who was old enough to drink alcohol, went to the bar while Barbara's eyes darted round the room looking for a space to hide. She'd memorised a false date of birth in case there was a police raid. Someone moved from a corner seat and she quickly moved into it.

Monica placed two bottles on the beer-stained table and two glasses on the soggy beer mats. 'It's black velvet, Guinness and cider mixed.' She poured the cider into the glasses, topping it up with Guinness, creating a frothy head, without losing a drop. *She's good at everything.* After a few long gulps, Barbara's nervousness evaporated. It was August. The air in the pub was stifling, but the place throbbed with a happy vibe, everyone laughing and talking about the Beatles.

Outside the Cavern, they stood near the end of the queue. 'They'll never let this lot in,' Barbara said. *I'll owe Dad ten shillings for nothing.*

'They'll have to, if they have tickets. It holds 500,' Monica said.

'God help us if there's a fire.'

Barbara stumbled down the steps and Monica grabbed her arm. Was it the heat, the frenzied fans inside the Cavern, or the black velvet she'd drunk so quickly in the pub? Packed more tightly than at lunchtime, the crowd was too thick to penetrate, heaving with bodies, damp and sweaty. She held onto Monica's arm as they edged their way around the cellar, the soaking walls dampening the back of her cotton shift dress. Monica manoeuvred into a space by the side wall, where they listened to the Merseybeats, one of the supporting groups.

On her tiptoes above the rows of heads bobbing up and down, Barbara could barely see the Beatles when they got onto the stage. She waved her hands in the air, her shouts buried in the deafening roar from the crowd. John tapped the microphone and everyone went quiet. 'OK, tatty head, we're going to play a number for you,' John said, and the screams and shouts got louder.

The lights went out. 'Oh God!' Barbara clung to Monica. The crowd groaned.

'It's the damp, it's fused the amps,' someone announced. 'Don't panic, they'll soon be back on.'

The mutters and moans got louder. Barbara gripped tighter. *Oh no! It's too hot and crowded, and dark.*

'John and Paul are going to sing with acoustic guitars!' someone yelled. The room breathed a deep sigh of relief and everyone clapped. Barbara relaxed her grip on Monica's arm, closed her eyes and listened, awestruck, to the words of 'When I'm Sixty-Four.'

She squeezed her eyes shut. *I'll wake up soon and it'll all have been a dream.*

The lights flashed back on and the spellbound crowd went wild again as John and Paul belted out 'Some Other Guy'. The heat, sweat, smell and discomfort were gone, the stage a distant blur; she was part of the sound, the energy and the vibe.

John sang 'Twist and Shout' to roars from the crowd. It ended suddenly and they were gone. Cries. Shouts. Moans. As though they'd lost something, everyone was sad. 'That's it,' someone said, 'they'll never come back.'

With smudged mascara and bedraggled hair, they clamoured for the last train back to Widnes, packed with teenagers from Warrington and Manchester.

When Barbara got home, her mother stood at the top of the stairs in her long flannel nightgown. 'What time do you call this?'

'I told you I'd be late.' Barbara sighed. 'It was the Beatles' last gig at the Cavern.'

'Your dad should never have given you the money. I don't know what you get up to down Liverpool at night. I don't know why you behave like this, I really don't!' Her mother sounded sad and confused as well as angry.

'Why are you causing such a fuss? I've only been listening to a group.'

'You've been drinking! I can smell it! You're still underage.'

'Everyone drinks underage. No one bothers, except you.'

'I don't know what that one who had you was like!'

'Oh shut up!'

Barbara banged her room door shut and flopped onto her bed. Her mother's words mingled in her head with the sound of John singing 'Twist and Shout'.

***

'Valerie's sick. She won't be in today.' Mr Sanderson stepped forward and helped Barbara take off her coat.

What's got into him? He's not usually so gentlemanly and Valerie's never off work.

'Oh! I'm sorry. What's wrong with her?' Barbara asked, stepping away from him.

'Woman's troubles.' He leered.

'Oh!' Barbara blushed and looked away. 'I'll make the coffee.' From the kitchen, she was relieved to hear noise coming up from the cellar: Patrick and Agnes were busy at their work. She placed the coffee on Mr Sanderson's desk. 'I've got loads of invoices to type. I best get started,' she said, quickly leaving his office.

He was busy with phone calls all morning, so she didn't see him. After she ate her sandwiches, she wandered round Liverpool glancing in shop windows, rather disturbed. He was always leaning over her desk when Valerie wasn't looking, breathing down her neck. Perhaps Patrick was right and he intended moving on to her. Thinking of it, she got a tingle in her stomach. *That'd be one in the eye for Valerie.*

Stood in the kitchen making afternoon tea, he came up behind her and put his hand on her shoulder. She looked round and flinched. 'Why don't you have your tea in my office. I've got some Cadbury's chocolate biscuits stashed away, but don't tell Valerie.' He winked and put his finger to his mouth. She was overcome with a strange excitement: flattered that he was interested in her.

There was a sofa at the far end of his office. Patrick joked it was where Mr Sanderson and Valerie had sex. 'Come and sit here with me.' He patted the cushion next to him, as she carried in the tea tray.

Compelled to do what he said, she sat as far away as she could, nervously gulping down her tea. As he opened the biscuits, he moved closer, his thigh pressing against hers. She took one, but it stuck in her throat. Coughing, she shook, slopping the tea on the front of her blouse.

'I'm sorry.'

He moved closer and patted her back. She forced herself to cough more violently. 'I'll get you a glass of water from the kitchen.'

Part of her was enjoying the attention, another part of her was repelled. *What's he up to? Should I make a run for it? I'll lose my job. But I love working in Liverpool. He can't do anything with Patrick and Agnes being downstairs, and the door isn't locked.*

'This'll clear your throat.' He handed her a glass of water. 'You're turning into a very beautiful woman, you know.' Fumbling in his pocket, he took out his handkerchief. 'You've wet your blouse,' he said, staring at her breasts.

'Have I?' She glanced down at the stain and snatched the handkerchief from his hand, dapping the front of her blouse as he watched.

'It's fine now.'

'It certainly is.'

Knock! Knock!

'Damn it! Hang on! Don't move!' Standing abruptly, he closed the door behind him. She heard Patrick's voice saying something about the barrel being ready. Silence. They must have gone to the cellar. She got up and went back to her desk, typing furiously until the clock said 5.30.

On the train home, Barbara dug in her bag for her cigarettes, offered one to Monica and told her about Mr Sanderson.

'You'll have to find another job.' Monica gave her a cheeky smile. 'Unless you fancy him. Is he handsome?'

'Yes, but he's too old.'

'He's bound to try it on again.'

'I know. I'm going to look for a job in Widnes. The fares are getting more expensive and I hate getting up so early for the train.'

***

On Saturday night, Barbara, slightly tipsy, hung onto Monica's arm as they left the New Inn and crossed the road to the Scala Ballroom in Runcorn, where a new circle of friends were waiting. They called themselves Mods and thought they were the in-crowd: exclusive and fashionable, they only danced with people in their group. Compared to her school friends, they were glamorous. The boys, as stylish as the girls, wore herringbone suits, paisley shirts and a layered haircut that framed their faces. She went with them to all-nighters at the Twisted Wheel in Manchester and parties where she listened to music until the early hours, creating more tension and distance between her and her mother.

'You're turning out just like *her*,' her mother said, when she got in.

Barbara lay in bed wondering if she would turn out just like *her*. Her mother was always quoting stories from the newspapers about the pill, teenage promiscuity and addiction, and she must have thought the worst of Barbara.

Purple hearts and pot were available in the coffee bars, but Barbara and Monica preferred alcohol and cigarettes.

Some of the girls she knew from the clubs were groupies. They scrambled into the back of vans or invited boys from groups back to their houses for sex. One girl bragged that she'd had sex through the keyhole in her dress with a member of a nearly famous group when they played in Runcorn. Fascinated, Barbara watched girls stand at the front of the stage and point to the group member they intended having sex with that night, sometimes arguing over who should have who. She wished she was reckless enough to act that way, just to spite her mother, but something stopped her. She didn't know what she wanted in life, but she knew it wasn't one-night stands. She could have reassured her mother: instead, she enjoyed her anguish.

***

Before going out to meet Monica, Barbara stood applying eyeliner in thick black strokes, in front of the same mirror where as a child, she'd watched her mother brush her hair.

Her mother stared over her shoulder. 'You're plain,' she said, her reflection in the glass mean, her mouth a hard, straight line.

Barbara flinched and the small black brush fell from her hand. They stared at each other through the impenetrable glass until Barbara bent down to pick up the brush and her mother moved away.

She was insecure about her appearance, always checking herself in the mirror, and her mother's words hurt her deeply. *I'm not plain. Why does she hate me? Is it because I'm not her real child?* Guilty, she blamed herself for being born – a naughty child who came from nowhere. She'd found an identity in fashion and music far removed from her parents. The more her mother criticised her clothes, hair and make-up, the shorter Barbara hitched her skirts and the thicker the black lines around her eyes became.

As she was leaving the house, her father looked up from his comic book with narrowed eyes. 'Them's cheeky eyes, they are. You're asking for trouble, you are. Mark my words.'

'You stupid old fool,' Barbara muttered to herself, and slammed the door behind her. Her breath quickened as she hurried to the bus stop. *He's getting as bad as Mam.* Lately, he looked at her oddly and it made her feel uncomfortable. *They both hate me now.*

***

'Bye!' Mam shouted, the following evening. 'I'm going to the bingo with Maggie.'

'Good luck.' Barbara sat at the square wooden table in the living room eating fish and chips while she watched *Ready Steady Go!* on the TV across the room. She stared at Cathy McGowan's long brown hair, dead straight, with a thick fringe that rested on her eyelashes. *I'd love hair like that!* 'The weekend starts here!' Cathy shouted, and the crowd cheered.

Without warning, her father got up from his armchair and switched the TV channel over to the BBC. Anger rose from Barbara's stomach, exploding in her chest. *How dare you! You old fool!* 'I was watching that!' She jumped up from her chair and ran at her father screaming, 'I hate you!' She thrust the knife she'd been eating with towards his face. He stiffened. As it scratched the surface of his cheek, he grabbed her arm and gripped her wrist tight to prevent it penetrating further. It hurt and she dropped the knife, but he held the grip and pulled her close, his face contorted, his eyes wild. *God no! He's going to kill me!*

His body sagged; the lines in his face softened and a tear formed in the corner of his eye. He released her arm, and the tear slipped from his eye, and mingled with a drop of blood seeping from the graze. He didn't shout: he looked at her as if he'd never seen her before. She couldn't bear the sadness in his eyes. She ran upstairs and cried alone, hating herself. *What have I become? A murderer? I could have killed my dad!*

Her body trembled as she lay on the bed, expecting shouts of anger, but there wasn't a sound. Disgusted with herself, she stood and looked out of the window at the sky, the blueness turning black, like the awful gloominess within her. She couldn't stop shaking. *How could I be so cruel to Dad, who'd always loved me?* Her heart banged in her chest and she wanted to be sick, but she couldn't go back downstairs. Sat back on the bed, she put her head in her hands. *I'm bad, like Mam's always saying. Where did she get me from?*

Her parents had never hit her and she'd never been violent before. *Why did I get so angry? Will Mam throw me out? Will they call the police and have me taken away to a home – back to where I came from, or even worse, put me in prison?* The house was quiet, and the tick of her alarm clock grew louder; she sat frozen, staring at the floral pattern on her carpet. Ten minutes – twenty minutes – an hour. A door rattled. Her mother was back. Muffled voices. A switch. The sudden burst of the television coming to life. *What's going on?*

Stood in front of her dresser mirror, she applied fresh make-up with shaking hands. *He must have told her. Why isn't Mam shouting? I'll leave before they throw me out!* Tense and ready to run from the house through the front door at the bottom of the stairs, she crept carefully down each step, clinging to the banister.

'Hello!' her mother shouted from the living room. Barbara jumped. 'What you doing hanging about on the stairs?'

'I'm on my way down.' She peeped round the door and saw her mother sat opposite her father watching TV.

'I won £10 at the bingo.' Her mother looked pleased. 'Well, it was £20 but me and Maggie share. Here, you can have a couple of bob.'

'Thanks.' Barbara took five shillings from her mother, slipped it in her purse and looked from one to the other dazed. Her father never turned his head. *What must he have told her about the scratch on his face?*

'I put those fish and chips you left in the oven. They're still warm.'

'I don't want it now, thanks. I'm going out with Monica. I won't be too late.' Barbara took a long deep breath and grabbed her coat. *He mustn't have told her.*

Chapter 9
Hitching a Ride

'I'm skint,' Barbara said to Helen, a friend she'd made at the Scala. 'How are we going to get to Chester?'

'We'll hitch a lift,' Helen said. 'It's not dark yet. We'll stand near the approach to the bridge.'

'But there's always a gang of us.' Barbara missed Monica, who she'd had an argument with.

'We'll be fine.'

It was late September and there was a slight chill in the air: they wore denim jackets over their mini dresses. Stood on a grass verge, they watched cars whizz by.

'You've got the shortest skirt, you hitch.' Barbara nudged Helen to the edge of the kerb. Helen stuck her leg out and waved her thumb. Her long auburn curls blew wildly in the strong wind wafting up from under the bridge.

A shiny black car pulled up sharply. 'Where you going?' Helen asked the driver, a man in his early forties with dark, slicked-back hair.

'Anywhere you want, gorgeous,' he said, in a posh voice, looking them up and down.

'Chester,' Barbara said. 'We're going to Quaintways?'

'Sure. I'm going that way.' He jumped out of his car and opened the back door for Helen, bowing mockingly as she got in.

Barbara attempted to follow Helen, but the man stood in front of her and shut the door.

He nodded towards the front seat, grinning. 'I need some company. The price of your lift.' *Oh no! I'll have to talk to him.*

He clicked the door shut behind her and she sank into the plush leather seat. Sat beside her, she noticed his crumpled suit and open-necked shirt.

She looked round at Helen and rolled her eyes. They'd had lifts in loads of cars, but there was something about this man. He was creepy and too anxious to please.

He asked their names. 'I'm Johnny, and I'm *very* pleased to meet such cracking-looking girls.'

Creep! Barbara turned her head abruptly and looked out of the window at the darkening sky. Although it was warm in the car, she shivered.

'Who's on at Quaintways?' He took his eyes off the road and stared at her.

'The Undertakers.'

'Are you groupies?' He lightly touched Barbara's knee.

She flinched. 'No!'

'Bet you are.'

'Well, we're not.' Barbara locked her knees together and moved her legs towards the door. *Weirdo! I need a fag.* 'Mind if we smoke?'

'Go ahead.'

'Do you want one?'

'No bad habits.' She could feel his eyes on her.

'I'll have one.' Helen leaned over the back seat.

Barbara lit two cigarettes, turning and handing one to Helen.

The man suddenly made a sharp turn off the A56 and accelerated down a country lane. *Where's he taking us?* Slowing down, he leaned towards Barbara and put his hand back on her knee.

'Please stop the car!' Barbara shoved his hand away.

'What's the matter with you?' He sounded surprised. 'We're not there yet.'

'This isn't the right way!' Helen shouted.

'We should get out!'

'No, you shouldn't.' He started massaging Barbara's thigh, moving his hand higher up her leg. 'This is a different way.'

Oh God! I'm going to be raped! 'Will you please stop that.'

'What's up? I'm sure you girls knew the score wearing miniskirts up to your backsides, hitching lifts. You're asking for it.'

Her mother's words came to mind but Barbara didn't want her to be right.

Helen rested her elbows on the black leather upholstery, her face red and creased with anger. 'We're not groupies and will you stop whatever you're doing to my friend?'

'Do you want to come in the front and join us, ginger?' he sneered.

'He keeps touching my leg.'

'Stop the car, you perv! Stop the car!' Helen thumped his shoulders with her fists.

'Hey! Take it easy. I just want a bit of affection.' He laughed and put his free arm under Barbara's arm, his fingertips touching her breast. Barbara tried to shove him away but he was broad-shouldered and kept his arm locked around her.

'Keep your eyes on the road. Get off me! You're going to crash the car!'

'Aghh!!!' Releasing Barbara from his grip, his hand shot to his neck. 'You bitch!' The car veered off the road onto a grass verge and jolted to a stop. 'She's stubbed her bloody fag into my neck!' he shouted, looking round at Helen. 'You bloody bitch!'

'Get out, quick!' Helen yelled, and jumped out as he turned off the ignition.

Barbara rattled the door handle but it wouldn't open. She banged on the windowpane. 'I can't get out!'

'He's locked the doors!' Helen shouted. 'Pull the button up.'

Barbara struggled with the button: like a trapped animal, her heart pumped blood to her muscles. *God, he's going to drive off with me!* Finally releasing the catch, she jumped and landed on the damp grass as he pulled away.

'Come on.' Helen grabbed her hand. 'Quick, let's run.'

'Bloody little whores.' He spat at them through the window and drove off in a cloud of exhaust fumes, leaving them on the deserted road, their nervous chatter filling the silence.

They walked as quickly as they could, the heels of their shoes sinking into the soil. 'There's no traffic down here.'

When they reached the main road, the noise of a distant engine became slowly louder. Brakes squealed and an enormous lorry pulled up. The door opened. 'You girls want a lift?'

'You're not a perv, are you?' Barbara asked, her heartbeat slowing. 'We've just had a narrow escape.'

'No, I'm just a lorry driver, name's Ted.'

'He looks OK,' Helen said. 'Come on, we've got no choice.'

Ted helped them climb up into the hatch and listened to their story.

'That was brave of you, singeing the swine in the neck.'

'I just did it without thinking.'

'Good for you.' He gave them cigarettes. 'You're both shaking,' he said, offering a light. 'I'd hate to think of my two teenage daughters hitchhiking.' His brow wrinkled and he shook his head. 'There's perverts like that beggar everywhere.'

'We won't hitch again, promise.' Barbara turned to Helen. 'You won't tell Mam, will you? She's promised to buy me a leather coat for Christmas.'

Florrie

Barbara sat opposite Florrie on the train to Liverpool, staring out of the window.

'What colour coat do you want?'

'Black,' Barbara answered, without turning her face away from the window.

Florrie wondered if trying to buy her affection would work. She remembered the warnings about adopting a child. Who'd have thought that beautiful baby she took from the orphanage would turn out to be so difficult? One day she was a kind and loving daughter and then the next day she changed without warning into someone Florrie didn't recognise. If only that psychiatrist had kept his mouth shut. She'd talked to Jim about it but he never said a word to Barbara. Typical of Jim. It was Florrie who had to deal with it all.

Sometimes she felt like telling Barbara to clear off and find her real mother. See if she'd put up with her staying out till all hours, drinking and smoking and giving cheek. Then she'd be someone else's problem. But losing her – that wasn't what she wanted. It had always been her worst fear, her baby running away. *I've done my best. Why does she hate me so much?*

She'd lost the battle and was ready to give up, but Lily had persuaded her. Lily said it was what teenagers did nowadays: rebel against their parents. She'd have to accept Barbara's modern style of dress, the short skirts, the heavy make-up, the panda eyes. Don't keep criticising her, Lily had warned, because society has changed. *Not for the better!*

In the store, Barbara stood in front of the full-length mirror and turned to look at the back of the dark navy coat with its semi-fitted skirt that reached down past her calves. 'I really like this one.'

'You look like one of those Mods off the telly. It's a perfect fit.'

'It feels so soft.' Barbara ran her right hand up and down the left sleeve.

'It's kid leather,' Florrie said.

'Can I wear it now, please?'

The coat cost 12 guineas but it was worth it to see the delight in Barbara's eyes.

'You're a lucky girl,' the shop assistant said. She bagged Barbara's woollen jacket and handed it to her. 'Is this your Christmas present?'

'Yes.' Barbara couldn't stop grinning.

On the escalator, Barbara self-consciously smoothed down the neat lapels of her coat as they made their way up to the café on the top floor of Lewis's. They ordered toasted teacakes and a pot of tea.

'I'll never take it off. Everyone dances with their leathers on at the Scala. It's a status symbol.'

'Well, at least it won't get stolen, if it's on your back.' They laughed. *She's just a kid trying to fit in with the crowd. They all dress like that now.* Florrie had been so poor growing up, buying new clothes had been unheard of, but Barbara wouldn't understand that. *Please God let this be a turning point.*

A few days later, Florrie lay on the sofa covered with a blanket, retching. She had the flu. Barbara approached the sofa as if she wanted to help, but Florrie felt uncomfortable and shook her head. 'I'm OK.' *I'm the carer.* When she retched again, Barbara sat next to her and held her hot forehead, with cool hands, as she vomited into an enamel bowl in front of the sofa. Lying back exhausted, her body too weak to resist, she let Barbara wipe her mouth and hold her hand. Florrie's skin was damp, and her clothes smelt of vomit, but Barbara seemed reluctant to move and stayed until she fell asleep.

When she awoke, Barbara was still holding her clammy palm. A sadness in Barbara's eyes told Florrie that her daughter was sorry for the pain she'd caused. *Was she growing up? Would things be different?* Florrie felt a previously undreamed-of connection, but would it last?

Barbara

'I've rang Mr Arya, who runs a yoga class,' Barbara said.

Her mother turned down the volume on the TV. 'Arya! That's a foreign name! What yoga class? Where?'

'He sounded Indian. I'm meeting him at Oxford Road Station in Manchester on Saturday. Have a look at this.' Barbara handed her mother the yoga book. 'It's supposed to make you calm.'

'Well, you could do with a bit of calmness, but I don't like the idea of you going off to Manchester on your own. You're only eighteen. He could be a villain, luring young girls to the city centre.' She flipped through the book and tossed it onto the table. 'It's heathen.'

'It's yoga, not devil worship, and I'm going.'

Barbara had spotted *Forever Young, Forever Healthy* by Indra Devi when she was browsing in a second-hand bookshop in Liverpool. She'd flipped through the pages, admiring images of peaceful faces and supple bodies bending into incredible postures. She wanted to find that kind of peace. Her mother said Barbara had a bothered conscience because she was always anxious about something. Perhaps the meditation would make her calm like Lily.

'How'll you recognise him?' her mother asked.

'He'll be stood on his head on the platform,' Jimmy, who had come home for his Sunday dinner, said.

Her mother and Jimmy laughed.

'No he won't!' Barbara said, annoyed at Jimmy making fun of her. 'I've described myself, and I'll be carrying my yoga book.'

***

Barbara sighed when she saw Mr Arya walking towards her on the platform. He wasn't stood on his head and he recognised her straight away. He shook her hand and introduced himself. 'We'll take the tram and then the bus.' He gestured for her to follow him.

Unsure of what to say, she stayed silent during the journey, and followed him to a row of large, bay-windowed Victoria terraces. He unlocked the door of a house with closed curtains, and her mother's warnings flashed before her. *Should I make a run for it?* She hesitated before stepping into the tiled hallway and was distracted by brightly coloured tapestries, embroidered with red and gold thread, hanging from the walls. Gods with elephants' trunks and goddesses with many arms and faces stared down at her. A spicy smell hung in the air.

She peeped past Mr Arya into an adjacent room, relieved to see people sitting cross-legged on huge flat cushions, meditating. They were older than her and they didn't resemble the young supple bodies in the book. *Perhaps they started too late.*

Sitting cross-legged was something she'd always been able to do easily. Chanting voices filled the room with an unfamiliar humming sound, relaxing her mind and body in a previously unexperienced way. For a moment, the turmoil inside her stopped and she became detached from her body, her mind at peace.

Why have I come all this way to do yoga? Will it make me a better person: kinder to Mam? I hate our arguments. What's my real mother like? Am I more like her than the family who've brought me up? She couldn't find the answer.

Mr Arya tapped her on the shoulder. 'Have you enjoyed the experience?'

'For a little while I felt so peaceful.'

'Good. If you practise, the peaceful time will last longer each day.'

Leaving her at the station, Mr Arya clasped her hands, looked her straight in the eye and told her softly, 'In your next life, you will find the Right Path.'

On the train home, she wondered if he was right, but decided that she didn't want to go through re-birth again and again until she was good enough to ascend to Nirvana. She'd never be that good. Not when she did so much to upset her mother. To stop feeling sad, she opened the yoga book on a chapter titled 'Diet'.

'No! You're not becoming a vegetarian,' her mother said the following day. She was frying steak and onions, filling the kitchen with a strong meaty smell. The fat in the chip pan bubbled on the back burner. 'Those Indians have put strange ideas in your head.'

'True yogis don't believe in harming any living creature. They believe in reincarnation, so they don't eat animals because they might come back as one.'

'We're Christians, we die and go to heaven or hell, and I won't be cooking any of that foreign-smelling muck.'

Her mother was always trying to fatten her up. 'You can't have a cup of tea without a cake or a biscuit,' she'd say. At five foot five inches, Barbara was taller and thinner than her mother and sister, and nearly as tall as her father and brothers. She was a shapely size 12 but wanted to be a size 10 or less, like the model Twiggy.

'You just don't understand.' Barbara's tummy rumbled as she watched the steak sizzle and the onions brown. 'Being a vegetarian is healthy and I want to lose weight.'

'You're not overweight and you'll become anaemic if you don't eat red meat.' Her mother placed the plate of steak, onions and chips on the table. Barbara licked her lips.

'Lily never dieted or caused any of this fuss.'

'I know! You don't know where you got me from!'

They both laughed.

Chapter 10

The Wings Club

Barbara left her job in Liverpool, and was working at a tyre factory in Widnes, sharing an office with Brenda, a comptometer operator, short with thick, waist-length dark hair, and a secretary, Barbara, a six-foot-tall redhead known as 'Big B'.

Shouts from the tyre fitters, and the smell of rubber and petrol fumes drifted in through the open window as the girls sat in the main office smoking and sipping coffee.

'Why did you fall out with Monica?' Big B asked.

'We were too different in personality and we started to argue, but we had some great times.'

Barbara remembered being on holiday with Monica – sitting pillion on multi-mirrored, multi-horned scooters making their way through the streets of Torquay – the warm summer breeze flapping the skirt of her flowered mini dress, cooling her bare tanned legs – the southern lads admiring their put-on scouse accents, saying they sounded like Cilla Black – watching Pete Townshend smash up his guitar on stage when the Who played at Torquay Town Hall …

'I miss her sometimes, we had a lot of fun.'

In the Wilton coffee bar, a few streets from their office, the girls ate lunch. The Beach Boys' 'I Get Around' played on the jukebox.

'I'm sick of my dad moaning about me staying out late,' Brenda said.

'Same here. My mam would like me to be married and settled like Lily, with loads of grandkids running around. Last Sunday, when I got up late, she had a real go at me.' Barbara imitated her mother's voice. '"We just get used to one and then he's gone and there's another one. I wish you'd settle down." She was almost pleading. I caught sight of myself in the mirror. I looked a wreck. Perhaps she's right.'

'What are you going to wear tonight?'

'I've got nothing to wear,' Barbara complained. 'I can't afford new clothes. I'm saving up to go to France with Rita in May.'

***

The week after her return from France, Barbara was sorting invoices with Brenda in the main office. 'I want to go and live in France,' she said. 'Rita won't leave her mum.'

'I'll come with you,' Brenda said.

'That's great. Paris was wonderful and the French men, ooh la la! Everywhere we went, we were chatted up.'

Brenda's eyes widened and she stopped sorting. 'Were there any special boys?'

'Yes, two waiters from our hotel, Pierre and Jacques. Pierre was mine. He was gorgeous, dark and tanned with enormous brown eyes and thick black lashes. They couldn't speak any English except a few phrases but it didn't matter. We communicated in other ways.' Barbara smiled.

'French kissing?'

Barbara blushed and carried on, 'Our last night was the best night of my life.'

'Tell me every detail. Well, perhaps not every detail.'

Barbara grinned and blushed deeper. 'I'd like to be an au pair or something like that.'

Brenda glanced at her watch, date-stamped the remaining invoices and quickly put them in a file. 'Should we go to night school and learn French?'

'That's a great idea. We'll get evening jobs as barmaids so we can save. Bet Big B will come with us.'

Brenda looked unsure. 'Don't know if my dad will like the idea.'

'Of you working in a pub or going to live in France?'

'Both.'

'He can't stop you. You've turned eighteen. I'm going no matter what my mam says. She'll probably be glad to be rid of me.'

***

Barbara wrote down the order on a small notepad and took it to the Wings Club bar, where she'd been working for a month. 'Two pints of bitter, a gin and orange and a Babycham,' she repeated.

The manager had given them jobs working the floor. On Sunday night, they attended the tables, took orders from the punters and then passed the orders to Big B through a hatch at the bar, before delivering the drinks back to the tables.

On Tuesday night, there was a beat dance, but weekends were for the old folks. She'd suffered the singer, the comedienne and the bingo. Now people were ballroom dancing to a trio. Barbara leaned against the hatch, puffing on a cigarette, staring at the fat middle-aged men in suits and the women with permed hair and crimplene frocks as they waltzed round the room. Words to the Who's 'My Generation' went through her mind: something about hoping to die before you got old.

Ignoring the punters who didn't give tips, she scanned the room until her eyes rested on a man beckoning her over who she knew was generous. She crossed the room and took his order while his hand slipped around her waist. He fiddled with the ties of her apron and patted her bottom as she walked away. *Randy beggar.*

Forcing a smile, she returned with the drinks. 'You've got a lot in there.' He tapped the large left-side pocket of her pop art pinafore. 'You've been working hard. Going to take me out tomorrow night, are you?'

His wife frowned and slapped his knee. 'Will you behave, George?'

'It's just a bit of banter, isn't it, love.' He turned his face to Barbara; red shiny skin creasing into a smile, teeth stained with tobacco.

Barbara grinned and gave him his change from the float in her right-hand pocket, slipping the shilling tip into her left-hand pocket. *Stupid old fool.*

'I earn more from my three nights' barmaiding than I do from my office job,' she told Brenda, as they counted their tips at the end of the night.

'Same here,' Brenda said. 'Have you told your mam and dad that you're going to France?'

'No, not yet,' Barbara said. 'I'm going to wait until I've saved enough and then just go.' *Will Mam care? We've been getting along better lately. Will she miss me?*

The following Friday, she heard loud laughter coming from a group of young men who'd come into the Wings Club bar for an early pint, kicking off their weekend binge.

'Hiya, Derick! How long have you been back?' Dave asked.

'About two weeks.' Derick, tall and tanned from hitchhiking round the South of England, smiled at Barbara, who was stood at the bar talking to Big B. Pleased with herself, she looked the other way. He'd asked her to go out with him three times, but she'd refused, although she didn't know why.

'He's really nice-looking.' Big B was washing glasses behind the bar. 'Why won't you go out with him?'

'I'm going to France with Brenda. I don't want to get involved with anyone.'

'You're not going till next year. You could have one date with him.'

'I suppose ... he's not bad-looking.' She glanced across at him. Sun-bleached hair and a beard made him stand out from the other lads, and his blue eyes twinkled when he laughed. *Why not?* she thought. As she was leaving with Brenda, he caught up with them walking down Peel House Lane and asked if he could walk her home.

They separated from Brenda at Fairfield Road. 'I know you'll probably say no, but Roman Polanski's *The Fearless Vampire Killers* is on at the Empire. Do you fancy seeing it?'

She hesitated. 'I love horror films. OK, I'll go.' *He seems all right and we both like horror films.*

In the back row, Barbara giggled at the comedy and cuddled up close to Derick at the horror.

'Can I see you again?' Derick said in between kisses as they stood at her back door. 'The Foundations are on at the Lion in Warrington. Their hit single "Baby, Now That I've Found You" has just come out.'

'Why not!' Barbara said.

***

Brenda shivered and stared at the calendar on the office wall. 'It's March, and your crosses are missing again, that's nearly two months.' She looked concerned.

'You're not, are you?' Big B asked, overly excited and eager for gossip.

'I don't know,' Barbara said, annoyed at their intrusion.

'We're not going to get to France.' Brenda looked sad. 'Are we?'

'Probably not.' Barbara thought of all the things she'd never get to do. 'Wish I'd gone on the pill. Lily said her doctor, a Catholic, didn't like giving the pill to married women, so unmarried women had no chance.'

'Are you going to get married?' Big B asked.

'Yes. He proposed, even got down on one knee.'

'He must love you. Do you really like him?'

'Yes. We have a lot in common. We like the same music. I introduced him to Bob Dylan and he took me to see John Mayall at the Philharmonic in Liverpool.'

'Good enough reason to get married,' Big B said sarcastically.

'But I've not told my mam and dad yet, so don't tell anyone.'

Barbara went back to her office and thought about what her

mother's reaction would be. Whatever the outcome, if she was pregnant, she would never give her child away; if they didn't get married, she'd bring it up herself. Some of her friends had got married young, already pregnant. Moira Smith's boyfriend wouldn't marry her and she'd been sent away to have her baby because Mrs Smith couldn't stand the shame. They'd made up some story about Moira visiting a relative in Ireland but everyone knew that she was having her baby adopted. She turned up six months later with a flat stomach.

Gently rubbing her hands across her tummy, Barbara resolved that wouldn't happen to her baby, but she had another worry. She didn't want to tell Derick that she was adopted because she felt ashamed.

Sat next to Derick in the Church View Inn that night, she sipped a bitter shandy. 'When I told my mam that I was pregnant, she breathed a sigh of relief. She's glad that I'll have to settle down, and she likes you.'

'Of course she does. Every time I go to your house there's sandwiches or cake or something.'

'She thinks you're too thin.'

Derick took a gulp of his pint and laughed. 'What a cheek! I'm a Catholic. I'm good-looking. What more could she ask for in a son-in-law?'

'She said my dad was disappointed but he's OK now. She's planning the wedding already, booked St Bede's and the Queens Hall for the reception. What did your parents say?'

'I told my dad to tell my mam. Too afraid to tell her myself.'

'Coward. She doesn't seem that bad.'

'You don't know her. They never said a word. Dad just whispered to me in the kitchen and slipped money into my pocket for a new suit.'

'That was it?' Derick nodded and they laughed. While he was at the bar, Barbara sat silent and tense, dreading having to tell him she was adopted, but she'd have to do it sometime. *Does it make me less of a person?*

'You've gone quiet and fidgety,' Derick said, when he returned. 'Is there something wrong?'

'No!' Barbara lied. 'I mean … yes. There is something …' Barbara's eyes darted around the room and she swallowed. '… Florrie and Jim aren't my real parents. I'm adopted!'

'That's all right.' He sounded relieved. 'I thought you were going to say that you'd changed your mind about getting married.'

'No.' Barbara forced a smile. 'But it's not all right.'

Derick looked puzzled. 'Florrie and Jim are great. It doesn't matter to me.' He put his arm around her shoulders.

'It matters to me,' she said, tears forming.

'Why are you so upset?'

'Thinking about it makes me sad.' She dabbed her eyes and finished her shandy.

'Do you want to find them? I'll help you to look for them. Do you know their names or where they're from?'

'No! I know they gave me away.'

'It might not have been that simple. Hasn't your mam told you what happened?'

'Not really.'

'They might be rich, aristocracy or something,' Derick grinned.

'It's not funny!' Barbara raised her voice and looked straight at him. 'She didn't want me then. Why should she want me now?'

'But you don't know …'

'I don't want to talk about it anymore. OK?'

Derick picked up his pint and drained his glass. 'All right, I won't mention it again unless you do. But it makes absolutely no difference to the way I feel about you, the baby or us getting married.'

***

Weeks before the wedding, her mother sat in her armchair looking through an old leather bag Barbara had never seen before.

'You're going to need this for the registrar,' her mother said.

'What is it?'

'Your birth certificate.'

Barbara stiffened, took the folded paper and held it in her hand, afraid to open it.

'You can't get married without it,' her mother said.

What's it going to tell me? Carefully, Barbara unfolded the paper. It was issued on 14 September 1948, a year after she was born. Barbara read her adopted name *Barbara Tiernan*, her sex, *female*, and the date she was born, *2 June 1947*. Nothing she didn't already know. *This must be a copy of the original.* It showed no evidence of her adoption or birth mother.

'You should have these as well,' her mother said – fingering the papers nervously, as though she was reluctant to let them go – 'your adoption papers.'

Barbara sat down in the chair opposite her mother, unable to speak; scared of what might be revealed, she hesitated before accepting the documents.

Her mother shifted in her chair, took a deep breath and looked up at Barbara. 'I never meant for you to find out. I thought you'd go off and leave me. I thought you'd try to find them – your birth parents.'

Why would I try to find someone who didn't want me? Barbara wanted to say, but her throat felt constricted.

'I've had you since you were six months old and as far as I was concerned, you were my baby, until that meddling psychiatrist told you different.'

Why are you telling me this now? You should have told me before the psychiatrist had a chance to. Barbara shut her ears to her mother's voice. 'I'll look at them upstairs later.'

In her bedroom, she scanned the adoption order. Carole Dalton: her real mother. *Who was she?* Barbara stared; tears formed as her eyes moved down the page, blurring her father's name. Blinking, she refocused. Thomas Fletcher: her biological father. *At least Carole knew who he was. Perhaps they'd had a relationship? Why did they desert me?* Barbara couldn't ask her mother.

She'd say bad things and remind her that Carole Dalton had left her in a home. *Why does it still upset me so much?* She touched her stomach and thought about the child growing inside her.

Glancing at the baby's name, Barbara Dalton, she realised that her mother had kept the name Carole had given her. Knowing how her mother liked to control everything, she was surprised. Her mother was sat downstairs, probably waiting for her reaction. Part of her wanted to run to her mother, sit at her knee and ask her a million questions, but she was afraid of the answers. The urge to retreat was stronger. She forced herself to detach from the child as though it was someone else, not her.

Perhaps Carole had been forced to give me up. Would knowing her fill the void that I always feel? That dark, empty place. She folded the papers and walked calmly downstairs. 'I'll just keep my birth certificate.' She handed the adoption documents back to her mother.

Her mother looked relieved. 'OK,' she said, with a weak smile, and put them back in the leather bag.

***

On the way to St Bede's Church, her father told the taxi driver to stop alongside Victoria Park. 'What's the matter, Dad?' *Is he going to kidnap me and stop me getting married?* Barbara grasped her bouquet tightly.

He took her free hand. 'Are you sure you want to go ahead with this?'

Barbara turned her head abruptly and stared at her father. 'Yes, of course I do.'

'It's not too late to change your mind, you know, you're only twenty. You don't have to go through with it. I'll support you and your mam'll help you look after the baby. You could even go back to work. We can turn round now.'

Her father's serious face worried Barbara. *Oh God! He really means it.* 'Don't you like Derick?'

'Yes, he's a nice lad, but is it what *you* really want?'

Barbara thought of Derick standing at the altar, looking over his shoulder, checking his watch. She couldn't back out now. She didn't want to.

'I'm OK, Dad.' She smiled and squeezed his hand. 'Don't worry, but thanks for saying that.' His words touched her and she felt truly loved. He would rather help her raise an illegitimate child than force her into a marriage she didn't want. Concern about her happiness was more important than what the neighbours thought.

The church was full and the organ started up with 'Here Comes the Bride'. Her father held onto her, proudly showing her off to smiling relatives and friends as they walked down the aisle. She wore a cream lace mini dress. Rita in her pink lace bridesmaid dress followed behind. Derick turned and smiled. She stood next to him. *What am I doing? Should I have turned tail with Dad? There's no going back now, not with everyone looking.* Derick took hold of her hand, squeezed it tight and looked into her eyes. That look said that he'd always be there for her. She smiled back knowing he would.

***

At 3 a.m. on 28 October, Barbara was woken up by a dream that her stomach was a huge water-filled balloon about to burst. 'My God!' She rolled off the double bed her mother had bought them, water running down her legs, soaking the carpet.

'Get up! My waters have broken!' she shouted to Derick, who was rubbing his eyes half asleep.

'What's happening?' Her mother burst into the room, wild-eyed. 'Don't worry about that, I'll clean it up. Have your contractions started?'

'No, I'm fine. It's just wet.' She stared down at the water seeping into the carpet.

'Get her off to the maternity home,' she told Derick. 'Jim will drive you.'

'Get my case.' Derick's face turned white.

At the maternity home down Highfield Road, about half a mile away, Barbara chatted excitedly and nervously, trying to cover her fears. 'Will it be a boy or a girl?'

'It'll be beautiful, no matter what it is. See you later.' Derick kissed her goodbye at the ward entrance, leaving her in the midwives' charge. *I'm terrified. Will it be as painful as they say?* She felt like a piece of meat as they stripped her down, dressed her in an open-backed gown, laid her on a bed, shaved her pubic hairs and gave her an enema. Alone in a labour ward that smelt of bleach, the contractions became stronger, as if an elastic band was being squeezed tightly around her middle then slowly loosened, leaving her with backache.

She pushed back the stiff white sheets and stared at the bare white walls, scared. 'Ouch! Oh God!' *They're coming quicker.* Panic! She shouted for the midwife.

Neither Pethidine nor gas and air made any difference to the pain wrenching inside her: the contractions reached a violent crescendo. 'One final push, Barbara. You can do it,' the midwife said.

God help me! My body's breaking in two.

'It's a boy!' the midwife said.

Barbara heard the baby scream. 'Is he OK?'

'Yes. He's a big healthy boy. 8lb 8oz.'

'Thank God he's all right.'

When they placed him in her arms, she fell in love, the birth pains forgotten. She gazed down at his perfect little body. *How could I produce something so beautiful?* She stroked the soft fair down on his head and held his tiny fingers, marvelling at their perfection and how tightly they gripped her finger. When she put him to her breast, she was overwhelmed. *I'll never let you go.* The tiny scrap of life she held close was her true blood relation, entirely dependent on her. She ached with love. 'Beautiful boy. My beautiful Shaun. I'll be the best mum you could ever want,' she whispered, smothering his smooth pink cheeks with kisses.

At night, when the nurses took the babies into a nursery, she longed to have him back. Unable to sleep, she thought about her mother. Now that she'd felt the magical bond between mother and child, she understood better why her mother had kept the truth from her. *I'll be a good daughter. It'll all be different now.*

The next day, massive mophead chrysanthemums – bright yellow – arrived from Eve and Fred, Derick's parents. The flowers were cheerful against the grey-painted walls, contrasting with the blood-red roses from Derick and the mixed bouquet from her parents. They made her smile.

Nearing the end of the ten days, Barbara looked at Derick for sympathy. 'I want to go home. They do everything for you in here. The only time I have him is when he's feeding.'

Derick took her hand. 'Never mind, you're coming home tomorrow.'

***

'Six months we've lived with my mam and dad, now. I can't stand it much longer. Mam won't use the sterilising unit, says it's a waste of time and that hot water was good enough in her day. How many babies died in her day? She won't do anything that I say,' Barbara said.

'Calm down.' Derick put his arm round her. 'It does have its advantages. We can go out whenever we want.'

'That's true. She loves to have him all to herself so she can put three spoonsful of sugar in his bottles when she knows I don't give him sugar.'

'And we do live here rent-free, which has helped us save a deposit. Lucky I got the job with the insurance company and we can get a mortgage with them. We'll start looking at properties next week.'

Twelve months later, Barbara was admiring their cosy three-bedroom terraced house, with its modernised kitchen and bathroom. 'At last we have our own home.' They had replaced the dingy wallpaper with a bright starflower design, lit up with an orange teak floor lamp. They'd bought a long, low brown sofa on hire purchase, and scattered it with brightly coloured cushions. The house was a few streets away from her mother and father, and a ten-minute walk from Derick's parents' house, so they always had a babysitter.

Two years old, but Shaun still refused to sleep. It was 2 a.m. Barbara's eyelids felt like lead and it was difficult to keep them open. In a dreamlike state, she remembered Derick's parents looking after Shaun while they went to the Isle of Wight Festival in the summer of 1970 …

It was hot. Young men, stripped to the waist, revealed torsos shiny with sweat and suntan oil, their chests decked with beads, crosses and tattoos.

Girls with long flowing hair, decorated with flowers and braids, love beads round their necks and bangles on their wrists, danced and swayed their arms above their heads. Brightly coloured see-through dresses fluttered in the breeze, revealing smooth tanned backs and arms painted with henna flowers.

Barbara thought her flared jeans and cheesecloth shirt looked tame compared to her New Age companions. In a queue for the toilets that stretched the length of the field, she spoke to two girls from Brighton whose parents didn't know they were there. That was the sort of thing she'd have done in her younger days to hurt her mother.

The sea of multi-coloured revellers stretched out before her as she made her way back, circling in and out of bodies. She was lost. Derick wore his hair long and had a beard, but so did every other man. Her confusion apparent, people beckoned her to join them.

A group of Dutch teenagers gave her an ice-cold lemonade and passed round a joint. 'You can stay with us, pretty lady.'

'Thanks, but I have to find my husband.'

After the smoke, she searched more calmly and eventually spotted a frantic Derick waving in her direction. 'You've been gone for two hours. It's Jimi Hendrix tonight.' …

Shaun wriggled in her arms, jolting her into consciousness.

She looked down at him, kissed his cheek and she placed him back in the cot. 'Please don't wake up.' As soon as his head touched the mattress, his eyes opened wide and he wanted to play. *I'm not having any more kids.*

In spite of the lack of sleep, she loved being a mum and they were inseparable. One day, Derick surprised her. 'We should have another child to keep Shaun company. We don't want him to be an only child, and I'd like to have a daughter.'

The following year, he got his wish. Although she'd been unsure about having another child, all doubts vanished when Barbara gave birth, and she fell in love with her beautiful, blue-eyed daughter, who they named Karen.

Barbara pulled back the shawl for five-year-old Shaun to see his new sister.

'When can I play with her?'

'Not till she's older.'

'Hope she grows up soon.' Shaun went off to play with his train set.

Barbara turned to Derick. 'It's a lot for him to deal with, starting school the same week that I bring a new baby home. He's had me to himself for five years. He's going to feel pushed out.'

'He'll be fine,' Derick said. 'He'll love it and he has a head start, with you teaching him the alphabet. Kids are tougher than you think.'

'Come on, son,' he shouted to Shaun, 'we'll go up Blundells Hill!'

Shaun's face lit up. 'Can I collect the dead bullets from the shooting range?'

'You certainly can.'

Karen was a calm baby who smiled and cooed at everyone, and she slept well. Barbara pinched her arm gently to make sure she was alive. Her head moved from side to side but she stayed asleep. Lying back in bed, Barbara thought how lucky she was to have a gorgeous baby girl, a clever little boy and a lovely husband. She was so busy with the children, it was now faint and hardly noticeable, but the feeling that something was missing from her life was still there.

She shopped with her mother and Lily every week. They loaded their large shopping bags with groceries from Lennon's, the first supermarket in Widnes. Barbara noticed that her mother and Lily chatted more, laughed more and, without knowing it, they made her feel left out.

She was different. Not just in the way she looked but in her attitude to life. She was quieter, more analytical and she wouldn't accept the limitations her parents tried to impose on her. They taught their children to be truthful and honest and to work hard, but aspiration wasn't encouraged. Barbara was ambitious and wanted her children to do better than she had. She wondered, as she had so many times in her life, if she was different because she wanted to be different or if she was inherently different because of her genetic make-up.

Since giving birth to Karen, she'd been thinking more about Carole. *She's got two grandchildren now. Would she want to know them?*

Chapter 11

Back to Work

'This bloody government!' Derick jumped up and switched off the ITV News. 'Interest rates keep going up and up! It was a bad time to move house.'

'I'll get a job.' Barbara sat at the table looking through the *Widnes Weekly News*. 'They need a secretary to the senior partner at a solicitors downtown.'

'Sounds interesting.' Derick sat down opposite her. 'My hours are flexible. Shaun can walk home from St Joe's and my dad will pick Karen up from St Bede's.'

'You've got it all planned,' she said with a smile. 'I've not worked full time since I had Shaun. How will I cope?'

She'd loved being at home with the kids, taking them to the park in the summer, for days out at the seaside and picnics, and planning birthday parties. Teaching them to read and write had come naturally to her, but drawing with them was what she liked best. They were both gifted at art and had won competitions in local papers, but Karen had won a painting competition in the *Daily Mirror* for a trip to the 1980 Olympic Games in Moscow, a trip of a lifetime.

The kids fought and squabbled like all siblings, but most of the time they behaved well. They were her world and she was proud of them. She'd done part-time work but going back full time was daunting. *Will I have the confidence?* She wrote a letter of application and walked to the postbox, hesitantly dropping it in. *No harm in trying.*

A month later, she started work at Fletcher, Rawlinson & Sons, Solicitors.

'Coffee's ready!' Jackie, the office junior, came in carrying a tray.

Lorraine grabbed two coffees, put one on Barbara's desk and sat down. 'How's the new house?'

'It's great and I love having a garden, but it's paying the mortgage that's the problem. Interest rates have rocketed.'

'Yes, 15 per cent and rising.' Richard, their boss, a labour counsellor, put his head round the door. 'Good for people with money in the bank, but families are losing their homes every day. Going into negative equity. You've got Mrs Thatcher to thank for that.'

'Well, I didn't vote for her.'

'Me neither.'

'The Tories only look after themselves. Come in for dictation, will you, Barbara, please?'

When Barbara returned to her desk with a notebook full of shorthand, she sighed.

'He lost another client's file,' Lorraine said quietly, sniggering behind her hand. 'Left it in the gents' toilets at the town hall. Someone just handed it in.'

'That's the third file he's lost,' Barbara rolled her eyes. 'The last time, he left one on a counter in Woolworths.'

'At least someone's handed it in.'

'He's completely mad,' Barbara said. 'Remember when I came in last winter and he was sitting behind his desk in his underpants with his trousers steaming on the radiator behind him? They'd got wet in the snow. If you'd have seen my face. I got out of that office quickly.'

'The best is when we have cream cakes on Friday.' Lorraine laughed and put her hand up to her face. 'He gets the cream all round his mouth like a child.'

'Then he holds his face up to me to wipe,' Barbara said. 'Ugh!'

Jackie walked in with an armful of files. 'I hate this job.' She pursed her lips.

'Don't complain,' Lorraine said. 'With three million unemployed, you're lucky to have a job.'

'What a start to the Eighties!' Barbara said. 'First John Lennon gets shot, then there were riots in Toxteth. All that burning and looting.'

'Ah, I loved John Lennon,' Jackie said, frowning. 'What were the riots about?'

'Unemployment,' Barbara said. 'The bosses introduced containers on the docks in Liverpool, which meant a lot of the dockers weren't needed anymore to load up the ships.'

'And the police were stopping and searching too many black people,' Lorraine said, 'which made it worse.'

'One morning during the riots, I was in here with Richard,' Barbara said. 'My hands were shaking and I couldn't concentrate on the contract I was typing. I was worrying about the riots spilling over into Widnes – Toxteth's only down the road. Richard saw how distressed I was and fetched me a cup of tea. "Widnes people don't riot," he said. "It's not in their nature." He was right, thankfully, but what a year.'

Barbara typed automatically, her mind elsewhere. *Am I a typical parochial person, cowed by authority, unable to rebel against my oppressors? Would I have been different brought up somewhere else by someone else? What sort of personality did my birth mother have? Am I more like Carole than Mam?*

***

Bored with office work, Barbara wanted a change of career. She was thirty-nine and didn't want to spend the rest of her life typing letters. Sat in the office of Social Services, waiting to be interviewed, she saw a poster for Halton College advertising for volunteer tutors to teach basic skills to people who had difficulty with reading, writing and maths.

'Take a seat, Mrs Attwood, and I'll run through your options. You work full time and you have a young family, why do you want to do voluntary work? Rather, how will you find the time?'

'I've got a lot of energy and I'd like to do something that helps people.'

'Right. We've got meals on wheels and …'

'Sorry to interrupt, but you don't need to go through the options. I want to be a volunteer tutor. As soon as I saw the poster, I knew that was what I wanted to do.'

'Great. I'll set up an interview with Kath at the college. If you're accepted, you'll have to do a short course in teaching basic skills, but I'm sure you'll be fine with that.'

After volunteering for six months, Barbara was offered two hours' paid work in charge of a class of ten students on a Wednesday evening.

'Mary, one of the tutors, said I was a natural and that I should give up work and qualify to be a schoolteacher,' Barbara said, 'but I know we can't afford that at the moment. It's a bit scary because some of the other volunteers are more qualified than I am.'

'Well, they wouldn't have offered it to you if they didn't think you could do it,' Derick said.

'I'm going to sign on for two night classes and get some qualifications.'

'That'll be three nights a week you'll be out as well as working full time. I'll help out but it's a lot to take on.'

'I can cope.' Being constantly occupied helped to keep the sadness at bay. It was as though she had to fill her mind up to the point of overload with activities, leaving no space for dark thoughts.

***

'Guess what? I'm going to train to be a teacher.' Barbara handed her mother a cup of tea.

'Good for you.' Her mother looked flustered. She smiled strangely, barely turning up the corners of her mouth; her eyes distant. 'I remember getting you, going round the orphanages with your Aunty Maggie.'

'Oh!' Barbara sat down. *What's triggered this?* Her mother never referred to her adoption. None of her family did. It was as though it had never happened.

'I'd seen an advert in the local paper asking for someone to foster a baby boy.' She relaxed back into her chair. 'I didn't want to foster. I knew if I took a baby, I'd not want to give it back, and I didn't want a boy. I already had two boys and a girl, so another girl would make it even. But we went to have a look at the children's home in Liverpool.'

'Did you?' Barbara took deep breaths. *I can't believe she's telling me this.*

'On the bus, Maggie admitted that she'd love to adopt a child, but Tom wouldn't agree to it. "You're taking on someone else's trouble," he'd said. "Be warned." I told her he was a miserable beggar and she agreed with me. I felt sorry for Maggie. She'd no children then, but she'd lost a baby, a little boy, the result of an affair with an Italian prisoner of war who worked at the Everite the same time as her. It was an ammunitions factory during the war and they put the POWs to work there. The baby only lived a few weeks. Poor little mite, but Tom was willing to bring it up as his own, give him his due. Fortunately, she had Jean two years later.' She paused, and sipped her tea.

What's she going to tell me next?

'We found the orphanage. It was on Brownlow Hill. There were a lot of older, bored-looking children hanging around. We took bags of sweets, but when we started to hand them out, the matron – a real stony-faced woman – shouted at us.' Her mother spoke in a high-pitched voice. '"We can't allow the children to have sweets. It wouldn't be right. They might expect to get them all the time." Me and Maggie were mortified. She shrieked at the children like a sergeant major, ordering them to give back the sweets. The timid ones handed them over resignedly, but she had to wrench the sweets from the clenched fists of the more defiant kids. The ones already chewing gulped them down before they were spotted. We couldn't believe that anyone could be so mean towards children – especially orphans – but we were too intimidated to protest.' She paused and sighed deeply.

'What did you do?' Barbara leaned forward, fascinated with the story.

'Most of the children there were for fostering. When I told the matron I wanted to adopt, she took my details and said she would pass them on to someone who could help me. We wanted to take the entire children's home away with us, and we cried all the way home, stuffing ourselves with sweets to cheer us up.'

Her mother smiled to herself and stopped to finish her tea. Listening to her talking with such ease and candour about Barbara's adoption was mesmerising. She sat motionless, watching her mother's eyes become distant again.

'It didn't take long before I was referred to a Catholic orphanage, run by nuns, in Bury. Off me and Maggie went again to an old Victorian building – red-brick – just like you'd imagine an orphanage to be. It was freezing. The winter started early that year, 1947, the year you were born.' She paused and looked directly at Barbara for the first time.

'Did it?' Barbara gulped.

'One of the Sisters of Mercy met us and ushered us into a cold waiting room. The benches were hard and it smelt of damp and disinfectant. You could hear faint cries. It broke my heart. As we were shown round the rooms, toddlers ran up to us stretching out their arms begging us to pick them up, but we weren't allowed to. The most distressing was the cries of the babies.' The lines on her mother's face deepened, and she looked down and cradled her arms around her blanket as though she was comforting a child. 'They were left lying in their cots. No one seemed to bother about their cries.'

Barbara was paralysed, struck by the image of a toddler tugging at her mother's coat with cold, pleading hands – babies left in sparse cots – tiny despondent faces looking up at her – sobs of despair as she moved away. Barbara's eyes watered, and gulping hard she bit her lip.

'I was determined I wouldn't leave until I was told I could have a baby. I thought, *I'll save one of them!*' Her mother sat up in her chair. 'They took me to see the babies ready for adoption. There were so many babies left in orphanages after the Second World

War that you could virtually take your pick. My age or the fact that I already had three children didn't seem to matter.'

Why did you pick me?

As if she read Barbara's thoughts, she said, 'I stopped by your cot, but the doctor warned me, "Take this infant and you'll have a lot of trouble." That settled it for me. I told him, "That's the child I want," and you smiled up at me, as if you knew.'

That's where we met. Would I have remained in care if she hadn't stopped by my cot that day? Moving about uncomfortably in her chair, Barbara wanted to get up and wash the cups, but was paralysed, compelled to sit back and listen.

Her mother's face hardened. 'In those days, the Church believed that if a young woman had a child out of wedlock, it was best for all concerned to have the unwanted baby adopted by a good Catholic family, and cut off all its ties with the past. That's what we were told by Father Donnelly.' Her mother's voice turned angry. 'That's what we were led to believe. We promised to provide you with a good Catholic upbringing.'

Struggling to speak, Barbara stuttered, 'You certainly did that.'

'If we hadn't taken you, you'd have been left there. *She* left you there, so she could have a good life. Meet other men without being burdened with you.'

Barbara's smile vanished. *I'm not listening to all that again.* 'Good job you took me then, isn't it?'

The story reinforced her belief that she'd been abandoned. She was indebted, but she suspected that her adoption was not a completely selfless act and that her mother must have desperately wanted a child. Seething with resentment, she went into the kitchen and washed the dishes, clattering them around the sink. *Did Mam bring it up to make me feel grateful that she saved me? Was my birth mother so bad or just an unfortunate girl who'd got into trouble? Do I really want to find out? What might I uncover? Would she want to know me now? It's too distressing.*

'You're making enough noise with them dishes; you'll crack them if you're not careful!' her mother shouted.

'They're fine. I've finished now.' Barbara fastened her coat. 'See you tomorrow. Bye.' Without looking at her mother, she hurried out of the door.

PART 2: THE SEARCH

Chapter 12

Awakening

Sorting out boxes of old toys, broken jewellery and books in the back bedroom, I came across the blue plastic cow. *I've not seen you for years.* No conscious effort had been made to protect it over the years, yet there it was. I held it, shook its rattle. It felt warm, almost alive. *What's your secret?* Mam had told me that an Aunty Carole, who I could hardly remember, had given it to me when I was a baby. From my adoption papers, I knew that my birth mother's name was Carole. *Was that just coincidence? Was she a different Carole?* My heartbeat quickened. Something inside me stirred. I woke up. No tears, just a sudden determination to find out who I was. I was coming up to my fortieth birthday. It was now or never. *I'll find out for myself why Carole left me, and what sort of person she was.* I rang Social Services straight away.

'Yes, since the Children Act 1975, adopted people have had a right to access their birth records,' an efficient-sounding lady told me. 'But the law says you have to be counselled by a social worker first.'

'Why?' *They're my birth records!*

'We have to assess your emotional state and the motives for your search. I'll send you an application form. But don't worry, it's just a formality.'

I was affronted, resentful that I wasn't given instant access and that a social worker would decide whether I should see what was rightfully mine. 'OK, thanks.' I put down the phone and flopped on the stairs in the hall. Awareness of the lack of control adopted people have over their destiny brought a lump to my throat. I swallowed, determined not to cry. *I'll get through this.*

The form arrived the next day: dismissing my worst fears, I filled it in. A torturous fortnight followed before I received a letter telling me to make an appointment. I hesitated for days, unable to pick up the phone: full of anticipation one minute, overcome with fear and dread the next.

I forced myself to ring and was given an appointment with a lady named Jane Black for 6 April. In ten days, I'd know the truth.

Panic set in as the days passed and I made up my mind to tell Mam what I was about to embark on. It was only right that she should know first. Fearing her reaction, my daily visits became an ordeal. I'd open my mouth to tell her but the words wouldn't come out. *How can I risk hurting an eighty-five-year-old? Would she feel it was a betrayal of the years of care she'd given me?* Each day, my courage failed, and I would return home tearful, wondering if it was going to be worth all the upset.

By the end of the week, I decided to broach it from another angle. 'I'm sorry, Mam, for all the trouble I caused when I was a teenager.' An invisible fist clutched my stomach but I carried on. 'Did you ever regret taking me ... taking on someone else's trouble, like Uncle Tom warned you? Was he right?' I swallowed hard.

She looked up from her armchair and stared at me through cloudy blue eyes. 'No! I never regretted it once. You were a lovely baby. You were no more trouble than the others.'

Does she really mean that? I couldn't imagine Jimmy or Lily – maybe Joseph – causing as much upset as I did, but being the youngest I hadn't been there to witness their teenage traumas. We'd never been openly affectionate, but I bent down, put my arms around her and kissed her lightly on the cheek. 'I love you, Mam.'

She turned her head and glared. 'What's brought this on?'

The fist clenched my stomach tighter, slowly twisting, but I stood up straight and blurted it out, 'I'm going to try to find my birth mother.' *There, I've said it.* I took a deep sigh of relief.

Startled, her eyes widened. 'Why do you want to go stirring all that up now?'

'You'll always be my mother,' I said quickly. 'I love you and I'd never turn my back on you.'

'But why now?'

She doesn't understand and probably never will. 'I want to know about the woman who gave birth to me.' I slowly emphasized each word, trying desperately to convince her of my motives. She didn't reply and stared into the distance. 'I'll put the kettle on,' I said, desperate to escape the tension.

The rain pounded mercilessly on the kitchen roof. It smelt of burned toast; blackened crumbs covered the worktop like dead ants. I mopped them up and filled the kettle. 'No good will come of it!' she shouted from the living room. When the water had boiled, I warmed the pot and scooped in two teaspoons of black tea, remembering how Mam used to tell fortunes reading the leaves left in the bottom of the cup. Waiting for it to brew, I leaned my back against the counter and squeezed my eyes shut. *How can I upset her like this?*

'It'll end in tears,' she muttered to herself, as I poured the dark liquid into the cups, watching the spirals of steam rise and disappear like wisps of smoke. We sipped our tea in silence, afraid to make eye contact, staring blankly at the TV screen until it was time for me to go.

'You should leave well enough alone,' she said, as I buttoned up my coat.

'I was hoping you'd understand.' My voice faltered.

'Why do you want to find someone who left you all those years ago?' Her face flushed; her fingers fidgeted. 'If she'd really wanted you, she wouldn't have left you, she'd have found a way.'

I gripped the back of her chair. *Maybe you're right. Maybe she won't want me.* I grabbed my bag and umbrella. 'We'll talk about it tomorrow.'

It rained again the following day. The grey sky reflected my mood as I walked to Mam's house, avoiding puddles in the street. I made tea and sat down, surprised to see the old leather bag lying open by the side of her armchair. Nervously, she fingered something in her lap. *What's she got there?*

'You can have these.' The sadness in her eyes was tempered with resignation.

'What are they?'

'They're your adoption papers. I showed you them before you got married, but you didn't seem interested then.' She frowned. 'Why you've changed you mind, I don't know.'

'Thanks.' *Looks like she's beginning to co-operate.*

'You can have this as well … it's from the lad who got her into trouble.'

I shivered thinking of my biological father, and opened the letter cautiously. Short and to the point, handwritten in a dark blue scrawl on lined paper torn from a jotter, dated April 1948, Thomas Fletcher gave his consent to my adoption if the authorities were satisfied that I was going to a good home. He finished the letter with the words '… and all my obligation ceases.' Rejected again, my thoughts turned as dark as the rain clouds outside. *Was it so easy for him to sign me away?*

'This is your baptism certificate, from St Joseph's in Bury.' She handed me a fragile piece of paper that I opened with care.

'I was christened Barbara Dalton. Why didn't you change my name?'

'I liked the name Barbara.' Her face brightened. 'It suited you.'

Simple as that. The 'Daughter of' section was left blank. *Did that mean Carole didn't want me to find her or was it the authorities, the church in this case, who didn't want me know who had given birth to me?*

'Bury's near Manchester, isn't it, about thirty miles away?'

'Yes. That's where you were born.'

'She could still be living there.' *Stay calm.* 'I was baptised by the Reverend R. Wearden on 6 June, four days after I was born, and I even had a godmother, Elizabeth Bevan – not Judy Garland as you once told me.'

'Did I?' Mam said, smiling.

'Who was Elizabeth?'

'Probably Carole's best friend.'

'Maybe they're still friends, like me and Rita.' I became hopeful. 'She might still be living in Manchester.'

'I suppose you should have these as well.'

'OK.' *What's she going to surprise me with next?*

She handed me five tiny photographs.

'What are they?'

'They're photos of Carole,' she said. I glared at Mam's face in disbelief. She looked down at her hands and fidgeted with her apron.

'What?' Startled, I stared at the small images, faded with age. My hands shook. *This can't be her.* I inhaled deeply.

'It's your mother.'

'Carole?' My eyes darted from one photo to the next, not processing what I was seeing.

'She worked on a farm, milking cows by the looks of things. Perhaps that's where she met your father.'

'When did you get these?' I asked, incredulous. 'Why haven't you shown them to me before?'

'You've never asked me about her before and I wasn't going to bring it up.'

'All you ever told me was how bad she was and how she'd abandoned me. That's why I never asked you.' *You lied and lied.*

Her head bent into her body and I could hardly hear her words, 'She sent them after I stopped her visiting you.' She looked up with guilty eyes.

'Visiting me!' Rapid thumping in my chest. 'Did you say visiting me? When was that?'

'Not long after I got you – you were toddling about. We were living in West Bank.'

I calmed my voice. 'So, she just turned up?'

'Yes, we had no phones then. She just appeared on the doorstep asking if I would let her see you. I let her in thinking that would be it, but she came back, staying a bit longer every time.'

'It must have been awful for her having to leave me. It probably would have been better for her if she'd never found out where I was.'

'Better for everybody, but at least she knew you had a good home and that you were being well looked after.'

Aware that I was losing control, I lowered my voice, afraid she might stop. 'Do you remember where she came from?'

'Colne, I think it was, so she was still in Manchester.' Beneath gently lifted brows, blue eyes pleaded for forgiveness.

For seconds, I was unable to reply. 'I can't believe you kept these from me!' I shouted. I wanted to scream and physically shake her. Instead, I escaped to the bathroom. A face white with fury stared back at me through the tarnished bathroom mirror. *Don't lose your temper. She'll stop talking. You have to find out more.*

When I came back into the room, she looked older than her eighty-five years, as though her frame had shrivelled into the chair. I spoke as calmly as I could. 'It's OK. At least you've told me now. And you don't know how she found your address?'

'No. They're not supposed to tell these girls where their babies go, but I didn't have the heart to send her away.'

I softened. It was typical of Mam's kindness. She'd adopted a baby for herself but she let Carole visit me, which must have been hard for her.

I pictured a young woman knocking on the front door of Parsonage Road, excited, apprehensive, longing to hold the baby she'd given away. Such sadness. A yearning to know that young woman possessed me. I fought to keep control of the turmoil in my head. 'Why did you stop her visiting me?'

'Because you were getting too attached. You were nearly four and your grandmother warned me, "That child'll be confused. She'll grow up not knowing who her mother is." So, I had to tell Carole not to come anymore. She was upset but what could I do? You were my baby by then.'

'I understand.' Exhausted, I eased back into my chair, forced to empathise with my mother. Why should she have risked losing me? I had to forgive her. She may have the clue to finding Carole. 'So, she just stopped coming?'

'Yes. That's when she gave you the cow, the day she left. Don't you remember Aunty Carole? That was her.' Her eyes widened, as though she was remembering.

'The blue plastic cow,' I repeated. Closing my eyes, I tried hard to remember the woman bending over me, kissing me goodbye. 'She was my mother?' *I'll find you, Carole. I would have looked for you sooner if I'd known the truth. If I hadn't been lied to all my life.*

'Did you never hear from her again?'

'Yes, she wrote letters from somewhere down south, Tunbridge Wells or Sevenoaks.'

'Letters!' My hopes rose. 'They'll have her last-known address.'

'In the last one, she said she was emigrating to Australia. Said she'd met someone working on a farm and that they were going on the £10 ticket. They were begging for people to go in those days, in the Fifties. It would have suited her working on a sheep farm, perhaps.'

'Australia!' I rested my head in my hand. *How will I find you in Australia?* I looked up and searched Mam's face. 'Where are the letters?'

She turned her face towards the window. 'I burned them.'

'You what!' I slid to the edge of my chair.

'After we'd had a row – one of your teenage tantrums – I burned them. I thought if you found them, you'd see her address and you'd go off looking for her.'

'I can't believe you did that!' I stood abruptly and leaned over Mam, bringing my face close to hers. She looked at me, afraid. 'You lied to me all those years! I can't believe she actually came to the house and was visiting me all that time and you burned the last link to her!'

She stared down at her hands, wrinkled and brown with age, and she shrank further into the armchair. 'Don't shout. I didn't want you to ever find out. I didn't want her taking you away from me.'

The poignancy of her words quietened my mind and I sat back down. 'All right.' I sighed. 'What was she like, Carole?'

'She was a nice girl, very tall, taller than you, with fair hair.'

Mam sat up, her eyes brightening. 'She had lovely blue eyes. You can't really see her properly in those photos, they're so small.'

I looked at them again. 'I can't see any resemblance. Do you think I look like her?'

'Yes, even though you're dark, you have a look of her.'

I lay back, defeated. *In the trauma of the years since I found out, would I have had the courage to look for Carole? What stopped me was believing she didn't want me. If I'd known the truth, would I have tried to find her?* 'But you kept the photos ... thankfully.' I glanced down at them, stunned, experiencing every emotion possible.

'I couldn't bring myself to burn the photos.' She looked at me helplessly. Her eyes begged me to understand. I didn't want to make her cry. *Why do I feel guilty? She's in the wrong. I've always felt guilty, just for being me.* Carole's sorrow was unimaginable; my thoughts turned to Thomas.

'Did you know anything about my father?'

'He was a soldier, but he came to the final court hearing.'

'I wonder why? Maybe they did have a relationship. If he hardly knew her, he wouldn't have been bothered.'

'He must have been concerned about the family you were going to. He didn't *have* to come. Seemed a nice lad, handsome in his uniform. He spoke to us briefly and he asked if you'd settled in.'

'That was good of him,' I muttered. *All my obligation ceases.*

'Carole didn't come, though. I don't know why.'

'Perhaps she didn't want to see him again – too much pain.'

'Maybe.'

Exhausted, I buried the papers and photographs in my bag. 'I'm off now. You should have told me all this long ago, but it doesn't matter now. Try and think if there's anything else, and remember you'll always be my mam and I'll always love you.'

'I know. I hope raking up the past doesn't cause you more heartache.'

'At least it's stopped raining,' I said, looking out the window, ignoring her last remark. 'There's even a bit of sunshine peeping from behind the clouds.'

Alone in my living room, light-headed with excitement, I examined the photos. This was my mother: a smiling, dark-haired stranger dressed in overalls, feeding cows; posing with a dog in a backyard; stood in a field with tall trees near a farmer's gate. In the last photo, I could see a resemblance to myself: her hair was lighter and she was wearing a twinset and lipstick. There was a photo labelled 'My pal Margaret'. *Who was Margaret? Why had Carole sent the photos? She must have wanted me to have them at some point in the future, together with the letters and her address, so that I'd be able to trace her. I have to find her.*

I tortured myself with the different scenarios. If she had been visiting me for so long, how could she have kept away all these years unless it was true about Australia and she had left the country to forget? The other possibility was she had died young, but I didn't want to dwell on that.

I looked at my adoption certificate. Although I'd seen it before, I hadn't been strong enough to examine it properly. Had Carole abandoned me at birth, then changed her mind? She must have known when she visited me that she could never get me back. The applicants, my future parents, had to pay the sum of thirteen shillings in costs – a pitiable sum. Saddened, I wondered if I was strong enough to cope with whatever was to follow.

I heard the door open. It was Derick. I blurted out everything Mam had told me.

'She should have told you but you can't blame her now. She's too old and she did what she thought was right. She didn't want to lose you.'

'She lost me anyway. I hated her for years, even though I loved her at the same time.'

'Illegitimacy was a disgrace then and no one talked about it.'

'I know all that. But I can't believe she's lied to me all these years.'

'Lied by keeping quiet.'

'That's still lying. Thankfully, she kept the photographs.'

'You can get them enlarged and you'll see her more clearly then.'

'There were so many unanswered questions. Mam said she burned the letters. Do you think that's true?'

'Yes. If she's given you this lot, she wouldn't have held the letters back. Not now she knows you've made up your mind.'

Lying in bed later that night, I wondered how Carole felt when she first saw me again as a toddler, calling a stranger Mummy?

***

Dad sat in his armchair while I tidied the house. 'Your mother's told me you're looking for the other one.' He spoke loud enough for me to hear, without having to look up from his paper. 'She's upset about it, you know.'

Lily had taken Mam out in her wheelchair and we were alone in their living room. 'Mm.' I struggled to reply and continued to dust the sideboard with increased vigour, avoiding eye contact.

'She's very upset,' he repeated, louder.

Deep breath. 'I'm not doing it to upset you or Mam,' I blurted out. 'It's just something I need to know about. It won't make any difference to us.' I turned to look directly at him. 'You're my *real* dad. You're the one who was there when I cried in the night. You've always been there for me.' *Even though I tried to stab you.*

Visibly moved, he nodded. Silence filled the air. I continued to dust until I couldn't stand the quietness any longer.

'What hurts is that she lied to me about Carole. She told me that Carole abandoned me and now I know that's not true.'

'She did it for the best reason.'

'I know.' I didn't want to argue with him and the conversation paused again.

'She lost a baby,' he said, breaking the silence. 'She took it hard.'

'Who?'

'Your mother.'

'No!' I put the duster down and stared at Dad. 'When? She never told me or Lily that she'd had a miscarriage.'

'She never told a soul apart from me. Flushed down the toilet. Never got medical attention.'

'Typical of her. She hates doctors.'

'You arrived on the scene shortly after.'

'That's why she wanted to adopt a baby? That's why you got me?'

'Yes, must have been. You know how she loves babies.'

I didn't have the courage to ask him any more, and I left the house filled with sadness for my mother and the lost baby. By way of compensation, she adopted me. *Did I make her life complete? Did I make up for the lost child? Perhaps for a while, until I found out.*

Chapter 13
Social Worker

Falling in and out of sleep, dreaming of Carole and what the social worker might reveal: darkness turned to light.

I told the managing director of the Runcorn factory where I worked as his PA that I had a dental appointment. Nervy and on edge, I drove my car over the bridge and parked outside the modern Social Services building, ten minutes early.

'Jane won't be long.' The smiling receptionist pointed to a row of chairs. It was a cool, bright day but the office was overly warm, with a smell of newness and lots of comings and goings. I flipped through a magazine, the pictures a blur, the words meaningless. I gave up and stared blankly at the posters on the wall.

A tall, slim woman, aged about thirty-five, opened the door and introduced herself. Dressed in a denim skirt and checked blouse, she shook my hand and asked me into her office. A frizzy, worn-out perm faded lighter towards the ends framed her face. Huge black-rimmed glasses rested on her nose. In spite of my nervousness, I smiled to myself. *A stereotypical social worker.*

She seemed friendly, but I sensed the power she held over me. Perhaps I was oversensitive, but in my mind, she represented the Establishment, which had for years withheld information from people like me. I was inwardly outraged to think that this stranger knew things about my past that I didn't know. *Am I brave enough?*

I sat stiffly on the edge of my chair as we discussed the errors of the past and how attitudes were changing towards illegitimacy and adoption.

'To avoid confusion, I'll call my adoptive mother "Mother"

because she is my mother, and my birth mother "Carole", if you don't mind,' I said with confidence.

'Of course.' She placed her elbows on the desk, interlaced her fingers and made strong eye contact. 'Why do you want to find Carole at this point in your life?'

Here comes the interrogation. 'I need to know my roots ... who I am. I'm at an age when I feel I can cope with whatever happened.' I looked down at my hands. 'No matter how upsetting it is – I *need* to know *everything*.'

'I understand.'

I fumbled in my bag for the adoption papers and photographs of Carole, handing them to Jane and relating the secrecy that surrounded my childhood. She looked up, surprised. 'It's very unusual for your birth mother to have found out where you lived. Once they signed the adoption order, they relinquished all rights of access to their child. Do you remember her coming?'

'Only vaguely.' *Say goodbye to Aunty Carole.*

When I'd finished my story, I felt a massive release of tension. I started to cry.

'Let it all out. You'll feel better after.' She handed me a box of tissues and ordered coffee.

Gradually, the sobbing stopped and my body relaxed. 'I don't know where that came from.' Embarrassed, I dabbed my eyes and blew my runny nose.

'It's common for people to come forward in their forties. Generally, they are settled and have their own families. Like yourself.'

'I have a wonderful family ... but I've always felt there was something missing.' A lump came to my throat and I was ready to cry again, but the entrance of the pretty young receptionist holding our coffee eased the tension. I became calm and told Jane about my family.

'Sometimes adopted people fantasize about their birth parents being rich or famous, but the reality can be quite different. Even if they're found, sometimes the birth parent doesn't want to know. You have to be prepared for whatever you might find, which includes having the door shut in your face.'

'Yes, I'm prepared for that,' I lied, knowing I was terrified.

'Worst-case scenario …' She paused, weighing up my reaction. '… The adopted person is the result of rape or incest.'

I gulped and gripped the arms of the chair. 'How awful. I hadn't thought of that.'

'That wasn't the case with you,' she said quickly. 'Quite the opposite.'

I took a deep breath. 'I've never fantasized like that. I shut myself off from it. Being rejected at birth must be the biggest rejection of all.' I swallowed hard to stop the tears.

'It's not usually a matter of straightforward rejection, you know. It's usually far more complicated than that.'

'Yes,' I said, reminding myself that Carole hadn't abandoned me.

'Your mother should have been more truthful with you. Keeping it secret has obviously been very damaging to your mental health.'

I didn't feel comfortable criticising my mother. 'She had no idea of the emotional trauma she caused me by not telling the truth. All my life, even during the turbulent teenage years, I knew deep down that she loved me. They all did. Not telling me was her only mistake, but even now she doesn't see it like that. She still believes that if the psychiatrist hadn't told me, all would be well and the secret could have remained hidden.'

'How do you feel about your birth parents?'

'It's my birth mother I want to find.'

'From the information I have here, she had a relationship with your father.'

'He left her … and me.'

'Well, he's a part of who you are as well.'

'I know, but he didn't want us.'

She stared, as if assessing my state of mind. 'Some adoptees want revenge. It can become very difficult to handle.'

'I'm not bitter.'

'Good.'

'I know someone whose adopted parents brought her up knowing the truth. When she was a teenager, they encouraged her to search, and she found her mother and half-sisters and -brothers who lived in the next county. Now she has two families who visit regularly.'

Jane smiled. 'That's how it should be in an ideal world, and nowadays adoptive parents are encouraged to be honest with the children they've adopted, but as I said before, it doesn't always end happily.'

She's preparing me for the possibility of rejection.

'If she was visiting me all that time, I think Carole would want to know how my life turned out – unless she's married and not told her husband.'

Jane nodded. 'Yes, that happens quite often. A child from the past popping up unexpectedly can cause all sorts of problems for a marriage. But let's concentrate on what we've got for now. Are you ready to start?' she asked, in a business-like manner. 'We'll take it very slowly. Stop me if you have any questions.'

I nodded.

She cleared her throat. 'Even though it was forty years ago, Social Services did keep records. Nothing like those we have today, of course, but quite comprehensive all the same. I've got a copy of their report here and there's evidence in it that having you adopted was quite a difficult decision for Carole.'

I sat up in my chair, immediately hopeful, of what, I wasn't sure.

'Carole was twenty-two years old when she gave birth to you.'

'Not as young as I'd imagined, but still too young to experience the trauma that having an illegitimate child must have caused at a time when sex outside of marriage was taboo – for women anyway.'

'Exactly.' Jane adjusted her glasses. 'There's no date of birth, which is a pity as it makes tracing easier, but there's a lot for you to go on.'

'I should be able to find her, then?'

'Let's hope so,' she said. 'Her occupation was ex-Land Army but she'd also been a companion/help to a doctor and his wife. Their name and address are here and you could check with Land Army people if anyone remembers her.'

'Does that still exist?'

'There's sure to be some kind of network.'

'This is quite sad.' She glanced over the rims of her glasses. 'Carole never knew her parents and had been brought up by her grandmother, who is now dead. You see why it would have been very difficult for her to keep you if she had no relatives.' She stared intently. 'Are you OK?'

'Yes. Please carry on.' Facts spun round my head in confusion but I had to keep going.

'Your father was twenty-one years old at your birth.'

'Younger than her.' *If he'd loved Carole, he wouldn't have signed me away, and I wouldn't be sitting here forty years later waiting for a social worker to tell me how my life began.*

'You look pale. Do you want to continue?'

'Yes, but I need the bathroom. Could you get me a glass of water, please?'

In the coolness of the bathroom, I stared in the small functional mirror hung over the sink. A haggard face looked back at me, blotchy and stained with mascara. *Why are you putting yourself through this?* I wet a tissue and rubbed the smudged make-up from my cheeks, reddening the blotches. *This is what you've been waiting for all your life. Be strong.*

'Feel better now?' Jane asked, when I returned.

I gulped the cool water. 'It's a lot to take in.'

She nodded. 'The next part, the case history, is written in more detail, so I'll read it slowly through for you. "Carole Dalton met Thomas Fletcher whilst in the Land Army, working on his father's farm at Nantwich known as Fletcher's Farm. When she became pregnant and had to leave the Army, Carole went to stay with Thomas's mother at the farm."'

'She stayed with his mother? That means all the family must

have known. If his mother had taken Carole in, she must have wanted to help her. But not enough to help her keep me.'

'No, but you must remember the taboos about illegitimacy at that time. If Carole had been her daughter, it might have been different. Many mothers brought their unmarried daughter's children up as their own, and no one was any the wiser, until they grew up and discovered the truth. It doesn't usually end with the child happily accepting that its sister is its mother.'

'Thomas's rejection of me wouldn't have helped.'

She gave a half-smile, as if to let me know she understood. '"The case was subsequently referred to a Miss Housden, Church of England Moral Welfare Worker, and she eventually went to a C of E Shelter."'

'Moral Welfare!' The words *Christian charity* flashed up in my mind. Abandoned by everyone, she was reduced to begging. I hated my father.

'"Carole became a companion help to a doctor and his wife, Mr and Mrs Cranshaw."' She paused and took a breath. 'The doctor placed you in a nursing home when you were five days old.'

'Five days old!' I closed my eyes. *It must have felt like having a limb torn from your body.*

'That's the way it was done then. She was fortunate to have you for five days.'

I sipped more water, feeling the coolness run down my throat.

'"On 9 December 1947, Father Donnelly contacted Mr and Mrs Tiernan, who were interested in adopting a child. Barbara was then aged six months."'

I pictured a six-month-old baby lying in a bare cot and two women who had lost a child – one flushed down the toilet, the other torn from her breast. I thought about fate and what had brought my mother and I together – a mutual need, her for a child she'd lost, me for a substitute mother. Jane's voice sounded distant as I tried to collect my thoughts.

'Are you sure you're OK, Barbara?'

'Yes, please go on.' I wanted it over, but I had to hear it all.

"'On 17 December 1947, Carole agreed to Barbara's adoption and on 22 December, Barbara was placed with her adoptive parents.'" Jane pushed her glasses back up the bridge of her nose. 'Now, here's the proof that she didn't want to let you go.' She looked at me, her eyes expectant. "'On 15 February 1948, Carole sent a letter to the Social Services explaining that she did not want Barbara to be adopted because she wanted her back.'"

'Wanted me back?' I repeated softly.

'Yes.' Jane smiled. 'It was obviously very difficult for her to part with you, Barbara. But on 24 February 1948, Carole signed the consent form for your adoption. Unfortunately, for Carole, her signature wasn't witnessed and she had to come back to Liverpool to sign it again. It says here that she refused to do so on numerous occasions, showing the struggle she had in letting you go, but obviously she did eventually sign.'

Jane's words became a background noise. She said something about a letter from the NAAFI in Oswestry and Carole's last known address being in Colne, but my only thought was that Carole had wanted me back. 'Why did she change her mind?'

'It doesn't say. But you know that she must have loved you very much.'

'It makes me determined to find her.'

Jane explained that Social Services do not help people search, but she gave me the names of organisations that could be of assistance. 'Take it very slowly,' she warned. 'It can take a while to adjust mentally to all this new knowledge. I'd start by sending off for a copy of your original birth certificate. There might be more information on that.' She wished me luck. I thanked her for her time and said goodbye, relieved to get out into the cool afternoon air.

I drove home through the rush-hour traffic, light-headed, hysterically happy. Derick's car was in the drive.

He'd returned home early, anxious to know the outcome of the interview. He wanted me to start investigating straight away. 'I suppose it's difficult to understand,' I said. 'After all those years of not knowing, you would have thought I'd be running off to Colne at the first opportunity, but Jane was right – I need time. The longer you've left starting the search, the more time it takes to adjust.'

I did nothing.

***

Two weeks later, the telephone rang. It was Jane. She sounded excited and said she had something else for me. Some letters that Carole had written to Social Services at the time of my adoption had been found. She said she'd drop them off and that I'd be reassured by their contents. I was ecstatic.

When I opened the door the next day, Jane greeted me with a huge smile. 'Please come in,' I said.

'No, sorry, I must rush.' She handed me a large brown envelope. 'You'll be pleased with the contents, but prepare yourself before you read them. It might be a bit upsetting, but don't worry, it's all good.'

'It's strange they kept them all this time,' I said.

'When you read them, you'll understand why. No one could possibly have thrown them away. They're yours, and they explain a lot of things about Carole. Do contact me if there are any developments.'

'Of course I will. Thanks.'

Settling on the sofa, Derick beside me, I opened the brown envelope and took out the bundle. My hands trembled as I unfolded the letters carefully so as not to damage the aged paper. There were two telegrams and eight letters, some written on thin, blue-lined note paper, others on cream faded sheets, torn from a jotter. Like the blue plastic cow, they'd survived for forty years. I looked for dates to read them in order, but some weren't dated. I traced the inky words with my fingers, feeling the pressure of her hand. Her writing was small and child-like, and reminded me of Karen's hand, especially the curl of the C. Carole was in the room with me.

Letter No 1

C/o Dr Cranshaw

Rochdale Rd, Bury, Lancs

1.1.48

Dear Father Donnelly,

Thank you very much for your letter about my baby being adopted.

I expect by now that Sister Gotharda will have sent the Birth Certificate and Baptism Certificate on.

I am naturally very upset at having to part with Barbara but feel that for her sake it is the best thing to do as I cannot provide a home for her.

But I should very much like to know something about the people who have her and what station in life she will have in the future.

I had a good education in a convent and have lost all my relations and feel very lonely.

It would comfort me a great deal to know that Barbara is with good people who can afford to give her a comfortable and happy life.

I am at present a companion help to a doctor's wife who has two children. I have been here since before Barbara was born.

I am very happy here and have good friends in Dr and Mrs Cranshaw, they have been very good to me.

Yours sincerely,

C. Dalton (Miss)

Letter No 2

Rochdale Rd, Bury, Lancs

15.2.48

Dear Madam,

I received the form which you sent the other day.

I find now I just cannot let her go and I want her back. I have been so unhappy this last 2 months wondering what to do, and then you send this form I wasn't expecting it till March, and now I feel I just cannot let her go. She is all I have and I shall work hard to keep her, please forgive me for the trouble I have caused you in finding a home for her and I hope the family that took her will understand. I am going to see the Sister at Facet to see if she can go back there till I can get somewhere else for her. I am returning the form and I hope this is alright.

Yours sincerely,

C. Dalton

Letter No 3

Rochdale Rd, Bury, Lancs

Dear Madam,

Thank you for your letter of this morning.

I am very sorry for the trouble I must be causing you, and I can see how unfair I am being to Mrs Tiernan who has so kindly taken her. I have been to our Priest and he says the same and that I was to fill that form in at once, so if you would kindly send it back I will do so if it is not too late.

When I said I would have her adopted I was definitely told I wouldn't know where she was and who it was that had her and that I would have to come there to sign the form in March. Please understand that is what upset me and made me change my mind. I am now going to join the A.T.S. and try and get away from here.

Yours sincerely,

C. Dalton

Letter No 4

338 N.A.A.F.I.

Birch Lines, Park Hall, Oswestry

18th March 1948

Dear Madam,

Just a few lines to let you know my new address in case you want me to come to Liverpool. I am hoping I don't have to come.

Yours sincerely,

C. Dalton

Letter No 5

338R N.A.A.F.I.

Birch Lines, Parkhall Camp, Oswestry, Salop

April 1948

Dear Madam,

I am writing to ask if you know what they are doing about my little girl. I have not heard from the court and it's worrying me very much. If I knew what was happening, I could put my mind at rest, but until I know I just can't.

Will you please help me?

Yours faithfully,

Miss C. Dalton

Letter No 6

338R N.A.A.F.I.

Birch Lines, Parkhall Camp, Oswestry, Salop

Monday afternoon

Dear Madam,

Thank you for your letter which I received this morning.

I am sorry but I refuse to sign another form of consent. Miss Housden came with me to sign that one and she said it would be alright, so did the Magistrate that signed it.

I don't know why I am being played about like this, you wanted me to let her go and still it's not over and done with yet. I am just miserable and very unhappy about it, it took all my courage to have that one signed. I don't think you know how much this is hurting me.

I long many a time to see my little girl. I have shed many a tear since I have been here.

Yours sincerely,

C. Dalton

Letter No 7

338R N.A.A.F.I.,

Birch Lines, Parkhall Camp, Oswestry, Salop

Dear Sir,

Thank you for your letter which I received yesterday. I am sorry I haven't answered before but I have been in hospital with a broken arm so have been unable to write. I told you I refuse to come and sign another adoption paper. I cannot afford to come all that way just to sign a paper. I am on the sick list and I get no money for another three weeks. I was told if I had her adopted, I shouldn't know where she was and that is why I am so unsettled because I do and it takes all my courage to keep away from her. I have known other girls have their babies adopted and not known where they are and they are quite happy about it, but me I am the unlucky one.

I am sorry I am causing all this trouble but I wonder how you would feel if you were in my place and all this fuss being made over a piece of paper.

I wanted her adopted so that she would have a home which I would never be able to give her, but I didn't know all this trouble would be caused.

Please excuse this writing as my arm is very painful.

Yours sincerely,

C. Dalton

Letter No 8

338R N.A.A.F.I.

Birch Lines, Parkhall Camp, Oswestry, Salop

Dear Sir,

Thank you for your letter of this morning. I don't want to come all that way as I shall want to see Barbara although I know it isn't allowed. I only wish I hadn't listened to other people. I regret it bitterly having let her go and never able to see her again.

If you send me the ticket I shall return the money as I have always been independent. I am alright to come any time now. I am not promising I will do any more signing if I come.

Yours faithfully,

(Miss) C. Dalton

On 24 May, Carole sent a telegram to Reverend G. Donnelly at 150 Brownlow Hill Liverpool:

= COMING TODAY = C DALTON +

Derick hugged me and held me tight as I cried uncontrollably, burying my face in his chest. 'She certainly didn't give you up easily.'

'All those years of fear and doubt,' I said, my tears subsiding. 'But the awful distress she suffered. It just tears me apart.'

Derick kissed my forehead, and left me to re-read the letters.

I re-enacted the drama, imagining her torment. The pressures of society, the figures of authority – doctors, priests, Moral Welfare workers and magistrates – all played their part.

The Cranshaws stole her baby under the guise of 'doing good'. The priest insisted that she fill in the form. Miss Housden accompanied her to make sure she signed: *parting us forever.* What chance did she have?

She was nothing to them. Just another foolish girl who'd got herself into trouble or a wicked girl who'd sinned. I longed to reach out and touch that young woman, hug her and ease her pain: tell her I understood why she left me.

'Knowing where I was must have tortured her. I wonder how she found out? And my mother, how she would have wept if she'd had to give me back,' I said to Derick later on.

'Florrie would never have given you up,' Derick said. 'She'd have hidden you in the coal shed before she'd have parted with you.'

'Or with the chickens.' We both laughed.

'You have to concentrate on finding Carole.'

'Those letters change everything. I'm starting right now!' I said, firmly. 'I'm applying to the General Register Office in London for a copy of my original birth certificate.'

Later that night, I read the letters again. My tears dampened the paper. We cried for the loss of each other. *I'll find you, Carole.*

I waited two weeks for my original birth certificate but it didn't give any more information than the copy, except to say that my birth was registered on 16 June 1947; Carole gave the Cranshaws' as her address in Bury, and the name of father column was blank.

'I was expecting more,' I said to Derick.

'Don't look so sad. It's a start,' he said.

***

I wanted to be honest with my children and answer their questions truthfully in a way that my mother was never able to do with me. If I'd been brought up knowing about my adoption, I'd have been able to talk about it freely to those closest to me. But I never could. Now things were set in motion, I knew I'd have to tell them.

Shaun, tall and handsome with the same blue eyes as his dad, sat watching TV while I paced up and down the living room, my body hunched, my palms sweaty. *Deep breath.* 'Can I have a word?' Shaun dragged his eyes away from the screen.

'What have I done now?' He rolled his eyes.

'Nothing!' I smiled. 'You know, I'm really proud of you getting good grades.'

'Is that what you wanted to say?' He turned back to the TV.

'Will you switch that off!'

He pressed the off switch on the remote. 'You're worrying me now.' His eyes widened. 'Keep still, Mum, and tell me what's wrong.'

I sat on the edge of the chair opposite him, clasping my hands. 'Your Nan and Jan aren't my natural parents. They adopted me as a baby.'

He frowned and looked puzzled, but he seemed relieved. 'Wow! You were adopted. When? How old were you?'

I gave him a softer version of my adoption story, and told him that I was going to search for my birth mother.

'I bet Nan's upset.'

'She's not very happy about it, so don't mention it to her unless she brings it up.'

'I won't, but why have you decided to do this now?'

'I was too scared to do it when I was younger, afraid of what I'd find out. But now I'm older, I need to know who I am.'

'Yeah, I can understand that. I'd be curious if it was me. And your father? Don't you want to find him?'

'Yes ... I suppose ... him as well, but he left her pregnant with me. I doubt if he'd want to be reminded of me or her.'

'He might regret leaving her. He might want to know how you are now.'

'Maybe, but it's her I want to find.' *It's thoughtful of him to give my biological father more credit than he probably deserves.*

'I've always wondered why you're the skinny one of the family.' He wrinkled his brow. 'It's weird to think that I'm not genetically related to the Tiernans. I've always thought of them as my family.'

'They are your family. Nothing's changed.'

'How come you never told us about this before?'

'I felt ashamed of being adopted. I know it's crazy, but I never talked about it to anybody, not even your dad until we were getting married.' I explained how I found out.

'My nan should have told you, but she was always kind to you, wasn't she?'

'Yes. She treated me no different than the rest of her children.' I remembered the unkind refrain, but didn't mention it.

When he looked at the photos and scanned the letters from Carole, his expression changed to sadness. 'It's weird thinking that I have another grandmother somewhere and a grandfather, but they'll never replace Nan and Jan.'

'Does Karen know?'

'No. I'll tell her in the café after I pick her up from her dance class.'

***

We inhaled the smell of freshly baked bread as we walked through the door and climbed the worn old staircase. The Sad Café, the name we'd given the café above Robertson's bakery, was bare apart from the bright red checked tablecloths decorated with chipped vases of plastic flowers. The low ceiling bowed at one end, making Karen, who was five-foot ten, stoop. There was more than a hint of dampness, but it was our favourite café because they made the best cheese toasties in town.

I scanned the empty room. The sun shone through the rusty window frames brightening the gloom. Karen sat by the window; we looked down on the people passing by in the main street. Aged fourteen, a skinny, pretty teenager with waist-length dark curly hair, Karen excelled at school and got straight 'A's in everything.

The stairs creaked and an elderly waitress appeared and took our order. I nibbled the toasted bread slowly. 'There's something I want to tell you,' I said, forcing a smile.

She looked up, startled. 'What?'

I leaned forward ... 'I'm adopted. Your nan and Jan adopted me just after my first birthday.'

Karen put down her cup and looked at me as if she didn't understand. 'Nan and Jan aren't my real grandparents?'

'They are your real grandparents. Nothing has changed.'

Karen listened to my story, interrupting with a thousand questions. She stared at the photos. 'She's my grandmother? This lady with the cows?' When she read the letters, tears fell. She moved to sit next to me, and we hugged and cried together. 'That's so sad ... I'll always love Nan and Jan, but you've got to find Carole.'

Lily was next on my list. I walked slowly round to her house in the fresh May sunshine, thoughts about Carole crowding my mind – was she still in Manchester, or did she go to Australia? An attractive young woman wouldn't stay single for long.

As close as Lily and I had been, I'd never discussed my adoption with her. After we had tea, I told her that I was going to search for my birth mother.

'Mam's already told me. She's not happy about it but I calmed her down.'

'Thanks. No matter who or what I find in this search, you know if I had to choose a sister, it'd be you.'

We hugged. 'I understand.' When she read Carole's letters, tears rolled down her cheeks and we cried together. 'The thought of having to part with one of my five would have destroyed me.'

Lily is my real sister. More than I could ever wish for. 'Do you remember anything about her?'

'I remember her coming to the house. Aunty Carole, we called her, and she gave you that cow, but I was only young – about seven or eight. Jimmy'll remember better. Ring him and ask to visit.' She handed me the phone.

'Hi, Jimmy. Suppose you know what I'm up to,' I said.

'Heard it on the grapevine,' Jimmy said. 'I believe Mam's upset?'

'Initially she was against it, but she's OK now, I think. Did she tell you?'

'No, Joe did. He met me in the Snig for a drink. He was angry, said it was a betrayal. "Why does she want to go off looking for that lot?" he said. "They left her in a home."'

'He's just protecting Mam.'

'Come down for a chat, and I'll see what I can remember.'

***

In their large terraced house in West Bank, Jimmy's wife, Jean, poured tea and sat beside Jimmy on the sofa: I sat opposite making notes. In spite of an unusually warm June, the high ceilings kept the room comfortably cool. Jean was house-proud and the smell of lavender polish filled the air.

'Yes, I remember her coming to the house,' Jimmy said. 'She was lovely. Tall, blonde-haired, very blue eyes. More heavily built than you.'

'What was she like, as a person, I mean?'

'Lively. Chatty. Very friendly.'

The picture of Carole I had in my head was laden with sadness. Imagining her being vivacious surprised me.

'She seemed happy, then?'

'When she was with you, yes.'

'Do you remember Mam stopping her coming?'

'Yes, Carole was upset, but Mam was afraid that you'd get too attached to each other.'

We were mother and child – how could we not get attached?

'And she wrote letters afterwards. Do you remember them?'

'Yes, Mam showed some of them to me, and the photos she sent.' *He knew all this. He never told me. I never asked.*

'Did you see the address on the letters?'

'They came from Sevenoaks, Kent. She'd been working there on a farm.'

'And is it true she said she was going to Australia with a man she'd met on the farm?'

'As far as I can remember, that's right.'

'I thought Mam might just be saying Carole was going to Australia to put me off looking.'

'No. Carole said they were going on the £10 ticket.'

Is Jimmy lying to protect Mam?

'You're not just saying that, are you? It's important that I know the truth now.'

'I wouldn't lie to you. She might have changed her mind, or split up with the man, but that's what I remember her saying.'

'I wonder if she married him before they left?'

'They probably would have had to get wed in those days.'

'If she did, she'd have changed her name and she'd be registered as Mrs-such-a-body in Australia.'

'I'm surprised you never went looking for her earlier.'

'Wish I had.'

Driving home, Jimmy's words replayed in my head. I saw Carole laughing, singing, teasing and hugging me, as though I still belonged to her. The shiny blue plastic cow; the rattle; Aunty Carole saying goodbye. Would my appearance disrupt her life, ruin her marriage, turn her children against her? Would I be welcome?

Chapter 14
The Search Begins

I'd read about people being traced through solicitors: Derick suggested we see his, Mr Clarkson. A middle-aged man with thinning hair, horn-rimmed glasses and a tired look invited us into his gloomy office. Dusty wooden shelves crammed with books lined the walls, papers and files covered desks, floors and tables. The lines on Mr Clarkson's face deepened as he read the report.

He's going to say it's hopeless.

'The best way to tackle this is to actually do some detective work yourselves and knock on doors,' he said after a long pause. 'You don't need to give the real reason why you're looking – if you don't want to – just make something up. You'd be surprised how helpful people can be, and you might feel inclined to tell them the truth.'

'I thought you'd suggest putting adverts in the papers the way they do for heiresses to come forward to collect the fortune a long-forgotten relative has left them in their Will.'

'That'd be expensive and is not always successful. My advice is to go to her last known address in Colne and ask the neighbours if anyone remembers her.'

'That makes sense,' Derick said. 'We'll give it a try.'

'Let me know how you get on and give me a ring if you need any further help.' He shook our hands and wished us good luck.

'That's given us a starting point,' Derick said, as he drove us home.

'But we know she moved away and might have gone to Australia,' I said.

'Or she might have come back to her roots.'

***

The autumnal mist slowly melted in the morning sun as we drove fifty miles to Colne, an old mill town nestling in the foothills of the Pennines, with its sloping cobbled streets and stone-built houses. It was an adventure and I was bursting with fear and excitement. 'We're looking for number 11 Hanover Street, her last known address,' I read aloud, 'where she lived with a Mrs Spencer according to the report.'

'It's real woolly back country this,' Derick joked, as we passed the numerous disused cotton mills, now warehouses or museums.

'You've just missed the turning,' I said, struggling to read the A-Z and balance the report on my knee.

'No! I can see it, next on the left,' Derick reassured me.

'Sorry, I'm so wound up.'

'That's understandable. You might be about to meet your mother.'

'If only.' I sat silently, imagining Carole walking the cobbled streets. We turned into Hanover Street and parked at the end of a row of tiny stone terraces with neat little front gardens. Sick with apprehension, I stood behind Derick as we walked up to number 11.

A young woman with a baby in her arms answered the door. Flashing his best salesman's smile, Derick apologised for the intrusion and asked if she knew of a Mrs Spencer, who had occupied the house in the 1950s. She gave us a surprised look.

'We've only lived here about five years, and the people we bought it from were called Pike. Sorry, I can't help you.'

'Thanks for your time,' Derick said.

She watched us walk down the short pathway; a pathway Carole had walked. Deep down I felt that she was long gone from here.

'Some of the older people in the street might remember her,' Derick said. 'Let's knock at the houses on either side.'

'I'll take this side,' I said, emboldened.

Curtains parted and curious bystanders stared at us.

'What you selling?' an elderly gentleman shouted from across the road.

'We're not salespeople,' Derick said.

Two women wearing headscarves stood talking by a lamppost. 'Who're you looking for?'

'Let's be honest,' I said to Derick. 'These look like decent folks.' Derick nodded.

Briefly, I told them my story. They immediately rallied round us with sympathetic interest, and we were directed to Mrs Hartley, now in her eighties, the longest-living member of the street.

'She knew everyone round here. I'll take you down there,' said a woman called May. 'She'll let you in if you're with me.'

Derick waited outside so as not to scare Mrs Hartley. I stepped into an antiques road show of mahogany and rosewood furniture – dark and shady – with a slightly musty smell. A fragile woman with dark wrinkled skin sat on a rocker by the fireside. She looked pleased to have visitors and perked up when May told her why I was there.

'Yes, I remember the Spencers, and Eric, their son.'

'That's great,' I said. *This is going to be a lead!*

'My son George used to play with him. My George is dead. So is Eric. It's awful to lose a child – unnatural for them to die before you.'

'I'm sorry,' I said. 'I can't imagine how terrible that must be.'

'When you get to my age, they're all dead. My turn soon.'

'You've got years in you yet,' I said. 'Do you remember them having a lodger called Carole, sometime in the 1950s?'

She looked thoughtful; a few seconds passed, then her cloudy eyes cleared. 'Yes, I think they did have a lodger, a young woman, but I don't think she was there long and I can't remember her name.'

It's Carole! It has to be her!

'Lily Farrow from number 33 might know something. She used to play with Eric and George.'

Mrs Farrow wasn't in so we left the street. 'I'll write her a letter,' I said, as we walked to the car. 'Looks like our detective work is paying off. I've seen a house she once lived in – walked on the same cobbled street.' I stared at the houses as we pulled away. *Would I ever find her?*

A few weeks later, I got a reply from Mrs Farrow saying that she couldn't remember Carole and neither could anyone who she'd asked. She suggested I put an advert in the *Colne Times* and the *Manchester Evening News* or write to Cilla Black on *Surprise Surprise*.

Disappointed but determined to continue, I placed an ad in both papers under the pretence of a Land Army reunion. I believed that if I told the truth, people may be reluctant to get involved in something so sensitive, aware of the problems an illegitimate child showing up after forty years could cause.

***

'Hi, I'm ringing about Carole Dalton,' a male voice, chatty and familiar, spoke down the phone. 'I knew Carole well.'

Wow! That was quick! Please let it be my Carole.

'Do you think it's the same person?'

'It's the same one.'

He sounded confident, which gave me hope. 'How did you know her?'

'She hung around with a group of ex-Land Army girls. They used to come into our local pub. A right lively one she was.'

'Oh! In what way?'

'The life and soul of the party, you know, full of fun.'

Jimmy said she was lively. It is her. The muscles in my neck tightened. 'When did you last see her?'

'In the 1950s.'

'Where was she living?' *Please remember where.* 'The exact location is really important.'

'Err ... round Rochdale ... that's where I was living at the time. I dated a lot of ex-Army girls back then.'

She must have moved to Rochdale – maybe had friends in the area – could still be living there. My hopes soared. 'What was your relationship with her?'

'Well, that'd be telling.' His voice became coarse.

Alarm bells rang. *Strange thing to say. I don't like the sounds of this.* 'What do you mean?'

'Do you want me to spell it out for you?'

Had she become a prostitute? God no! This is the worst-case scenario. Dizzy. Sick. I forced myself to carry on talking. Was there some grain of truth in what he was saying? 'What did she look like?' I asked.

'She was a good-looker,' he said, his voice becoming more excitable.

'What colour was her hair?' *Fifty per cent chance of him getting it wrong.*

'Err ... brown.' He paused. 'Long and dark it was, and sometimes she wore it up in curls on the top, but I liked it down round her shoulders. Dark and smooth, like chocolate.'

Is he lying? Can I call his bluff? 'No, she was fair.'

'Women dye their hair,' he said, without hesitation.

That was true, evidenced by the photos of her with dark hair. Even if she'd been a prostitute, I have to know the truth. 'What colour were her eyes?'

'Err ... brown, to match her hair.'

The bastard's lying.

'No. They were blue.' *Strikingly blue.*

'It was years ago. You forget these things,' he said slyly. 'It wasn't her eyes I was interested in. Make no mistake about it, I knew Carole. She was all right.' He laughed crudely.

I was sickened, but had to keep going. 'Was she tall or short?' *This is the clincher.*

'Err ... average height ... but she was a little tart. Are you a tart? She liked to wear stockings and suspenders, black lacy ones, and she ...'

'Pervert!' I screamed down the phone, slamming it back on

the receiver. I felt stupid, dirty and furious with myself for letting a depraved individual take advantage of my vulnerability. That was the only response I got to my newspaper advertisements in Manchester. *I won't let that idiot stop me.*

***

I spread the information across the dining room table. 'We'll work methodically through the extract from your birth records,' Derick said. 'Carole lived at 10 Rochdale Rd, with the good doctor. Pass me the phone book.' Frantically, Derick flicked the pages. 'You won't believe this, he's still in it. Ring him.'

My heart thumped as I dialled the number. *This is the man who separated us.*

'Doctor Cranshaw speaking,' a fragile voice answered. He sounded about 102 and I could barely make out what he said.

'I'm sorry to disturb you, doctor, but I'm trying to trace someone. Do you remember a young woman named Carole Dalton who stayed with you as a companion help to your wife in 1947? She had a baby she named Barbara, who was adopted. I'm Barbara. I'm trying to trace Carole, my birth mother.'

'Carole who? Can't quite hear you.' I repeated my story until he grasped what I was saying.

'I'd like to be of help, dear, but it was so long ago.'

'Please try to remember. She'd been working on a farm in Nantwich. That's where she met my father, Thomas Fletcher. He left her and you took her in … please.'

'If she'd been alive, Phillis, my wife, would have been able to help you, but I was always busy with the surgery. My wife and I helped so many girls but I can't remember any particular one. I'm sorry.'

Yes, you separated them from their babies. Was he telling the truth? Did he believe I'd no right to be looking for her? I hated him for not remembering but I thanked him for his time. He probably had little left. Another dead end.

'It's back to the drawing board,' Derick said.

'I was baptised on 6 June 1947 at St Joseph's R.C. Church in Bury by the Reverend R. Wearden and my godparent was Elizabeth Bevan.'

'Elizabeth Bevan, must be a strong link,' Derick said. 'She must have been close to Carole if she was your godmother.'

'You'd think so, but Dr Cranshaw had already taken me away from Carole and dumped me in an orphanage, and it was Mrs Cranshaw who took me to be baptised at St Joseph's, so Elizabeth Bevan could have been a friend of hers. It's all so murky."We'll check if the church still exists. There might be some clues. It's worth having a go.'

The church did still exist, and Derick wrote to the parish priest, a Reverend R. Morrow, asking for information. He replied a week later saying that he'd searched the parish registers from January 1942 to December 1952 and had found no trace of either Carole Dalton or Elizabeth Bevan. There was no record of any Bevan children being born or Elizabeth Bevan marrying in the church. He suggested checking the voters' lists at Colne Registrar's Office to see if she married about the time she ceased to be registered as a voter at that address.

The following week, Derick arrived home late. 'You look worn out,' I said.

'I've not worked today,' he said, hanging up his overcoat and sitting down in the living room. 'I've been on a mission.'

'What mission?' *What's happened?* 'Why haven't you been in work?'

'Come and sit down and I'll tell you.'

'OK!' Confused and fearful, I sat down next to him.

'I've been to Bury and Colne looking through the electoral rolls for evidence of Carole's time there. Bill tagged along.'

'You're a dark horse,' I said, relieved and curious. 'Did you tell him the whole story? He'd understand, having two adopted children himself.'

'Yes. He was keen to help.'

'I'll ring him and thank him. But what made you go off like that when you should be working?'

'I want to solve the mystery of Carole for you.'

'Aww. Thanks.' I leaned my head against his shoulder, and a lump formed in my throat. 'Did you find anything?'

'Depends how you look at things. We found Bury Town Hall, a typical old Victorian building, and we parked up. Inside, we located the Electoral Roll office and began searching. I'd taken a notepad to write down any information. It was fun at first. We spent a couple of hours looking through the registers, but after a while the excitement began to wear off. So, we went to a local McDonald's for lunch. We did find out that Bury is the birthplace of Robert Peel.'

'At least you found out something,' I said, smiling.

'After we ate, we went on to the Colne office and carried on for another couple of hours, covering the years of her stay either side, but there was nothing – not a trace.'

'What a shame.' The familiar sinking feeling started in the pit of my stomach. 'Thanks for doing that.' He hugged me. 'It's probably because she only lodged with people and didn't have a permanent address. She sounds like a bit of a gypsy, with no roots, moving from place to place.'

'You do have a Romany look about you.'

'Is that a compliment?'

'Of course,' he said, smiling. 'As for whether we found anything, we now know that she never resided in Bury or Colne for a long enough period to be put on the electoral registers.'

'That's something.' I smiled to mask my utter disappointment.

'So, she remains elusive – for now – but there has to be someone, somewhere who knows her.'

***

The social worker had given me a list of organisations that specialise in finding and reuniting lost relatives. I started with Searchline, who had a contact register. They checked, but Carole had not registered as a contact. Searchline told me about NORCAP (the National Organisation for Counselling Adoptees and Parents) based in Oxford, which supports and helps unite adoptees with their birth parents. I immediately joined.

The phone rang. 'Hi, I'm Suzanne, I'm your NORCAP contact.' The voice was warm and welcoming. 'We work on the same principle as Alcoholics Anonymous. We support each other. Most of us have been adopted ourselves.'

'It's great to speak to someone who understands.'

'Exactly. How did you find out about us?'

'From Jane, the social worker who counselled me and gave me a list of organisations who help people. You were on it. Carole hadn't registered with Searchline, so I placed my name on their register, in case at some future date she might contact them.'

'You never know,' Suzanne said. 'I've checked the NORCAP contact register for you, but there was no entry for Carole on that, either.'

'Perhaps she doesn't want to be found.' My voice reflected my thoughts.

'Don't be downhearted. Carole might not know such registers exist. Did you know?'

'No, I didn't.'

An hour passed quickly. We laughed and cried. 'It's a shame you haven't got her date of birth,' Suzanne said. 'It makes it easier, but you have other information. Every three months, NORCAP organise a trip to St Catherine's House in London where records for all the births, deaths and marriages in the UK are kept. The date of the next one will be in our monthly magazine. Did you receive it?'

'Yes. Thanks,' I said. 'I like the adoption stories and hints about searching.'

'NORCAP are trying to get the government to set up a national contact register, so write to your MP. After the Childrens Act 1975, we were inundated with thousands of desperate people who wanted to find their blood relatives. The government set the Act up on the cheap and provided no support, so they all came to us, a voluntary organisation.'

'Typical of the government,' I said, full of regret. 'Wish I'd had the courage to search for her back then.'

'No use fretting about that. You're doing it now. That's all that matters.'

When I put the phone down, I wrote to my MP asking the government to set up a national contact register. I sat at the table and stared through the patio window. It was November and the backyard was littered with leaves. *If Carole had been in the UK in 1975, she would have heard about the change in the law. Did she hope that I'd find her? Was she disappointed that I didn't, or did she live in fear that I'd turn up and destroy her life?* No matter what the outcome, I knew I had to go on. *Why did I leave it so long?*

The NORCAP magazine lay open on the table in front of me. I flipped through, pausing at an article about the Department of Health and Social Security (DHSS). It said they would forward a letter to a missing person. I immediately wrote to the DHSS.

Two weeks later, I received a reply:

> *...I should explain that information contained in our records is confidential.*
>
> *In cases involving adoption or similar situations we are unable to offer our usual letter forwarding service because of the risk of causing distress or embarrassment to the person receiving the letter.*
>
> *...I regret that I cannot help you. I am so sorry – NORCAP were wrong to refer you to the Department as we cannot help.*

After every setback, the longing to find Carole intensified. I wrote the same day to Catholic Social Services in Liverpool, who had arranged my adoption. I told them I was having difficulty tracing Carole, and asked if they had any further information. They promptly replied that the facts I'd already been given by the social worker were comprehensive and that there were no further details on the file, no date of birth for Carole Dalton, no address for Thomas Fletcher and no name or address for Carole's grandmother. The authorities appeared to be cold and unwilling to help. I felt like a persistent fly constantly being swatted away.

FIND CAROLE DALTON I wrote in large red letters on the yellow foolscap file I'd bought to hold the increasing records, notes and correspondence relating to the search. Every week, Derick and I sifted through the papers like detectives examining evidence.

'If Florrie was telling the truth about the letters, Carole's last known address was in the Tunbridge Wells area,' I said to Derick. 'I'll write to Tunbridge Council and ask if it would be possible to look through the electoral roll.'

A week later, they replied saying that the electoral registers were not in alphabetical order so it would not be possible to check whether Carole Dalton resided there in the early Fifties. They suggested I contact the *Kent and Sussex Courier*.

'As with Manchester, she was probably only in the Kent area for a short time, working casually on a farm,' I said.

'She may not have been registered at all,' Derick said. 'A newspaper ad might be more promising.'

'I'll use the Land Army reunion story.'

I wrote to the *Kent and Sussex Courier*:

> *I was in the Land Army in 1946/1947 at Nantwich in Cheshire. I am planning a reunion of my 'old pals', but have had great difficulty in locating the whereabouts of a lady named Carole Dalton, who was last heard of as living in the Tunbridge Wells area in the early 1950s.*

> *Would Carole, if you are still there in Tunbridge Wells, or anyone who knows of her please give me a ring on—*

I had three replies, but nothing concrete emerged.

'If she did meet a man from that area while working on a farm,' I said to Derick the following week, 'he must surely have had some family or friends who remembered them, even if they did go to Australia, unless he was a stray, wandering through life with no roots, like Carole,' I said, aware of the disappointment in my voice.

'Don't get disheartened,' Derick said.

'I'd be able to reach more people if I contacted the radio with the reunion lie. I'd like to tell the truth but imagine how Carole would feel if she was driving along in her car, with her husband, and she heard me on the radio saying I was her daughter. She'd be furious.' *How would she react if she knew I was looking for her? Would she welcome me?*

***

'You're listening to *Radio Kent*. This is Dave Raymond. It's time for that moment in the show when we help to reunite people with lost loved ones or friends, and today we have Barbara Attwood, nee Tiernan, from a town called Widnes in the Liverpool area, who's planning a Land Army reunion for her mother, Florence. Come on, all you Land Army girls, get listening. This might concern you or someone you know! And can I just say what a grand job you girls did, working on the land while your men were away fighting for their country. But I'm sure there were lots of good times as well – country hops, local lads, Yanks! Yes, I thought so. I'm living proof of the good times, along with a few million other 'baby boomers'. Perhaps we'd better not go into that, but I'd like to be a fly on the wall at this reunion. Well hello, Barbara! How's things up there in sunny Scouseland?'

In spite of my bravado, I was nervous about being on the air. The fact that I was lying and could be caught out made it worse, but I forced myself to do it.

'Hello, Dave, I'm great.' The receiver shook in my hand. 'We live twelve miles outside of Liverpool, but we're still thought of as Liverpudlians by southerners, because of the accent.'

'No offence meant – salt of the earth. So tell us about your plans, Barbara, and who you're hoping to contact through the show.'

'Thanks. Err … Mm …' I swallowed.

'Don't be nervous now, Barbara, speak up.' *I'll never get through this. Deep breath.*

'My mother, Florence, known as Florrie, was in the Land Army working on a farm in Nantwich, Cheshire around 1946–47. She had a friend there named Carole Dalton. They were very close and my mother would love to meet up with her again.'

'I'm sure she would. Does she know what happened to Carole?' Dave asked.

'A little bit. After leaving the Land Army, Carole went to live in the Sevenoaks, Tunbridge Wells area, working on a farm. My mother had letters from her in the 1950s, but in the last letter she said she was going to live in Australia with someone she'd met on a farm. I know it's a long shot, but I thought someone down there might remember her or be related to the person she met on the farm. Maybe she never went to Australia, and still lives in the area. My mother never heard from her again after that.' *I did it!*

'Well, come on, folks, does anyone remember Carole Dalton, who came down here from Cheshire in the 1950s? Barbara, I'm sure my listeners will do their best, and if anyone does know anything, you know the rules, please don't contact the show, contact Barbara on the following phone number: 0151—. Thanks for talking to us today, Barbara.'

'Thanks for having me on the air. If anyone thinks they know anything about Carole, no matter how insignificant it may seem, please let me know.'

'Good luck with the reunion. My listeners would love to know how it goes, and if you find Carole. Hope you get some good news soon.'

'Phew! That was scary but exciting,' I said afterwards, full of adrenalin. 'Now that I've been on the air, I'm going to go on BBC Radio Suffolk and Radio Essex, and I'm going to write to all the local papers. She has to be somewhere.'

***

Over the weeks, I accumulated numerous letters from kindly ladies who'd been in the Land Army. I'd eagerly open them with excited fingers but no one remembered Carole Dalton.

I received a letter with suggested avenues of exploration from the Citizens Advice Bureau in Tunbridge Wells. Most of them I'd already been down, but one of the names on the list was the Council for Voluntary Service in Tunbridge Wells. I wrote to the General Secretary, Mr John Heywood, who was interested in my story and said he would do everything he could to help. I sent him copies of all the information I had and he spent months making enquiries in the area, but they all came to nothing. With every negative response my mood plummeted. The continual disappointment was hard to bear.

Chapter 15

Surprise Caller

The phone rang. I was working as a personal assistant at a shipping company while studying to get my A levels at night school, with the aim of eventually becoming a teacher.

'Are you busy?' Derick sounded excited. 'Guess what?'

I sat erect. 'What?'

'I've just spoken to your father, to Thomas.'

'To my father ... to Thomas?' I repeated, stunned.

'Yes, Thomas.'

'Derick's just spoken to my father!' I shouted to my colleague, Vera. My shoulders drooped and the phone slid from my hand.

'Are you still there? Are you OK?' I could hear Derick's muffled voice.

'My God,' Vera said, rushing over to my desk and handing me the phone. She was a gentle, understanding woman who knew my story. 'I'll put the kettle on.'

Confused, I put the phone back to my ear. 'Why? How? Where did you find him?' My heart thumped in my chest. 'Did he speak to you?'

'Calm down while I tell you.'

'I can't think straight! What made you go off like that?'

'I know it's Carole you want to find, but he must hold the key. Even if he doesn't know where she is now, I thought he'd remember something about her past. So, I went to his last known address on the social worker's report and just knocked on the door.'

'Oh God!' I said, my heart still thumping. 'Was he still living there?'

'Just listen. There was no reply, so I knocked at the adjoining house. An elderly lady answered. I made up a story about him being a distant uncle. I could feel her weighing me up, but she must have decided that I was legit, and she told me that he hadn't moved far, just round the corner. She gave me his address. It was as easy as that. I screeched round the corner, rang the bell and again I just knocked on the door. No one answered, so I started to walk round the side of the house.'

'I can't believe you did this,' I said, my mind whirling. 'What happened?'

'I heard barking and a small dog came running up the side path, followed by a man of about sixty. He was shouting at the dog, telling it to shut up.'

My hand shook as I held the phone.

'Do I look like him?'

'He was dark with brown eyes, like yours, but no striking resemblance. Tall, medium build, still had his own hair, healthy-looking for his age.'

This is the man who abandoned me.

'What was he like?'

'Oh! He was likeable, on first impression.'

'Likeable?' *I'd not imagined him being likeable.* 'What did you say to him?'

'"Are you Thomas Fletcher?" "Yes, that's me," he said. He gave me a look as if to say *Not another salesman.* "What can I do for you?" "Do you remember Carole Dalton?" I asked him straight out. "No, I don't," he said firmly. "Who *are* you?" He looked genuinely puzzled. "You remember Barbara, don't you – the baby – and Carole," I said.'

'Did he remember?' I asked, my heartbeat rising up to my throat.

'Not at first, and I started to have doubts. But then he went quiet and his face changed. In a split second, his eyes registered shock. He looked straight at me and said, "Carrie ... It was Carrie – not Carole." I was so relieved, it *was* him.'

'Carrie,' I said, my stomach tightening. *And we've been looking for Carole.*

'I asked him if he remembered you. He said he last saw the baby in Widnes at the court hearing.'

'The baby,' I repeated. 'That's me.'

'I introduced myself and offered my hand. He shook it reluctantly. I told him the difficulty we were having finding Carole – now Carrie. I stressed that you don't want anything from him, and that we won't cause him any problems, you just want to find your mother. He said he understood that, but that he has no idea where she is now.'

'He didn't know anything?' I said, my body wilting.

'No. He said he'd put it all out of his mind. I asked if he'd talk to you about it, maybe meet up with you. Initially he said no, that he didn't think he could. But I continued with my salesman's persistence. I said that he owed you at least one phone call. He kept prevaricating. "She won't bother you again," I said. Perhaps he sensed that I wasn't going to leave until he agreed to a phone call.'

'Did he agree?' My heart was bursting.

'Yes, grudgingly. I got him to write down his number before he could change his mind. He scribbled it down like a man signing his life away. "Leave it a few days before you ring," he said, guilt written all over him. "It's a long time since I've thought about any of this." So, there you have it. I found Thomas.'

'He must have been stunned, after forty years.' Relieved, I slowly sipped the tea Vera had made extra sweet to help me get over the shock. 'But what would you have done if his wife or someone else had come round the corner?'

'I'd have crossed that bridge if I'd come to it. I did ask him if his family knew about you, and he said his wife, Dorothy, knew.'

'That'll make things easier. I wonder what she'll think of all this. Did he say he had children?'

'Yes. He has two daughters, but he stressed they don't know about you.'

'No.' *Both born in wedlock and much loved. Why would he tell them about his bastard?*

'Are you OK?'

'I'm in a state of shock, too, but I'll be fine.'

'I'd gone off naively thinking that Thomas would be able to tell me where Carole was, and that I'd be able to surprise you.'

'I'm certainly surprised, Private Detective Attwood. If only finding her was so easy.'

'When he's had time to think, he might remember something, and tell you what really happened.'

'If he's willing to tell … the truth, I mean.'

'Are you sure you're all right? I'll have to get back to work.'

'This is such a big step forward. My mind's all over the place but I'll be OK. Vera will look after me. She's dying to hear the tale. Bye! I love you, and thanks.' I put down the phone and thought how lovely Derick was.

'Well, what's happened?' Vera asked. 'Are you well enough to tell me?'

'Yes,' I said, but before I could give her the story, I burst into tears.

***

'When are you going to ring him?' Derick asked two weeks later.

'It's hard for me. I want to do it myself but the fear of him putting the phone down and rejecting me again scares me.'

'Let me make the first phone call.'

'OK.' I felt such a coward, but I couldn't make myself do it. In typical secretarial style, I typed a list instructing Derick what he should say if Thomas's wife, daughters or anyone but him answered the phone, and a list of questions to ask him.

'You've covered just about everything,' Derick said, poking fun at my office-like efficiency.

Derick sat at the dining room table and I sat opposite with a notepad, paralysed with emotion. He pressed the speakerphone.

'Hello! It's Derick Attwood, Barbara's husband? I'm sorry to have surprised you like that the other week. It must have been quite a shock to have the past brought up so abruptly after all those years.'

'Oh! Hello! Yes, it was. I've been thinking about it a lot since you came. How is Barbara?'

I sighed, relieved he hadn't put the phone down, encouraged by his concern.

'She's OK, but it was a bit of a shock for her as well. I didn't tell her beforehand because I wasn't sure of the outcome. Barbara's a bit shy about talking to you just yet, but do you mind if I ask you some questions?'

Quickened heartbeat: acid rising from my stomach. *He's going to refuse.*

'No, I don't mind,' he said, pausing, 'but I haven't thought about this for a long time.'

'We've been searching round the Colne area, her last known address. Do you know where Carole came from?'

'It's Carrie. I called her Carrie,' he said, firmly. 'She wasn't from round here. She was from Essex.'

Wrong name! Wrong place!

'From Essex,' Derick repeated, looking at me for a reaction. 'We just assumed she was a local girl.'

'I don't know who she'd be living with in Colne, but she wasn't local. She came up north with the Land Army.'

'Yes, we knew about the Land Army. Whereabouts in Essex? Which town?'

'It was the Lowlands, the Fens, but I can't remember the town. It was all so long ago.'

I made notes and Derick studied the sheet for the next question. 'Did you know her birthday?'

'No, I never bother about birthdays.'

'Not even the month or the time of the year?'

'No.'

Why should he remember someone he'd rather forget?

'That's a shame. Date of birth is important when you're trying to trace someone, and it wasn't on the report.'

Derick must have seen the disappointment in my face, and gave me an encouraging smile.

'Did you know any of her friends or a woman called Elizabeth Bevan, who was Barbara's godmother?'

'Sorry, no. That name doesn't ring any bells.'

'How long did she live in the area?'

'About three years, as far as I know. We were together for about two years.'

'When did you last hear from her?'

'Oh! I never heard from her after all that trouble.'

All that trouble. That was me! I felt furious.

Derick thanked him and asked if he'd thought any more about meeting me.

'I'm not ready for that,' he said.

Neither am I.

I wanted him to know my feelings: I wrote him a letter and enclosed a photograph of my family.

16 August 1988

> *I hope you will read this letter. I won't write again and I don't want to intrude into your life in any way. I will respect your privacy ... I do not want to upset your wife and I would never embarrass you or try to see you without your permission, but I would like you to understand how I feel ...*
>
> *My husband, Derick, said that you seem a good, decent sort of man, and he immediately liked you ... When you have been adopted you often wonder what your natural parents are really like – they could, after all, be anything. Even if we never meet, I feel so much happier knowing the sort of person you are ...*

I wrote in detail about my adoptive parents, my family and my search for Carole.

> *...Although I have a secure and happy family, the past still haunts me and I will not be able to settle until I have found Carole and found out what happened, even if it means me finding out things which may upset me. I really need to know ...*

> *... The reason I have not tried to find either of you earlier was the fear of having the door shut in my face. Thank you for not doing that ...*

> *...You seem to have had a happy family life and are fortunate in having two daughters. I hope Carole found similar happiness ...*

> *...I cannot think of you as my father, although you are my biological father, as a father is the person who brought you up, who loved you and who was there when you needed him, and Mr Tiernan, my adopted father, will always be that to me. I loved him very much. I know you can't love someone you don't know, and I would not expect that, but I have a very strong need to know who I am. Can you understand that need? I don't know if it is curiosity; no, I think it's more than that, and it is very important to me. I know we would be like strangers and it would be awkward but it would mean so much to me if we could meet. Perhaps you are curious too or maybe I am something you would rather forget. If that is the case, I will not pester you, but if you ever change your mind, maybe sometime in the future, I would love to hear from you. If only one meeting could be arranged, it would set my mind to rest. I do not feel bitter about anything, but I would love to know the circumstances of my birth and why you did not marry*

Carole. Maybe sometime you will find it in your heart to tell me, even if only in a letter. I think you owe me that at least. If you decide to see me, I would like it to be because you want to see me, not out of a sense of duty, and I won't try to contact you again – I will leave it up to you.

He never contacted me.

Chapter 16
St Catherine's House

Encouraged by Suzanne, my NORCAP contact, Derick and I drove down to St Catherine's House in London, where all the records of births, deaths and marriages are kept. We met up with Freda – a NORCAP counsellor – and her small group of members in the foyer. It was a cold November morning and we were glad to get inside. Freda explained the system and introduced us to the group – so many tales of loss and desertion.

'Are the records on microfilm?' I asked.

'No!' Freda said, looking Derick up and down. 'Lucky you brought him with you. The entries are written in those.' She pointed to rows of tall shelving holding enormous hardbacked books.

'Looks like hard work,' I said, laughing nervously.

'The more often you come, the more you get used to handling them,' a man named David said.

'It's going to be a difficult one, this,' Freda pointed out after scanning through my report. 'You don't have her full date of birth, and the fact that she had no living relatives, and moved about a lot, is very difficult.' Seeing the disappointment on my face, she forced a smile and added, 'But you never know, it's worth trying.'

The place smelt stuffy, like a library, but it buzzed with private investigators; experts who must have known the books back to front; journalists looking for gossip; retired gentlemen researching their family trees, and the unmistakably desperate-faced adoptees.

Derick spent most of the afternoon swinging down the great volumes at the request of elderly or vertically challenged searchers.

We had no town where she'd resided long enough: no use looking at the electoral role. The purpose of the visit was to find an entry for her birth. If we could find an entry for a Carole Dalton born in 1926 it would give the place of birth. We searched entries for the five years before and after that date. It was a laborious job; there were hundreds of Carolyns but not too many Caroles or Carries.

Freda approached. 'Do you want to break for lunch?'

***

Sat crowded in a coffee house round the corner, Freda asked how we were getting on.

'Not very well,' I said, staring into my coffee cup, the crumbs of sandwiches scattered on the table. 'We've not found anything yet.'

'There's a possibility,' Freda warned, 'that she could have been illegitimate herself. It does suggest that in the report. Her mother may never have registered her birth. It did happen then, especially in rural areas; some slipped through the net. It also says she never knew her parents and was brought up by her grandmother, so it's certainly a possibility. That could be why she's so difficult to trace.'

'If her birth wasn't registered, she wouldn't know her date of birth, and maybe that's why she didn't put it on the documents. But that's unlikely,' I said, still optimistic.

Some successes had been made. David had found a marriage certificate for his birth mother dated 1959 in Swansea. Knowing the date and place of the marriage, he could go to the electoral roll in the town where they lived. Jackie had found the entry for her birth with her birth mother's name and address on it.

Simon, a good-looking forty-year-old, had been coming to St Cath's for five years and had found entries for his birth mother and all her family. He had a sister and two brothers who had five children between them. He'd obtained copies of all their birth certificates and knew exactly where each of them lived. He had even visited their streets, and stood looking at their houses from afar, but had not made contact with any one of them. Today he had found a death certificate for his grandfather. His boyish smile couldn't hide the sadness in his eyes. I understood his reluctance. Would he ever overcome the fear of rejection and pluck up the courage to knock on the door?

'You've all done well.' Derick swigged the dregs of his coffee. 'I'll have bulging muscles by the time we leave.'

Encouraged and disturbed by their stories, I took Derick's hand as we made our way back to St Cath's through the cold streets, the sky grey and cloudy.

By mid-afternoon, the air, gobbled up by searchers, left the building hot and stuffy. We found no record of her birth. Through the windows, the autumn sky had darkened and we noticed it was nearing five o'clock. Tired and frustrated: we were reluctant to give up.

Freda approached us. 'They'll ask everyone to leave shortly.'

'We've not found anything,' I said.

'She could have changed the spelling of her name,' Freda said.

'My biological father called her Carrie, but Carole is the spelling she used on the adoption order and my birth certificate; surely she would have used the correct spelling on legal documents.'

'You'd think so, but not necessarily,' Freda said. 'Under stress, people do strange things.'

I looked at her, bewildered. Derick put his arm around my waist. 'We'll find her somewhere.'

'You can pay to have any further searches done,' Freda said, 'and they'll post the results to you.'

I made a quick grab for an application form and filed for a Search in the Deaths Register for Carole's grandmother, who, according to the report, had died in 1948.

We thanked Freda. She'd found her birth mother, who'd refused to see her. Freda was hoping that one day she'd change her mind. In the meantime, helping others eased her pain.

We shook hands, kissed goodbye, wished each other luck and left carrying our secrets with us.

***

Through the patio doors, a thin layer of snow covered the garden and rested on the branches of the trees. A robin stared, beady-eyed, feasting on a fatty ball hung from the bird table. Christmas had been and gone, and I was eager to resume the search.

'I wonder if she did go to Australia?' Derick said.

'I've always doubted my mother's version, but Jimmy confirmed her story,' I said.

'Leaving the country would take away the temptation to try and see me. She could break off all ties and start afresh. There seems no trace of her anywhere else. If I wasn't here, I'd swear she never existed.'

'You're definitely here,' said Derick, gently pinching my arm.

'Ouch!' I said. 'The people from NORCAP give me the address for International Social Services in Sydney. I wrote to them three times last year but I never got a reply.'

'I remember you checking the post and being disappointed.'

'I've got NORCAP's latest mag here,' I said, flipping through the pages. 'Look at this in the small ads.'

> *Jenny, Oxford Contact Leader, will be away in Australia from 1st February – 14th March 1989. She has kindly offered to do a little research for members whilst in Sydney.*

I wrote to Jenny immediately. She rang me as soon as she got my letter, touched by my search and Carole's sad plight. Her kindness and understanding assured me that she would do whatever she could to help me. She wrote to me twice from Sydney. In the first letter she told me that she'd drawn a blank at the State Library in

Sydney, where they had no records after 1905. In the office for the registration of births, deaths and marriages, there were no books where you could look up records. You had to fill in a form with all the details and the relevant certificate would be posted in two to three weeks. As I had no idea who my mother married, or if in fact she did get married, it would be futile trying there. She wrote again on 9th November:

> *I heard today of the Australian Archives – an office where records of people coming into the country are kept. I rang up and found they have lists of passengers entering Sydney by ship, the public is allowed access so I've been there today. All the lists are in date order and are on micro-film. I only found a few Daltons, none of which were Carole. There were a large number of ships each month and though only a small number of them came from England there was no way of picking these out from the rest. The details given were the nationality of each person, age, occupation, and the state they intended to settle in.*
>
> *However, I thought later that even if I'd managed to find her it would only prove that she had emigrated, I don't see it would be a great help in finding her now. As I said before, it doesn't seem possible to look up and see if she married. Also, the records in Sydney only showed the ships going to Sydney, she could have gone to Perth or Melbourne, etc.*
>
> *So, I'm sorry I've not been much help, but I'll give you the archives office address. It might be worth writing.*

It was kind of Jenny to try – the NORCAP people were wonderful – but it all seemed hopeless. *Don't you want to be found?*

Chapter 17

Margaret

Thomas was never going to ring me: I had to do it. My longing for knowledge of Carole conquered my fear of rejection. I picked up the phone, my stomach in knots, the list of questions on my knee. He answered quickly, before I had time to change my mind.

'Oh! Hello, Barbara.' He sounded older but he was friendly enough, with a country accent, and a voice rough like gravel. 'I don't know what you must think of me.'

'It was a long time ago.' My hands shook but I tried to put *him* at ease. 'Everyone makes mistakes. I just want to find Carole – sorry, Carrie.'

'Yes, Carrie.'

'Is your wife OK with me ringing? Derick said she knows.'

'Yes, I told Dorothy about Carrie and the baby when we first met.'

The baby! 'It's best to be honest,' I said.

'I wanted to be sure she found out from me and no one else.' He sounded self-assured. 'She accepted it, and we courted for three years before we got married. Dorothy bares no animosity towards you.'

She sounds like a good woman. Her support should make a difference.

'You have two daughters, don't you?'

'Yes, Diane and Judith. We were married for three years before Diane was born.'

He's letting me know there were no more babies out of wedlock.

'We had a grand wedding – top hat and tails – and a honeymoon in Llandudno.'

I gripped the phone tighter. 'I wonder if Carrie found such happiness?'

'Carrie'll have done all right. She was that sort.'

What sort does he mean? I didn't ask. 'Have you told your daughters about me?'

'No,' he said abruptly, 'and I'd rather keep it that way.'

'Of course.' Filling an awkward gap, I told him I'd been on the radio and advertised in all the papers.

'Maybe she wants to stay hidden,' he said.

'Can't you remember the town she came from?' I stared down, finding my place on the list of questions.

'Somewhere in the Fens, but I'm not sure where exactly. I went with her to visit her grandmother. We stayed at the grandmother's house. Strange people … very strange. There was a chap staying in the house. A scruffy-looking fellow, not too clean. Didn't talk, just grunted, very odd. Whether something was going on with the old lady, I don't know …' He laughed. '… Or if he was helping her out. But he disappeared. I don't know where to. He slept in the barn. Best place for him.' He laughed again. 'They're a different breed down there you know, inbred, not a bit friendly.'

I'd read *Waterland*, a novel about the Fens and the strange phlegmatic people who inhabited them, but barely knew where it was on the map. I imagined the strange country folk – my relations – and I smiled to myself.

'What was the name of the village?'

'It's so long ago now.'

'What about any landmarks?' I was starting to get impatient.

'Well, come to think of it, there was a church there and it had no steeple. It was on the floor and the bells were in a sort of wooden building – a cage.'

'Great!' *Talking about the past is stimulating his memory.*

'Yes, it's coming back. I … err … think it was called Brookland … something … Holts … Brookland Holts … but I could be wrong. There was a railway station there, and the church was famous because of its steeple, so you should be able to look it up.'

I made hurried notes. *If not the exact town, I've got an area where we could make enquiries.*

'Did she ever speak about her parents?'

'No, she never did, and I never liked to ask.'

'The report said she didn't know her parents and was brought up by her grandmother, probably the one she took you to visit.'

'Yes, that's likely. She was a very independent girl.'

'What do you mean by independent?'

'Err ... sure of herself. She could look after herself.'

Not that well.

'And you don't know what happened to her after she had me?'

'No. We went our separate ways.'

Feeling bolder, I asked him why they'd split up. He didn't answer – I immediately regretted the question. 'Hello? Are you still there?'

'Yes ... well, it was all to do with religion ... you see, she was a Catholic and our lot were Methodists. It would have caused problems.'

That made sense. She wanted me brought up with a Catholic family. I accepted his explanation, reluctant to delve further into such a sensitive area. I thought about Conor, my first boyfriend, and how religion separated us. 'Religion causes more problems than it solves.'

'It does. I'm not religious. No time for any of them.'

'Same here,' I said. *Why did he let religion come between them if he wasn't religious?*

'She wasn't a typical farm girl. She was well spoken, more accomplished. She had big ideas, Carrie, wanting to do this and that and go places, whereas I just wanted a simple life on the land. It caused arguments.'

'Is that why you left her?'

'No, not really ... She liked people, Carrie, and she was always writing letters or sending cards, usually religious cards.'

'She must have kept in touch with some of the people she was writing to. Don't you know who they were?'

'No, I never bothered much about her friends. But she was writing to my mother for years after we split up.'

'Was she?' *This might be a lead.*

'It's a pity you left it so long. My mother would have told you everything – given you all the sordid details – but she's dead.'

'I'm sorry about that. Where did the letters come from?'

'I don't know.' He answered in a flat voice. 'I didn't see them.'

'That's a shame.' *At that time, you'd have had a wife and family to occupy your thoughts: the woman and child you'd discarded long forgotten.*

'I'm sorry, I can't remember.' He sounded genuinely apologetic. 'Margaret, my sister, might still have the letters.' His voice was brighter. 'She never got married, and lived with my mother and my two brothers, George and Robert. My mother never threw anything out. I bet Margaret's got them.'

I sat up straight. 'They'd give me her last known address. She lived in the Manchester area for a few years after I was born. She found out where I lived and my mother let her visit me, which was very kind of her, but she was that sort of person.'

'She must have been to take on someone else's kiddy.'

Yes, your kiddy.

'Where does Margaret live?'

'In Cheshire. I'll give you the address. You look like her – in her younger days – from the photos you sent with the letter. You look like our side of the family.'

'Do I?' I said, curious.

'I can't see much of Carrie in you.'

'My mother gave me photos of Carrie, on a farm somewhere.'

'I'd like to see them,' he said softly, as if talking to himself. 'I wonder where she got to?'

'Should I call Margaret first?'

'No, she doesn't like phones. Just go. She'll know who you are as soon as she sees you. We had a family business going, but I fell out with Margaret and left the business, and haven't spoken to her for years.'

'It's sad when families fall out.'

'I'm the black sheep, always have been. The three of them run it together, growing mushrooms – her, Robert and George, none of them ever married. Go and see her.'

After half an hour, exhausted with stress and elated with the new information, I ended the call.

Wow! I paced up and down the living room. *Carole may still live at the address on those letters. Old people never throw anything out.* My monkey mind jumped from branch to branch. *What do Margaret and the rest of my genetic family look like?* I wondered how I'd feel if a person turned up on my doorstep saying Derick was her/his father. It takes a big heart to accept your husband's love child. By the time Derick came home, I was elated and related every detail.

After that first phone call, I rang Thomas every few weeks after the six o'clock news, and to break the ice we talked about what was happening in the world. He was right wing and opinionated: I was left wing and liberal. It was pointless arguing with him, so I never said much. When he grumbled on about disputes with neighbouring farmers, I'd gently bring the conversation back to Carole. In one conversation I asked him about my medical history and if there was anything I should know about.

'No. All my family are fit as fiddles and most of them lived to a ripe old age.'

'What about mental illness?'

'There's nothing like that in our family,' he insisted. 'We're pure-bred Cheshire stock.'

'What about Carrie?'

'Well, she was a fine-looking, healthy girl, and she loved the land and farming, but I can't tell you about her ancestry. She didn't look Irish or foreign. I'd never have had anything to do with her if she'd have come from anything like that.'

You bigoted old beggar.

***

We drove through Cheshire lanes, canopied with magnificent trees, to the farmhouse in Bunbury where Margaret and her brothers lived. Karen sat in the back seat: it was July and the Sixth Form holidays.

'What a beautiful place to live,' I said, as we pulled up further down the road on the opposite side.

'See what you've missed,' Derick said.

'I'm not so sure I've missed anything, if they're all like him.'

'Are you nervous, Mum?' Karen leaned forward from the back seat and hugged me.

'A bit, but I'll be fine. Don't worry.'

'Do you want us to come with you?'

'No, it's too much. It might scare her.'

I gave Derick and Karen a kiss and stepped out of the car, breathing in the earthy farmyard smells.

'Good luck, Mum!' Karen shouted through the open car window. I waved back at them as I approached the house, hesitating before I knocked. No one answered at the front, so I walked round to the back door, took a deep breath and knocked as loudly as I could, half hoping they'd all be out. A lady in her early seventies peeped through the window, before opening the door.

'Hello, I hope you don't mind me calling on you like this,' I said as calmly as I could. 'I'm not selling anything. Are you Margaret Fletcher?'

She obviously didn't see any astounding resemblance between us, and eyed me coldly as I stood at the doorstep of her beautiful old farmhouse. 'Yes, I'm Margaret Fletcher. Who are you?'

'Thomas told me to call – Thomas, your brother.'

'Did he now!' She frowned deeply. 'What does *he* want?'

'He said you might be able to help me.'

'Help you?' *This isn't going well. Just tell her the truth!*

'Yes, I'm Barbara,' I blurted out. 'Do you remember Carole – you'd know her as Carrie – and the baby, Barbara – Thomas's child – I'm she – I mean that's me – I'm Barbara.' Sweat dripped from my armpits, dampening my cotton summer dress.

'Oh!' She stared with wide eyes, her mouth slightly ajar.

'I'm sorry – I didn't mean to shock you – but I've been trying to find Carrie for years now, without success.'

'You took me by surprise,' she said, recovering her composure. 'It's a long time since I've thought about Carrie.'

'Thomas said you might still have some letters that Carrie wrote to your mother years after I was born.'

'Mother never threw anything away.' Hovering on the doorstep, she scrutinised me, but didn't ask me inside.

'I don't want anything from anyone, and I'm not bitter. My adoptive parents were wonderful people who loved me. I just want to find my mother.'

Her face softened. 'I can understand that,' she said, her mouth curling into a half-smile. 'I've still got a lot of Mother's stuff upstairs. I'll have a good look. You might be lucky.' She stared at me with sympathetic eyes.

'Oh, would you, thanks.' I yearned to escape, suspecting that Thomas had set me up for this. He must have known the shock it would give her. I should have ignored him and telephoned first. As I was writing down my telephone number and address, a dark-haired man with muddy boots walked towards us from behind one of the barns. I recognised my features in his face.

'This is Robert, my younger brother.' She explained to him why I was there.

He adjusted to the situation far more quickly than she had, and he smiled warmly as he weighed me up.

'He's a bit of a rogue is our Thomas, you know, and he's loaded. Got money he never spends.' I resented the inference that I was after money. There was obviously no love lost between the brothers.

'I just want to find Carrie. I wouldn't have contacted Thomas if I hadn't had such difficulty finding her. My husband and daughter are waiting for me in the car, so I'll have to go. It's been really nice to meet you both. Let me know if you find the letters, please, Margaret. Bye for now.' We exchanged phone numbers, and

I hurried down the driveway, my heart thumping. A feeling of weary relief came over me as I slumped into the car seat, fastened my seat belt and explained through my tears my first encounter with my biological family.

When Margaret hadn't rung a week later, I phoned her. 'I've searched through everything but I couldn't find any letters. I'm really sorry, dear.'

Another vital link lost. Would I ever find her?

***

We had a happy distraction from what was becoming a futile search for Carole: Shaun got excellent A Level results. He came home from Sixth Form College, sad-faced, telling me he'd failed. I believed him until I saw the glint in his eyes. 'I'm in!' he shouted, ecstatic, face lighting up. 'Liverpool has accepted me. I got a Grade 1 in the Special Economics Paper, higher than Susan Wilson, who's going to do Economics at Oxford.'

'Well done! You'll be the first member of our family to go to Uni.' I hugged him.

It was all down to Mr Dillon, his Commerce teacher, who had let interested students take part in the purchase of British Telecom shares, heralding the beginning of Mrs Thatcher's privatisation of the country's utility companies. Being socialists, Derick and I refused to lend Shaun £50 to buy the shares. Determined, he borrowed it from Derick's mother, Eve, a staunch Tory. The shares doubled in value. Shaun was hooked and decided he'd be a stockbroker.

It was the late Eighties, and the economy had started to grow: Shaun would sing 'Opportunities (Let's Make Lots of Money)' by the Pet Shop Boys. Out went his short spiked punk hairdo of the Seventies and in came a perfectly coiffed George Michael big hairdo. Out went the school trousers sewn up so tight he couldn't get them off at night without considerable help and in came designer gear.

To celebrate Shaun's success, I booked a meal at the Barge, a restaurant by the canal in Runcorn, taking Karen, Shaun's girlfriend, Amy – who had equally big hair – Mam and Derick's parents, Fred and Eve.

Large French windows opened onto the canal, cooling the warm August air as we sat in the lounge, sipping pre-dinner drinks.

'Are you going to be one of them yuppies?' Fred asked Shaun.

'Certainly am.' Shaun smiled at his girlfriend from beneath an enormous suspension of highlighted hair.

'What's a yuppie?' Mam asked.

'It's a Young Upwardly Mobile Professional Person,' Derick said. 'They have more money than sense, spend it on frivolous things, and look down on everyone less well off.'

'Yuppies don't sound very nice,' Karen said.

'They're not nice,' Eve said. 'I've read about them in the *Daily Mail*. All they're interested in is making money to buy designer clothes and fancy cars.'

'That'll do me,' Shaun said.

Through an open door, I could hear Starship's 'Nothing's Gonna Stop Us Now' playing on the jukebox in the adjacent room.

Will Shaun make it as a stockbroker? Glancing round the table, I reminded myself how lucky I was to have this loving family. *Why do I always feel there's something missing?*

Chapter 18

Desperate Measures

'I was so desperate, I wrote to *Surprise Surprise*,' I told Susan, Derick's younger sister who lived in America.

'Somehow, I can't imagine you with Cilla Black,' Susan replied, laughing down the phone.

'Neither can I. Ron, one of the managers at work, did some research for me on Ancestry. He was convinced he'd find Carole, but he couldn't, and *he* suggested Cilla. I've watched the show and they don't usually help with straightforward adoption searches, for obvious reasons. It's more brothers and sisters who've been separated in the care system. In a way, I was relieved. I think programmes like that exploit people by putting their emotions on show to feed a voyeuristic public.'

'But they might help you find her. That's all that matters, isn't it?'

'Yes. I'd like my reunion with Carole to be private, but honestly, I'd do anything to find her. I'd have gone on their show but I never got the chance. They said they'd look into it but they never contacted me again. It was a mistake being truthful; a Land Army reunion is more their style.'

'Never mind. Leave it to me.' Susan sounded eager to help. She understood because she'd given up a baby daughter, Sarah, and desperately wanted to resume their relationship. She'd found out where her daughter was living, and was hoping to contact her on her next visit home. 'Carole must have had a National Insurance number, everyone does.'

'Yes, I've tried that. The DHSS won't give out information

about anybody, but they will forward a letter to the person you are looking for, and then it's up to them if they want to reply. That's the good news. The bad news is, they don't get involved in cases of adoption.'

'When did you write to them?'

'Oh, it was about two years ago.'

'Good, then they probably won't have a record of your enquiry. I've got a plan.'

'What plan?' I wondered what Susan's lawyer brain had come up with.

'I'll write from America to the DHSS, but I won't say it's about adoption. I'll pretend I'm planning a Land Army reunion for *my* mother who lives in England, and that I've found most of her old pals, but not Carole Dalton. To put them off any scent I'll also throw in Lorraine Murphy's mum.'

'What do you mean, throw her in?'

'I'll say I'm having difficulty finding them both and see what they come up with. Brilliant, don't you think?'

'Yes, I've got to admit, it sounds good.' A surge of hope made me smile.

Six weeks later, I received a phone call from Susan. The DHSS had found a record for Vera Murphy, Lorraine's mum, and said they would forward one letter to her. For Carole Dalton, they said they had been unable to trace a National Insurance account.

'All it really proves is that there's no National Insurance number for a Carole Dalton at this time,' Susan said. 'If she got married and changed her name, she'd be registered under her married name.'

'It's hopeless,' I said.

Susan wrote again to the DHSS from America asking if they could supply her with the names of other bodies that may help in tracing Carole. They replied saying that without knowing more details such as full date of birth and/or Army Service number, they were unable to suggest any organisation which would be of help.

It was a moment of incredible despair and I pushed thoughts of Carole away and got on with my life.

Keeping busy, almost to distraction, helped to ease my disappointment. I worked full time and attended evening classes three nights a week. My ambition was to become a teacher. My mind was filled with lesson plans and organising work for the volunteers in my Wednesday evening group, but Carole was never far from my thoughts and I frequently scrutinised what information we had.

'She joined the Auxiliary Territorial Service, the women's branch of the Army, in March 1948, nearly a year after my birth,' I said to Derick. 'The Army must have records of who joined, but, of course, it doesn't tell us where she went after she left.'

'There might be a forwarding address.'

'It'd be nice to see a record of her existence somewhere.'

Derick found the address on his laptop for the Women's Services Record Office, based in Chester. I wrote using the reunion story, telling them she was based at the NAAFI in Oswestry, which no longer exists, and asking if they had the files there in Chester. They replied promptly, saying they had been unable to trace the person from the limited information given.

'Another avenue closed.' I filed the letter away in my methodically kept folder and put it back in the filing cabinet in the back bedroom. *There must be some vital clue that we are missing.*

'What about Ireland? You have a look of the Irish about you,' Derick said the following day.

'I don't think so, but anything's worth a go. We know she was a staunch Catholic. I'll apply to the General Register Office in Dublin.'

They replied saying there was no entry corresponding with the particulars we had given for that period of time. I wrote to the General Register Office in Northern Ireland and Scotland requesting the same. All the results were negative.

'In one of Carole's letters, she wrote that she'd lost all her relations and was brought up by her grandmother. Maybe Grandma was ill and she spent some time in a children's home,' I said.

'Sounds very likely,' Derick said.

'I'll contact Dr Barnardo's.'

They could find no trace of her, but sent me a list of relevant organisations. I wrote to them all. None of them knew her.

'It's like banging my head against a brick wall. Of course, none of these institutions, even if they had information about her ever being there, would be able to tell us where she is now. I just feel like giving up.'

'We'll find her somehow.' Derick kissed my cheek and left for work. I wasn't reassured.

Every morning, I opened my mail with trembling hands expecting to see the words, 'We have information about Carole Dalton.' My folder was bursting with negative replies. With each one, I became more disheartened. So many of the correspondents wrote similar words:

> *It is clear from Carole's letters that she found parting with you a deeply distressing experience and I feel sure she will never have forgotten you ... Sorry we are unable to help.*

Will she have forgotten me? I wondered, in a dreamlike state. *Is she somewhere thinking about me now?* The memory triggered by the cry of a child aching for its mother's touch. *Is her torture worse than mine?* I fantasized about her meeting my children, seeing her face light up, asking Karen about her dance classes, Shaun about college. I wanted her to meet Derick and Lily and Lily's children ... *will it ever happen? Will we like each other or will we have the typical mother and daughter relationship, loving each other one minute, hating each other the next?* No matter what we were capable of feeling after years of living apart, I wanted to feel it.

People hinted that I was luckier than most adoptees, because I had proof that my mother loved me and didn't want to give me up. I didn't feel lucky: I felt angry with people who didn't understand. How could they? Good or bad, they knew who their parents were.

***

'Let's have a look at the Essex connection,' Derick said. 'We could go down there?'

'I'll do some research first. Thomas said she came from the Fens, the Lowlands of Essex.'

I rang Essex Tourism Board. There was no Brookland Holts in Essex, but there were a number of churches with sunken steeples due to the marshy land. There was a place called East Bergholt north of Colchester with a Church of England church that had no steeple, and the bells were kept in a cage in the grounds of the church, just like Thomas had described. *Could this be the place? Please let it be the place!*

A helpful lady at East Bergholt post office said there was a Brookland Estate at Brantham. The Catholic church was still there but the convent was sold twenty years previously. I suddenly felt hopeful.

'That's where Thomas must have got the Brookland from, and the holt from East Bergholt,' I said.

'Yes. He could have just got the names confused,' Derick said. 'Sounds promising.'

'It must be the place. The church will have records of births, deaths and marriages. Even if she wasn't registered by law, she must have been baptised in the church. This is exciting. I feel we're getting close.'

I rang the Diocesan Office, and Father Knight told me to write to St Mark's Church in Ipswich, where all the records for the area were kept. I wrote straight away telling the Father Guardian the true story, enclosing the extract from the social worker's report. I got a reply from Father Simon:

'... The various clues that I get from your letter have not, as yet, produced any result. The baptismal records I hold from Brantham/East Bergholt do not give anything. But I have a few contacts, and I will let you know as soon as anything turns up, if it does.'

I convinced myself there was still hope, if just one of his contacts could find some proof of Carole having been born or living in Essex. I received a further letter from him:

'... I have now checked with the Office of Registration of Births and Deaths in Ipswich (for Suffolk) and they checked with their office in Colchester (for Essex), but your mother is not recorded for births in either office.

There is an estate on the edge of our Parish of Brantham called Brooklands, but discreet enquiries amongst a few of the older parishioners has produced nothing.'

I rang Father Simon, and we talked at length. He was sympathetic and said he would continue asking round the district, and contact me if he found any information. Too frustrated to cry, I thanked him and said I would send a donation to his church.

'Guess what?' Derick said the following week. 'That training course I'm going on is at Head Office in Colchester next month, and I'll knock on a few doors myself.'

I knew that if Carole was down there, Derick would find her. He went to the Brooklands Estate and the surrounding area, but no one he talked to knew of a Carole/Carrie Dalton.

***

I hadn't rung Thomas since late 1989 because he was useless. He didn't want me in his life, and wouldn't tell his daughters that they had a sister. If I rang, he'd talk to me for hours, rattling on about the farm or politics. Sometimes, I thought I could be anybody at the end of the phone, and when we did talk about Carole, he referred to 'the baby' as though it was someone else, not me, but he was my only link to Carole. I rang him.

'My grandfather was killed by a bull, you know,' Thomas said down the phone.

'How awful! How did it happen?' I asked, wanting to know my great grandfather's fate.

'My Uncle Ernie liked a drop of drink after dinner, well more than a drop, and sometimes he'd fall asleep and forget to do things – important things. One day my father told him that my Uncle Arthur was bringing a new bull over that day, but Ernie hadn't got the bull coat set up.'

'What's a bull coat?' I was becoming interested in the story.

'It's a pen you keep 'em in so they can't get at the cows. I told him I'd help him put it together, but he fell into such a deep drunken sleep that I couldn't wake him. He snored so loud they must have heard him in the village.'

'Oh no!' I laughed.

'I saw the cart come trundling down the lane, and shouted to my uncles, "It's here! The bull's here!"

'"We'll have to put it in with the cows," Ernie said.

'"But it's been kept in a bull coat for the past three months," Uncle Arthur warned him. "It'll go mad for the cows!"

'"This is all your fault, Ernie. You drunken fool," my granddad said. I told them that I'd open the gate and I ran down to the field. The cows had been quite content munching at the grass, until the black menace was put in with 'em. It went daft and started fighting with the cows – tussling 'em like hell, which wasn't surprising after three months' enclosure.

'My granddad lined up with me and his brothers in the field, waving wooden sticks in the air to distract the bull. It turned, looked straight at us and started to run in our direction. Its speed increased, forcing us to run behind a row of large oak trees.

'When it got close, Ernie jumped from behind the trees and whacked the bull on the forehead. It looked surprised, but stood its ground while the four of us took it in turns to hit the creature as hard as we could and then spring quickly back to our hiding places.'

'Good grief!' I laughed. 'It's like a scene from a movie. Perhaps it's as well I wasn't brought up on a farm.'

'It can be dangerous. Anyway, I remembered that there was a load of rubble on the side track, left by the workmen who fixed the road, and I pointed it out. I ran breathless and gathered hands full of the concrete mix.'

'"That'll shift you, you black bastard!" I shouted, pelting him with the heavy lumps. The bull backed off and started to run out of the gate, down the road. But the cows were deeply distressed and followed in a stampede round the back of the farmhouse.

'"Leave 'em, Granddad, the bull will settle down," I pleaded with him.

'"It's too dangerous," Arthur warned him. "We'll get the cows out later."

'But my granddad was headstrong. "I'll finish the job now," he said, and grabbed a pronged picket from the barn, determined to separate the bull from the cows. As he went into the back field, the bull put down its mighty head, dug its heals in – just like in the comics, steam came from his nostrils – and he charged. Granddad stabbed it with the picket. The prongs are very sharp and blood spurted from its forehead, but it kept charging until it flung him in the air, and he fell, banging his head against a brick wall.'

'The dangers of country life.'

'Yes, but he should never have risked his life. We could have got the cows out. His head looked as though it had been gashed with a turnip slasher. The doctor came and stitched it up, but he died shortly after.'

'That's sad. I can imagine what a machine used for cutting turnips could do to a human skull.'

'He was eighty, mind you, and he'd had a good life. Nobody told him what to do. He was a character – wiry and fiery. They all were, my uncles. Farming was a good life then, not like now. It was a man's life, you know, drinking, gambling, working hard on the land. I loved it,' he said with enthusiasm. Then his voice softened as he recalled. 'It was all that mattered to me – the family and the land.'

Yes, I thought. *And the women? What did they do? Cooking, cleaning, helping with the more arduous farm tasks, and giving birth to legitimate heirs who'd help on the farm, while the men had all the excitement and danger. What would my life have been like if he'd married Carole? How would I have fared in this alien world that I could only imagine: the stench of manure; tractors and fences; barns full of hay; cows, pigs and chickens.*

Of all the stories he'd told me, that was the scariest, but it was Carole I wanted to

know about. Where did she fit into all this?

'Will you meet me?' I blurted out.

'Yes,' he said. 'You'll have to come on your own though.'

Chapter 19

Meeting

Derick looked disappointed at not being able to accompany me. He, of all people, knew how much this meant to me, but he understood. 'You'll be franker with each other alone.'

I'd arranged to meet Thomas at the Baptist Chapel car park near the village green at Wharford. I drove slowly, following the written instructions from Derick, trying to remember signposts from the trial run we'd carried out the week before. The leaves – red, gold and brown – kept a fragile hold on the trees that witnessed my journey down lonely lanes, in my quest for the truth.

My thoughts were everywhere: to my father's death from liver cancer, a void in my life which Thomas could never fill. He'd died painfully, crying out to Our Lady the Virgin Mother to take him. If there is a heaven, Jim will be there. He was my real dad, the one who had provided for me, cared for me and loved me, not this stranger: all we shared was our biology.

I concentrated hard on the directions, trying to dispel negative thoughts about the man I was going to meet. I arrived half an hour too early, got out of the car and looked furtively around, relieved he'd not arrived before me. The sun shone, but in the shady churchyard the chill of autumn crept up my spine. I got back in the car, fidgety with fear. To steady my nerves, I picked up the A4 pad containing the carefully written instructions for the journey, turned to a fresh page and started to write a letter to Shaun, who had gone to live in America. After the first sentence, I stopped and thought of him. He'd graduated with a 2:1 Honours degree. Even Mam, who thought education was not for the likes of us, congratulated him and rewarded him with £10, telling everyone who visited the house that her grandson had got a degree.

His ambition was to be a stockbroker, but England was by that time in recession, and jobs in the stock market were difficult to come by for a lad from a working-class background with no contacts. To help him achieve his dream, Derick's sister Susan had invited him to go and live with her in America. 'The US market is more open and willing to give anyone who'll work hard a chance,' Susan had told him.

I remembered driving him to Runcorn Station, sad to see him go, but optimistic for his future …

'Who knows? Perhaps Carole went to America and not Australia. I may come across her,' he said, as we pulled into the station.

'Well, there's around 528 million people living in North America, but let me know if you bump into her,' I said, trying to keep it lighthearted.

He kissed my cheek and looked down at the battered suitcase, secured with a large leather strap, and smiled up at me. 'Everything I own, the contents of my life, are in this case.' Tears formed in my eyes. 'Don't worry about me. I'll be a millionaire before I'm forty – you'll see …'

Terrified, I scribbled feverishly:

> *In half an hour I will meet my biological father, Thomas … he is going to take me to see his land and the cows and 'Billy the Bull'. I'm getting butterflies in my stomach. I must keep calm because I don't want to make a big emotional scene when he arrives. It was Karen's birthday yesterday. She was seventeen. We bought her lots of silver jewellery, and she went to the Black Horse celebrating with her friends from Sixth Form. How is your new job going? Oh dear, I can't concentrate. Once the initial meeting is over, I won't feel so bad. I don't think I can write any more. It's 1.50 now. I hope he hasn't changed his mind. I feel sick. I think this is his car now …*

My hands trembled and I tried to compose myself. I straightened my hair, buttoned my jacket and took deep breaths, determined not to embarrass him with tears. Anyone watching might have thought it was a secret rendezvous – an older man, a younger woman, two parked cars. My eyes scanned the churchyard and beyond. Everywhere was deserted. I'd read about genetic attraction: relatives who had been brought up apart being attracted to each other. *Will it be like that?*

He waved gently as he got out of his car. *Restart the engine and drive away. He's nothing to you. Leave now!* As he walked across the grass towards me, my body became so tense, I wanted to throw up. *He's here now. You can do it.* He smiled and kissed me awkwardly on the cheek as I got out of my car. I turned my face away from him abruptly, fighting back the urge to cry. I took a deep breath and swallowed.

'Did you find it all right?' he asked lightly.

'Yes, just about,' I said with surprising calm. 'It's beautiful round here. Very different from Widnes.'

'Yes.' He smiled. 'We'll leave your car here and go in mine, if that's all right.'

I followed him to his parked four-wheel drive and he held my arm as I climbed up into the passenger seat. *Don't cry – don't cry.* I peeped at him shyly as we chatted, driving through the Cheshire countryside.

He didn't look seventy. His skin was smooth and ruddy. A typical farmer, in a flat cap and tweed jacket, with brown trousers and boots; new ones worn specially to meet me. My stomach flipped when he said that.

He pulled off the road into a dirt track and stopped the car. 'I own about sixty acres of land just here.' He opened the gate. Green fields scattered with oak trees stretched as far as I could see. It was deserted. No one would hear our conversation, except the cows – beautiful, tawny-coloured creatures, sleek and healthy, about thirty in number.

'Come and meet them.'

'I'm not sure about that.' The tale of his grandfather's death came to mind.

He stared at me as though he couldn't believe I was real.

'You'll be fine with me. They're very friendly, even Billy the Bull is gentle.'

He climbed a fence and I followed him, stepping carefully. 'Your mother would have jumped over that fence, no problem.' He laughed and took my hand to help me down. 'She was a big, strapping girl, robust she was, taller than you are.'

I pictured them together, working on the farm. The affectionate tone of his voice when he spoke about Carole made me soften towards him. *He's going to tell me about her, about their relationship.*

A faint smell of manure drifted on the breeze as we walked across the field in the sunshine. The cows recognised him and slowly moved in our direction, their tails slapping their backs, their mouths salivating as they chomped grass.

'They're like children. It's the way you bring them up,' he said. 'If you're cruel and beat them, they learn to distrust humans and attack out of fear.'

'Cow psychology?'

'Yes, I suppose.' He smiled. 'They've never been beaten or ill-treated.' The enormous creatures nuzzled him and he patted their backs. 'Aren't they beauties? They groom themselves like a cat would.'

'Really!' I stared at their cream-coloured fur, spotless and shiny. Their gentle brown eyes looked in my direction but I didn't move. Seeing my discomfort, he shouted and waved his hands, giving the more curious creatures a gentle push, sending them off like children. 'Get a move on, girls! Off with you!' They lumbered away, bending their heads to chew grass as they went. I sighed, relieved, and looked across the field. There was Billy, magnificent in his masculinity, turning his enormous head as if to see what had disturbed his harem.

'Oh my goodness!' I shouted.

'Don't worry about Billy. He's the happiest bull alive. He got all thirty cows pregnant last year. No need for artificial insemination with Billy around.' Billy ignored us and carried on chewing the grass. The animals and the land were fascinating, but I was there to find out about Carole.

'I've brought the photographs of Carrie that I told you about.'

'Let's sit down for a minute and I'll have a look.' He pointed towards a tall oak tree spreading its branches in perfect symmetry above a weathered log. 'I like to sit out here, just me and the cows.' *He's more thoughtful than I imagined, or maybe he prefers the company of cows to people.* The midday sun shimmered through the leaves, making a shadowy pattern on the damp soil surrounding the log. My feelings towards him were ambivalent. I wanted to like him but I couldn't forgive him for abandoning me.

I handed him the tiny photos, together with some enlargements a photographer friend had made. He stared at them for a long time, smiling sadly, before he said anything.

'She changed her hair colour!' he said loudly.

'It might have been bleached.'

'No! She was naturally fair. Looks to me like she was a picker, down in the fruit fields of Kent. They call it the Garden of England.'

Yes, reduced to fruit picking because you'd abandoned her.

'If you do ever find her, let me know. I'd like to see her again.'

I looked at him and frowned. 'Just to see how she is?'

'Yes, I'd like to know what happened to her.'

Bet you would, you old devil.

'You're right about Kent. She sent them with letters from Tunbridge Wells or Sevenoaks, but my mother destroyed the letters because she didn't want me looking for Carole.'

'That's understandable. She'd adopted you.'

'Yes, but they were the last link, apart from the letters she sent to your mother, which Margaret can't find.' Frustration turned to anger and I stood and looked out across the fields, taking deep breaths to slow my racing heartbeat.

'Sorry about the letters,' he said, with genuine sympathy.

'Carole was writing everywhere in the Fifties – then it all stopped. Maybe she met someone and gave up on me.'

'She was an attractive woman. She'd soon find someone else.'

He stood and we walked on in silence. *Stay calm. Don't spoil things.* There was so much I wanted to know but my thoughts circled: sad, sorry, angry, hopeful, liking him, hating him. I had to keep control.

'What did you do … after I was born?' I blurted out.

'I joined up.'

'My mother said you came to court for the final hearing in uniform. Why did you come?'

'I wanted to be sure you were going to a good home. Then I could rest easy.'

So you could forget about me and live the rest of your life.

'That was good of you,' I said, but he didn't get the irony.

'They seemed like good people.'

'They were. Carrie didn't come. Do you know why?'

'Didn't want to see me again, I suppose.'

Not after what you'd put her through.

'I saw her after you were born but it was too upsetting.'

'Was that the last time you saw her?'

'Yes,' he said with a sigh, as if it was painful to recall. 'She sent us a card via my mother at the birth of our first child, Diane. There was a mix-up at the hospital and we thought we had a son.' His voice faltered. 'If you'd been a boy, I'd probably have come looking for you.'

'What!' *You didn't want a useless girl.* Furious, I struggled to keep my temper.

'I thought I had a boy. Dorothy put the baby bath in the living room, right in front of me. That's how she told me. I jumped and shouted bloody hell when I saw it was a girl.'

She must have been too terrified to tell you. 'A baby girl! What a disappointment,' I said, hating him.

'It was,' he said. 'Ian Thomas, we'd called her. We sued the hospital. We had photographers climbing in through the windows.

It was in all the papers, and Carrie must have seen it and sent us the card.'

'Oh my God!' I shouted, my heart racing.

He looked at me, startled. 'What's up?'

'When was Diane born?'

'1957, I think.'

'That's ten years after my birth. Carole – I mean Carrie – must have still been living in the UK. My mother told me she was going to Australia on the £10 ticket, with a man she'd met.'

'That sounds like Carrie. She wanted to see the world. Probably running a sheep farm in the Outback by now.'

'Don't you see?' I stopped and looked him in the eye. 'I can't see your story making the Australian news, phone calls were expensive and the post took forever. Surely, if the card had come from Australia you'd have remembered?'

'Yes, I probably would have been curious about that, but I can't remember.'

He looked down and scuffed the earth with his boot, and we carried on skirting the field. With no use pursuing that further, I asked him again what Carrie was like.

'I didn't care for her at first,' he said, his face animated. 'She seemed stuck-up – from the South, you know.'

'The North–South divide existed then, did it?'

'Well, I was a local lad. I'd never been anywhere … didn't want to go anywhere … and she was … different.'

'In what way?'

'She was more outgoing than me, very sociable, and she liked meeting people.' His expression softened. 'She looked at you under her eyes … blue eyes … lovely eyes.'

I felt embarrassed, as though I was intruding on his memories. He must have loved her at one time and I didn't know what to say.

He looked at me with a sad smile. 'We could have made a go of it, if things had been different.'

How different my life would have been if you had.

'You see, the family had different opinions about her. My

father thought she was lovely in the beginning ...' He looked into the distance. '... But then he changed his mind ... influenced by my Uncle Ernie, I think.'

'Ernie the drunk?' My body stiffened. 'Why? What do you mean?'

'I don't know, they had different ideas then ... but it was a rotten thing to do ... leaving her like that.' He paused and looked down at the grass.

I appreciated his admission. But he'd said previously that they'd split up because of religion, and now he was suggesting something else. I didn't believe him. 'I have to look to the future and finding Carrie.'

'I wish I could help you more.'

I couldn't bear the sadness in his eyes, and I changed the subject and told him about my childhood on the banks of the Mersey. He spoke of life on the farm with his eleven brothers and sisters.

'I'll take you to see Margaret now,' he said, as we walked back towards where he'd parked the car. 'You can meet my eldest brother, George.'

'Have you told Margaret that we're coming?' I asked, shocked.

'No. Haven't spoken to her for years.'

In view of what I knew about his relationship with his family, I had reservations, but he insisted. He was that kind of man. He helped me into his car and we drove away, the afternoon sun fading. I gave the tawny cows and Billy the Bull a goodbye glance, wondering again what my life would have been like if they'd stayed together.

'One time I visited my mother's house, years after all this with Carrie, years after she'd thrown me out, and Robert came to the door with a shotgun,' he told me, as we drove along. 'Admittedly, I was drunk, but he chased me off with a bloody shotgun.'

'Oh great!' I said with a shiver. 'Is a surprise visit such a good idea?'

'He'll not chase me off while I've got you with me.' He gave me a cheeky sidelong glance.

I was apprehensive as we pulled up outside, and followed him timidly round the back of the farmhouse. He pushed the back door open. 'Anyone home?'

Margaret appeared and her eyes jumped from me to Thomas with shocked surprise. There was no show of affection between them, and glancing my way, she gave me a weak smile. 'Hello again. Come in,' she said coldly, without looking at Thomas. We followed her into a large living room with a low ceiling and oak beams. It smelt of fresh herbs and wood smoke from the open fire spitting in the grate. An elderly man dozed in an armchair by the fire. 'George!' Margaret gave him a gentle tap on the shoulder. 'This is Barbara. Remember I told you about her, Carrie's child.' His skin was yellow and wrinkled, and he appeared unmoved by my presence, grunting an acknowledgement.

A door creaked open. 'Good afternoon!' a shout came from the kitchen. It was Robert, who must have seen Thomas's car outside. Thankfully unarmed, he nodded towards Thomas and smiled at me. 'This is a turn-up, brother.'

'Aye.' Thomas turned to me and smiled, as if to reassure me.

'You'll stay for tea?' Margaret asked.

'That would be lovely,' I said, 'but don't go to any trouble.' In spite of the awkwardness, I wanted to stay and find out more about the family I'd nearly been a part of.

Robert relaxed into an armchair and nodded towards Margaret. 'She's made some scones this morning,' he said, grinning, obviously enjoying everyone's discomfort. Thomas paced up and down, and I sat at the sturdy oak dining table, scratched and worn with time. Margaret spread a white lace cloth and served tea from a Royal Doulton teapot. 'You'll have a scone?' She handed me a matching red-and-gold-patterned plate. Far too nervous to eat, I nibbled at the scone, easing it down with tea.

Thomas continued to pace, stopping now and then to slurp his tea or take a bite of scone. He talked about the old days and they all joined in; even George roused from his nap. Thomas and Robert spoke loudly, outshouting each other with tales from the past. Like a spectator watching them joust, I sat speechless. I couldn't relate to the people they were talking about: Carole wasn't mentioned. At Margaret's request, I told them briefly about my family, but I was relieved when Thomas said we'd have to leave to avoid the rush-hour traffic.

Margaret touched my arm as I walked through the door and handed me a small photo. 'I'm sorry I couldn't find the letters from Carrie, but you might like to have this.'

I stared down at a photograph of Thomas and Dorothy on their wedding day. A strange thing to give me under the circumstances. Was it an act of kindness or did she do it on purpose to make me feel uncomfortable? I couldn't decide. Thomas looked handsome in his tailcoat, and Dorothy was beautiful in her white gown.

'It was a posh wedding. No expense spared,' Thomas boasted as he drove me back to the church car park. *Carole and her baby conveniently forgotten.*

Chapter 20

Greater Manchester County Record Office

'I've got two letters.' With eager hands, I ripped open the first envelope. 'It's from the General Register Office.' I scanned the words and looked up at Derick. 'Carole hasn't registered with them.' Saddened by another negative response, I handed the letter to Derick.

'She was a country girl, and not all older people are into technology,' Derick said. 'She might not have a computer or know how to get onto a contact register, or know that they even exist. She could still register sometime in the future.'

'You're right,' I said, trying to be positive. 'It's great that NORCAP's canvassing for a general register has paid off. It'll help a lot of people, but not me, not now anyway.'

I opened the second envelope slowly. 'It's from International Social Services.' *They've found her in Australia! If only!* Derick looked up, eyebrows raised. 'Don't get excited,' I said. 'Their Australian colleagues haven't made any progress with their enquiries.'

'We're not even sure that she went there now.'

'She must have changed her mind, but she obviously didn't want to let go.'

'It must have taken some doing, congratulating Thomas on the birth of his first child – his legitimate child – considering he'd abandoned her.'

'She must have been a forgiving person.'

'Or still very much in love with him.'

'She obviously wanted to leave a trail for you to follow somewhere down the line.'

'Maybe.' I buried my head in my hands. 'Why did I leave it so long?'

Looking through my files later in the day, I spotted a clue. 'Why didn't we think of it before?' I shouted to Derick, who was sat in an armchair watching the news.

'What?'

I stared down at the social worker's report. 'Jericho, the home where Carole gave birth to me. They must have asked the mothers who gave birth there for their date of birth. Carole's date of birth is bound to be in their records.'

'You wrote to them a while ago, didn't you?'

'Yes, and the letter was returned marked "gone away", so it must have closed down, but the records of my birth must be kept somewhere.' I rang Rochdale Social Services and was told that the records did still exist and were kept at Fairfield Hospital. A receptionist at the hospital said, 'I'm terribly sorry, we only keep the records here as far back as the Sixties. Just hang on and I'll go and enquire.' *Nothing is ever straightforward. The only easy part of it has been finding Thomas.*

'The other records are kept in the Greater Manchester County Record Office, who hold the original entries of all the births at Jericho Hospital prior to 1960,' she said. 'My colleagues assured me that a record of the mother's date of birth will be written in the ledgers.'

'Oh! Thank you! That's brilliant news.'

'How long have you been searching, if you don't mind me asking?'

'Since 1987.' I told my story as briefly as I could, hoping she might know someone somewhere who had information. 'Will you ring me back with the result of your investigations? I'd love to know how you got on. It's such an interesting story.'

'Let's hope it has a happy ending.'

'Good luck with it.'

***

It was late October and an autumnal fog hung around Widnes Station, like the impenetrable barrier keeping me from Carole.

'If I can get her date of birth, I can go back to St Catherine's House to find her birth records,' I told Lily, who'd volunteered to come with me. As we walked through the station, I noticed the plaque commemorating the singer Paul Simon having written 'Homeward Bound' while sitting on the platform, after appearing at the Howff folk club in Widnes in the Sixties. 'I went to the Howff every week. I must have seen him, but I can't remember,' I said, happy to be distracted.

'He wasn't famous then,' Lily said, as we boarded the train.

We got off at Oxford Road, walked across the road and boarded a bus to the Records Office. 'This is your stop, ladies!' the conductor shouted as we approached a renovated warehouse in a deserted part of the city. The fog had lifted to reveal a watery autumn sun. We walked across the cobbled streets, linking arms and chattering, full of nervous expectancy.

Inside the building, the air seemed trapped, stale and dated, as if fresh air would make the records disintegrate like ancient parchment.

Individuals and couples sat hunched, staring intensely at the microfilm on the screens. A middle-aged woman with short grey hair and a kind smile approached us. *Joan Smithers* was written on a tag pinned to her neat cream blouse. 'Nineteen-forty-seven, Jericho, yes, we still have the entries,' she said. 'They're written in their original form, in the registers the hospital kept at the time. Well, it was a workhouse then.'

'Imagine keeping them all this time.'

'We've not got round to putting them on microfilm yet. I presume it's your birth records you want to see?'

I told her my story and got the usual reaction of helpful interest.

'They're upstairs. If you'll just excuse me for a while, I'll go and get them.'

Lily looked at me and touched my hand.

We watched Joan tread carefully down the stairs carrying two large black books, which she placed on the table in front of us. I'd known Jericho was a workhouse, but reading the cover of the books, *Register of Inmates* and *Register of Births* – seeing it in black and white – made me incredibly sad.

'You'll find the entry for your birth in the *Register of Births* and information about your mother in the *Register of Inmates*. As you can see, they are in date order, so look for the date of your birth in the first column.'

'Sounds straightforward enough. Thank you.'

Joan left to attend to someone else, and I stared at the huge black books, scuffed and dog-eared. Lily stood close by my side as I opened the *Register of Births*. *This is it! I'm going to see a record of my birth.* Carefully, I thumbed the worn pages, expectant. I held my breath, while invisible fingers squeezed my stomach and my heart thumped in my chest. There it was scrawled in black ink. The entry dated: '2nd June, 1947', Child: 'Barbara Dalton', Mother: 'Carolyn Dalton', Father: 'unknown'.

'They've spelt her name wrong or she gave them the wrong name.'

Lily rubbed my back. 'Are you OK?'

'Yes.' I smiled. 'I've already got this information. This is the most important book.' I ran my hand over the cover of the *Register of Inmates*, opened it and turned the page, glancing at the headings of the columns. 'Yes!' I shouted loudly, distracting searchers, who looked up in surprise. 'Sorry,' I whispered to the onlookers, before turning to Lily and saying, 'Each page has a date of birth column with the mother's details written in it.'

'Oh great!' Lily said.

This is definitely it!

My heart beat faster and my hands trembled as I flipped over the pages until I reached a page headed '31st May, 1947'. I squeezed my eyes shut and turned the page. Opening them wide, I stared down at the information.

'She was admitted on 1 June 1947, the day before my birth,

and discharged on 16 June 1947. Confined for two weeks, but it confirms that at five days old I'd been taken away from her by Dr Cranshaw.' I was confronted again with the agony she must have suffered through those remaining days, watching the new mothers tend to their babies, breastfeed them, hold them close. The muscles in my stomach tightened again as I followed the inky-black writing stretching its way across the pages. I pointed to the entry and repeated the words out loud to Lily. 'Her name's been spelt Carolyn not Carole in this one, too.'

'This mix-up of names is worrying,' Lily said.

My head spun with confusion over the names as my eyes darted from column to column. 'There's nothing in the next-of-kin column; her address is Bury with the Cranshaws.' Thud, thud, thud in my chest. 'I don't believe this!' I wanted to scream. 'Date of birth: 1926. It doesn't give her full date of birth!'

Lily hugged my shoulders. *Defeated.* Too numb to cry, I stared at the column. The elusive Carrie, Carole and now Carolyn: a girl who wouldn't give her date of birth or her real name. *Did you never want me to find you?*

'It's a wonder they didn't insist,' Lily said. 'Even if she was born out in the wilds of the Fens and never registered, her mother must have given her a birthday. I'd have made one up if it'd been me.'

We smiled at each other.

'It's strange, isn't it,' I said. 'When she first had me, she mustn't have wanted to leave a trail for me, although we know she changed her mind later.' We both looked down at the entry. Carole's loneliness and vulnerability accentuated in the missing information.

Joan approached, smiling, eyes expectant. 'How are you getting on?'

'My birth's recorded but there's no entry for my mother's date of birth. Why?' I asked, feeling hopeless.

'They must have asked her.' Joan frowned. 'I can't think why she didn't give it. That's disappointing for you.' She looked straight at me. 'You've really got no further then, have you?'

'Not really, no.' I was ready to cry.

'But it was worth coming,' she said quickly, 'because you've seen the actual entries, and I can tell that means a lot to you.'

'Yes, it does.' I stifled the tears. 'Can I have photocopies of them, please?'

'I'm terribly sorry, but it's not allowed. The books are so old, you see, it would damage them. But you can write all the information down. Shout me when you've finished.'

I took a large jotter and pen from my bag and copied the words from the ledger while Lily stood and watched.

'It's so sad, no next of kin column. It looks so bare.' Lily wiped a tear but I was too traumatised to cry. *I'll never find her, that's clear now. I may as well give up.*

'Have you tried advertising in the local press?' Joan asked when she returned.

'Yes, I've done all that. I've done everything anyone could possibly do!'

'Don't give up hope.'

'I won't,' I said, but knowing I couldn't go through any more of this. 'Thanks for all your help.'

On the journey home, Lily's chatter sounded distant. The dark black lines of the columns dividing the yellowed pages of spidery writing were etched in my mind. Date of birth: 1926.

Chapter 21

Mam

'What was the trigger for the First World War?' I said aloud to myself while balancing an A4 pad on my knee and chewing the end of my pencil.

Mam woke from her doze and sat up, her cloudy eyes wide. 'The assassination of the Archduke Ferdinand in Sarajevo in 1914. He was the heir to the Austrian throne. A Serb shot him. That's what started it all off, and then all those lives were lost – young men sent to die – all for nothing.'

'Wow!' I looked at her, startled. 'You've got a good memory.'

'I was only twelve when war broke out.' She relaxed back into her armchair, her eyes distant. 'But I remember it clear as a bell.'

Mam was ninety-three years old and over the last year mini strokes had little by little taken away parts of her personality. Her short-term memory had gone; she asked repeatedly what she was having for dinner. But her memories of the past were vivid: the poverty of her upbringing; the bugs in the bed; unable to afford shoes; the treat of a hen's egg at Easter.

The years of night school had paid off and I'd gained enough qualifications to get on a degree course in English and Psychology at Hope University in Liverpool. I was looking after Mam while doing my history project.

'Why are you studying?'

'I've told you, I want to teach Psychology when I've finished.'

'I've no time for psychologists or psychiatrists. I don't know the difference, but the one you saw ruined our lives.' Mam's face crumpled.

That still haunts your unconscious as much as mine.

'If you'd told me the truth earlier it wouldn't have mattered.' I immediately regretted what I'd said, and quickly continued, 'A psychiatrist's medically trained and can prescribe drugs, but a psychologist has whatever qualification they need in their area, such as counselling.'

'They're all interfering troublemakers,' she grumbled.

'Events from our childhood can affect us all our lives.' Again, I regretted my words.

'You shouldn't dwell on stuff like that.' The lines in her face deepened. 'We are what we are. You just have to get on with it. I don't worry about things, not like you, old bothered conscience.' She looked at me with a half-smile.

She'd called me that before. Perhaps she understood more about my anxiety than I realised.

'People who study Psychology are usually crazy.' I laughed to myself and thought of the eccentric tutors and neurotic students, including me.

'What's Karen studying?'

'French and English, a four-year course, with a year in France.'

'That's a long time to be at school.' With heavy eyes, she dozed off and started snoring softly.

I stared at her sleeping face. *You'd be proud of me, Mam; a typical mature student: I attend all my lectures; hand my coursework in on time; and sit in the lecture theatre before anyone else gets there, thinking how lucky and privileged I am.* Her snores got louder and I returned to the First World War.

***

'She's fading fast, you best hurry,' Lily said.

I covered the speaker with my hand, and shouted to Karen, who was watching television in the living room. 'Lily thinks your Nan is dying. We must leave now.'

Karen's face turned white and she wiped a tear from the corner of her eye.

'We'll be there in a minute, Lil.' I slammed the phone down and grabbed my car keys.

'We were expecting this but it's still a shock,' I said to Karen as I drove too quickly down Peelhouse Lane. 'Don't be so sad. I think she's had enough and is ready to leave us.'

'But I'll miss her.'

'We'll all miss her.'

Mam had deteriorated over the last few months and could no longer live on her own. 'You're just in time,' Lily said, as we walked through the door and into the parlour, where Lily had put up a bed for Mam. It was a warm September day, the 19th, but Lily's pre-war house in Neil Street was pleasantly cool.

Close to the bed, I could hear the gentle rattle in Mam's throat. We sat round her bed with Lily's children, Tony, John, Lynne, Sue and Gill. I held Mam's hand, the skin thin and brown with age spots. Her face relaxed and all tension dissolved as she breathed her last breath. The grandchildren, red-eyed and tearful, kissed their nan goodbye.

'Goodbye, Mam.' I kissed her cheek, warm and soft. *I love you, Mam. No one can replace you, but I still have a mother somewhere. I'd never love her in the way I love you, she'd be a different kind of mother, but I want to know her. I have to find her. You understand that now, don't you?*

She'd taken me in, someone else's child, and loved me like her own. Now her love was gone, I felt a void and guilty for not loving her enough. I looked around the sad crumpled faces, tears running down their flushed cheeks, eyes uncomprehending. 'I'll put the kettle on,' Lily said, through her tears.

Relieved Mam's suffering was over, but sad she'd no longer be the pivot on which the family revolved, I cried for our loss. We had all often met up at Mam's house. It was the one place in the world where I knew I'd always be welcome; that my mother would protect me and be on my side no matter what I'd done.

'Don't be sad at her funeral,' Father Faye said. 'It's a celebration of a long and happy life.'

Mam had enjoyed life, in spite of the hardships. Her family had been desperately poor, but her eight brothers and sisters, my aunts and uncles, were a merry gang. I remember the fun and laughter whenever they were around. Perhaps their sense of humour saw them through. They were all in it together – the suffering, the fear of their violent father. Mam was the eldest and looked after them all.

She'd survived a miscarriage without postnatal care. Found her own solution. Me. You can get yourself better without doctors, she'd say. Tablets were thrown in the bin and medicine washed down the sink. She was a remarkable woman. *I have another mother somewhere. What is Carole like? Will I ever find out?*

***

When I'd finished my degree, I went back to see Jane, the social worker. 'I can't believe you've done all this yourself,' Jane said. 'You should get a job as a private detective.' She raised her eyebrows above large black glasses after thumbing through the two green dog-eared files I'd placed on her desk. She looked older – not an easy job, social work. A short dark bob, streaked with grey, replaced the frizzy perm.

'After my disappointment at the Jericho hospital, I gave up looking.'

'Her reluctance to give her full date of birth is strange,' Jane said.

'I've been busy since I last saw you.' I said, smiling. 'I've done a degree course in English and Psychology and I got a 2:1.'

'Congratulations! That's certainly an achievement. So, what's stimulated you to start searching again?'

'In my final year, I took a free writing course and I wrote about Carole and Thomas, or how I imagined them meeting, falling in love and separating. I wrote 10,000 words and I got a 70 per cent mark for it.'

'Well done! That must have been cathartic for you.'

'Yes, it was, but it triggered all kinds of emotions. I've been going over everything again, trying to find clues. But I'm no closer to finding her. I've come to ask if there's any way you can help me? Is there anything we haven't done? I get more and more depressed with each sorry-can't-help-you letter that arrives.'

'You've worked hard. I'm really sorry that you haven't found her.' Jane sounded sympathetic but she looked uncomfortable. 'I wish I could help you more.' She paused and looked intently at me, as if weighing me up.

I told her about Derick's sister Susan writing to the DHSS from America.

'That was certainly inventive.' She shuffled through the papers again, with an embarrassed look.

'All for nothing,' I said, deflated.

'No, not for nothing!' Her face lit up. 'You must think of the positive things that have come out of this. You've met your father, and through him found out a lot more about your mother and their relationship, and you know that she loved you.'

'Yes, that's true. But even that's a double-edged sword. If she'd left me without looking back, I wouldn't want to find her, but knowing how hard it was for her to give me up makes me desperate to find her – I want to see her – touch her – tell her I've had a good life.' I could feel the lump in my throat. 'Although Thomas will chat to me if I ring him, he doesn't really want to know me. He won't tell his daughters. I did say when he agreed to meet me that that was all I wanted – one meeting – but now I can't help wanting more.'

Tears forced themselves from my eyes. She passed me a box of tissues and sent for some tea. By the time it arrived, I'd composed myself. She handed me the steaming cup and studied my face. 'You might find this hard, but you've got to accept the fact that you may never find her.'

I sat up straight, returning her gaze. 'Why? I don't think I can do that.'

'You're going to make yourself ill if you don't. This has become a bit of an obsession with you, hasn't it? That's perfectly understandable, but it's not doing you any good mentally.'

'But I'm running out of time. She could be dead already.'

'If I want to know what I think, having read those letters …' Jane looked directly at me. '… I don't know how she could have kept away from you, especially after finding out where you were living and visiting you for all that time. It must have been a terrible wrench. She's either emigrated or started a new life, possibly not telling her partner, or …' Jane's look softened. '… You have to accept that she's dead. To have so much contact and then suddenly to have none is unusual.'

'Yes, I know it's hopeless but I can't accept that that's it.'

'You have a very supportive husband and family. You have two lovely children and you must think about them.'

'You mean I should give up.' A heaviness settled in the pit of my stomach.

'No, not completely, but you need to take things a little easier. Think about what's good in your life now – don't live in the past. It would be wonderful if you found her, but learn to accept the situation as it is. You've done everything you can. You've got a degree now. Feel pleased with yourself. Get on with your life.'

I left the building feeling fobbed off. But when I got home, I was overcome by a sense of relief. *If I follow Jane's advice, there'll be no more disappointments.* I collected my course books from the shelf, spread them out and planned the following week's lessons for the outreach classes I taught in the community at schools in Widnes and Runcorn.

I loved teaching on the ten-week courses in Psychology, Sociology and Criminology, which earned me the title of 'the Ologies woman'. My students, mostly in their twenties and thirties, had young children of their own who they dropped off at a crèche run by Sure Start while they attended my class.

The following week at my Psychology class, we did Freud. 'At the phallic stage, aged three to five, the child begins to have unconscious longings for the opposite sex parent.' I looked around the room at the shocked faces. 'Little boys want to possess their mothers. It's called the Oedipus complex.'

'Freud's a pervert!' Jackie shouted.

Everyone laughed.

At break time, we sat around Formica tables in the kitchen area sipping hot drinks, and eating cakes baked by my students.

'Did you use all this psychology stuff on your own kids?' Joanne asked. Ten faces turned towards me. Like sponges, they soaked up information.

'My kids were grown up by the time I qualified. But I wish I'd known more about child psychology when they were little. Shaun started school the week I gave birth to Karen, and I don't think we handled his jealousy as well as we could have done. He never got over it.'

'He must have felt pushed out.'

'Yes. He was quite a handful and psychology would have given me more understanding of his behaviour.'

'But he's all right now, isn't he?' Jan asked, her brow furrowed.

'Oh, yes. He lives in America with his partner Debbie and our first grandchild Xavonya, who is gorgeous, and he's doing really well as a stockbroker.'

'Oh wow! Does he have a swimming pool? All Yanks have swimming pools in their back gardens, don't they? Like on TV.'

'Yes, he does,' I said, smiling, feeling proud. 'Which is nice when we visit every year.'

'What's your daughter doing?'

This is getting to be twenty questions, but if it encourages them with their education then what the heck. 'After she finished university, she went to Japan and is teaching English there. I'm a little bit jealous of her travels. I'd have loved to have travelled before I settled down, but it didn't happen. But we're going to visit her before she comes back.'

'You must miss them.'

'Yes. Sometimes Shaun arranges conference calls from his office and we all speak to each other if we can time it right.

Phoenix, where he lives, is eight hours behind and Japan is six ahead.'

'What clever kids you have.'

'I'm very lucky.'

While the students completed an exercise, I remembered showing Shaun's partner, Debbie, the letters Carole wrote documenting the trauma she had suffered in giving me up. Debbie got angry. 'You should check out the mental homes,' she said. 'I know that having my baby taken away like that would have sent me crazy.'

I have to try Thomas again …

Chapter 22

Dorothy

Thomas recognised my voice even though it had been three years since I'd rang him. 'I was only thinking about you the other day,' he said.

'Were you?' I said. *What were you thinking? You always sound pleased to hear me, but you never make the effort to call me yourself.*

'How are you keeping?'

'I'm fine. Just wondered how you are?'

Silence. He coughed and cleared his throat. 'I lost Dorothy last June,' he said, in a voice heavy with sorrow.

'I'm so sorry.' Even though I'd never met Dorothy, I was saddened and remembered her kind voice on the phone. It would have been easy for her to reject me, fear me, hate me even, but she didn't appear to. I wouldn't have expected him to inform me. Why should he? I wondered if anyone would tell me if *he* died.

He talked and talked about his grief and the pain of losing Dorothy after nearly fifty years together. Being happily married myself, I empathised with his plight. He sounded old and confused, no longer the strong, confident man I remembered. For the first time in our strange relationship, he needed me; if only to listen to his grief. Emboldened, I asked him if he'd told his daughters about me.

'No.' Silence. 'Dorothy may have told them but nothing was ever said to me. The photos you sent were left in the drawer and our Judith often looked in there but she never commented, and you know what that means? If they don't ask, they must already know.'

'Then why can't you talk to them about me? I'd really like to meet them.'

'We'll sort it out sometime.'

'When?' *You'll never tell them, you old devil.*

'It's very difficult for me. We never discussed sex or anything like that with the girls. When it came to them having sex education in school, Dorothy wrote and said we didn't want it for them. They find out about sex soon enough without telling them – that's what I always said.' He laughed.

I disagreed with everything he said, but laughed weakly at his attempt at humour.

'I brought them up very strictly, so it's difficult to admit I had a child out of wedlock.'

Were you afraid they'd do the same? I wanted to shout down the phone *You're a bloody old hypocrite*, but instead I said, 'Yes, very difficult.'

'If they saw the photos, they'd guess, because you're the model of our Margaret.'

'How are Margaret and your two brothers, Robert and George?'

'George died. Robert and Margaret sold up the farm in Cheshire and moved to Wales. That's three of my brothers dead – George, Walter and Albert.' The tone of his voice suggested fears for his own mortality.

Will this change his attitude towards me? I doubt it. He's given me all he's capable of giving. What do I want from him, now, if he can't lead me to Carole?

'I never found Carole,' I stated. He went quiet and I thought something was wrong.

'Hello, are you still there?'

'Yes … I've something to tell you.'

'What?' I froze.

'It was three days to go …' He spoke so softly, I barely heard.

'Sorry, what was that about three days?'

He coughed. 'It was three days before our wedding when I called it off.'

'Your wedding to Carrie? There was a wedding planned?'

'Yes. I called it off, three days before.'

Every muscle in my body turned to jelly and I almost slipped from the chair. 'You and Carrie were almost married?' Thoughts whirled. I hated him for what he'd just told me – not the sad old man who was on the other end of the phone, but the young selfish Thomas who had refused to do the right thing. My hands shook as I thought of Carole planning for the big day.

'Are you still there, Barbara? Are you OK?'

'No! I'm shocked. How could you do that? She must have been devastated.'

'She wasn't happy about it, that's for sure.'

I didn't appreciate his joke and remained silent.

'It was my mother, you see. She was a very devout Methodist and she had it all planned, but I couldn't go through with it.'

'Why didn't you marry her?' I asked. 'Please tell me the truth. I think I at least deserve to know.'

'It was complicated. I was young – only nineteen – and you know what you're like at that age, selfish.'

'Yes, I know. Derick was only nineteen when we got married. We had some problems but we got through it.' *There's more to this than he's telling me.* 'What's the real reason? Please, will you be straight with me!'

'Well, you see, my father was against it and so were my uncles … and I idealised the Fletchers … all strong men. I looked up to them.'

'It's not a good enough reason to have jilted Carrie … to have abandoned us.' Tears stung in the corners of my eyes but I refused to cry. 'If you'd loved her enough, you'd have defied them. You don't seem the kind of person to take orders from anyone.'

'Yes … I've always had a mind of my own.'

'Well? What was it then?'

'You see, Carrie … she was a manipulative sort of person. She could get people to do whatever she wanted.'

'It didn't work on you then?'

'Oh, it did! Most of the time, she could twist me round her little finger.'

'But not in the end, when it really mattered.'

He took a deep breath and sighed it out. 'She had a past … if you know what I mean.' There was a long pause while this sank in. *Was he telling the truth at last?*

'Yes, I think I know what you mean.' I hadn't expected this. It didn't fit in with the image I had of her. I'd imagined her as an innocent girl, falling in love and giving herself for the first time. I berated myself for thinking less of her, if only for a moment.

'There were rumours. Things about her past.'

'What things?' I asked, aware of what he was implying.

'Dorothy was a virgin.'

'And Carrie wasn't. Oh, I see! Having sex before marriage was OK for you, but not for Carrie?'

'Things were different then … men expected girls to be virgins when they married.'

Dismayed at his prudery and double standards, I fought to keep control. 'You called it off not because of religion, or your father, or your Uncle Ernest – you never really loved her. If you'd loved her, her past wouldn't have mattered. She was having your baby and you deserted her.' My voice croaked and I started to cry.

'Don't get upset. I did love her, but we wanted different things and I wasn't ready to settle down. Maybe it was all for the best.'

'No!' I fought back the tears. 'I'll bet Carrie didn't think it was for the best. I've got letters, evidence of her suffering, and what about me? I was just the unfortunate by-product.'

'That's not true. We were in love, your mother and me. We could have made a go of it.'

'But you didn't,' I said.

'No, I left her pregnant with you and I'm not proud of that.'

Hurting him was hurting me. I had to calm the thumping in my chest. I took a deep breath. 'It was brave of you to tell me all this,' I said, calmly.

'It's only right that you should know what happened. Like I said, it wasn't my proudest moment.'

A strange sadness spread through my body, a feeling of defeat. 'I'm really sorry about Dorothy,' I said, remembering her inviting me to their house.

'Thanks. She wouldn't have done anything unless I'd agreed to it, but if she'd really wanted something, I'd have given in.' He obviously regretted the years of dominating his compliant wife.

'I know,' I said sadly. 'I wish I could have met her, but it's too late now.'

'It took me a long time to get over Carrie, a long time. I suffered a lot over all that business.'

That business? You suffered! You self-pitying old beggar. What about Carrie? What about me?

'We all suffered.' My stomach tensed. 'I've had a lot of problems with depression over the years.'

'I'm not surprised. Dorothy said to me, "If Barbara's a Fletcher, she'd never understand being rejected."'

Rejection! I couldn't stop the tears. Dorothy had understood everything. I tried to tell him through the sobs what a good woman she must have been.

I heard him crying gently down the phone. We cried together. But I realised his sobs weren't for me, they were for himself and his loss. And my sobs, who were they for? A mother and father? I'd had both of those. A happy family life? I had that. I was crying for an identity that was never meant to be mine – an existence somewhere else – another life – in the countryside with them. With one selfish act he had changed the course of my life forever – casting Carole and myself aside – left to find our own way through this world without him, and worst of all without each other. I couldn't bear to continue. The tears dried up and I tried to think logically and concentrate on now. I told him that we'd booked a cottage in the Cotswolds for the following week and that I'd ring him when I got back.

I went to my computer and wrote up my conversation with Thomas while it was still in my head, and emailed it to Karen. She replied immediately ...

I feel very angry that he can be so selfish and ignorant, still even now. He has been in the wrong all this time and yet hides behind meaningless moral mores that were always hypocritical and are now worthless ...

I think you should definitely contact your sisters. He has not behaved in an honourable way throughout and you have every right to meet your sisters. I think you should forget about not doing things because Thomas doesn't want you to. He has been abominable in his behaviour to you and you have the right to get to know your sisters.

Chapter 23

Hypnotherapy

A colleague of mine recommended Sophie, a hypnotherapist who had helped him with his eating disorder by regressing him back to his childhood. In one session, he remembered sucking at the breast. He saw his mother looking down at him and actually tasted the milk. I wondered if I could resurrect the memory of Carole visiting me in West Bank. Would it be the closest I'd ever get to her? I rang the lady and explained my situation.

'Come in.' Sophie smiled, and I stepped into a scented, candlelit room, an Enya CD playing softly in the background.

'Take a seat.' She pointed to a maroon velvet sofa, a multi-coloured throw draped over the back. I sat on the edge, with my knees tight together, my stomach tense.

'Don't worry, there's nothing to be afraid of. You'll be fine. Would you like a drink?'

'Just a glass of water, please.'

I looked around. Everything in the room was there to create calm, including Sophie. Her dress, in soft muted shades of purple, flowed as she walked to the kitchen. She was fine-boned and petite, with long, wavy brown hair, a friendly face and welcoming manner. She placed the water on a carved wooden side table and told me to lie back, seating herself in a nearby armchair. 'Take deep breaths and relax,' she said. 'Ree-lax … ree-lax …' Sophie repeated, her voice soft and soothing. My eyes became heavy. She coaxed me into the safety of an imaginary garden. I felt the warmth; smelt the flowers; lay in the grass, drifting into deep relaxation – conscious sleep.

'You are conscious and can wake at any time,' she said, firmly. 'You are safe and nothing can harm you. Do you understand?'

'Yes.'

'How did you get on with your father?'

'He was very kind to me. As a small child I was the apple of his eye.' I saw him smiling, taking my hand.

'What about your sisters and brothers?'

'They were all older than me. I suppose I was a novelty. They all spoiled me, especially Lily.' I smiled, remembering.

'What was your relationship with your mother like?'

I cried. Somewhere in the darkness, Sophie got up from her chair and handed me a box of tissues. 'We love tears in this room, we absolutely love them, so let them flow.' I cried and cried.

'She did love me,' I repeated numerous times between sobs, as if to convince myself. '"I don't know where I got you from ... that woman who had you was a bad one," she'd say, but she didn't mean it.'

'She didn't know the damage she was doing,' Sophie replied. 'Have you forgiven her?'

'Yes, long ago. When I was a child, I blamed myself. I thought I was bad because I came from something bad. That feeling of being bad – not good enough – has never left me.'

'When something happens in childhood that we find traumatic, it can remain hidden deep in the subconscious, causing anxiety which leads to depression.'

'Yes, I'm very anxious and I get depressed.'

'Are you on medication now?'

'No. I hate the mushy feeling in my brain. I've been off tablets for a while. I like to be in control. I want to manage without drugs.'

'Repressed emotion has to come out somewhere. It's like a boiling kettle with the lid held tightly down; the pressure builds up and the lid bursts off.'

'I can't live the rest of my life feeling like this. I need to get to the bottom of it all, and let all that steam out.' When Sophie woke me at the end of the session, I felt as though I'd only been under for a few minutes.

'No, it was forty-five minutes,' she said.

At the beginning of each session, Sophie used the same techniques and I responded more quickly each time. 'The most likely cause of your anxiety and depression is finding out that you were adopted at a difficult age, in such a brutal way, and your mother's handling of the situation increased your trauma,' Sophie told me after the fifth session. 'Then you buried all that emotion, compounded with the fact that you've not been able to find Carole, so you've no closure. Retrieving her memory, if we can, will help you. Are you ready to try?'

'I feel anxious about it.'

'You won't when I regress you. It's in there somewhere, but you may not be able to retrieve it. Be prepared for that, and if you don't remember, we can try again.'

'Right, we'll go for it next week.'

'Bring the blue plastic cow – it could stimulate the memory.'

The following week, I held the cow in my hand, as Sophie took me slowly through the relaxation.

'Now I want you to concentrate on blue. Think of blue, the colour blue. Nothing else matters except the colour blue ... light blue.'

'Yes, blue ... blue ...'

'Now, think of blue plastic. A small blue plastic object ... a toy ... a blue plastic cow. A blue plastic cow that rattles. You're holding it in your hand. Shake it and hear it rattle. Concentrate on the cow ... on the blueness of the cow ...'

'She's sitting on the floor,' I said.

'Who is?'

'Carole.'

'Where are you?'

'At Parsonage Road, in the parlour. It's dark but I can see her. She's sitting opposite and playing with me.'

'What does she look like?'

'She's so lovely. She's wearing a blue dress, clean and fresh-looking, with tiny white flowers dotted all over. It's got square shoulders, short sleeves and a white belt. The collar's white as well. Her hair is light and rolled back off her face.'

'What is her face like?'

'… It's not clear, but I can hear her laughing … she's laughing at me, but I can't see her face clearly. It's fuzzy.'

'How do you feel?'

'Happy. I'm laughing with her and we're very happy and close … so close … happily playing together … no one else matters …'

'… And what's happening now?'

'She's holding out her arms. She wants to embrace me … but I can't get any closer. I'm trying to move but my legs feel heavy … so heavy … I can't get to her.'

'How does that make you feel?'

'I want her to pick me up, but I can't get any closer … Now she's holding something behind her back, and I want to get it.'

'What is it?'

'I can't see … she's hiding it from me.'

'How does that make you feel?'

'It's all right. It's just a game of peekaboo. She keeps hiding it. I can see it now. It's blue.'

'What is it?'

'She's shaking it and we're laughing, and I'm grabbing at it, and she's teasing me, holding it back, but I can't move my legs to get closer to her.'

'Can you see what it is now?'

'Yes! A blue plastic cow.'

'What's happening now?'

'She's bending over me and handing it to me. We're laughing, and I'm shaking it and examining it, but I want her to hold me. She's going! I don't want her to go – she's sad – she's crying – my mother is picking me up – holding me tight – too tight – it hurts and I'm struggling. "Kiss Aunty Carole goodbye, kiss her goodbye." I'm screaming and wriggling in my mother's arms, outstretching my little arms, but I can't touch Aunty Carole. She's gone.'

Sophie handed me another tissue. 'It's all right. You're safe and warm. Ree-lax … ree-lax.'

When I awoke, I wasn't sure if I'd had a dream. Did I conjure Carole up in my mind because I so desperately wanted to meet her?

'It was so real – the subdued light, the dark carpet and mahogany furniture – the sense of being a child looking up at her.'

'You were actually shaking the cow about.'

'But I couldn't get close enough to hug her. My legs wouldn't move.'

'It's your inability to find her. You know she's there somewhere but you can't have her.'

'Not yet.' *Is this the closest I'll ever get?*

'You've made good progress. I want you to enjoy your life now, enjoy your family, just be happy. Even if you never find her, you will always have that memory of her. Treasure it.' She hugged me as I was leaving and asked me to ring her if I found Carole.

When I got home, I told Derick every detail. 'You know those dreams where your legs feel as though they're stuck in treacle? That's how I felt.'

'It doesn't take Freud to figure that one out,' Derick said.

'There was an overwhelming togetherness, which excluded everyone else. I could feel the emotional bond between us even though we didn't touch. My mother must have witnessed the same scene many times in Parsonage Road. Watched that bond develop, jealously looking on at our play as we grew closer. I think I understand now why she stopped Carole coming.'

'It was worth doing then.'

'Oh, yes, but I'm not sure if I just imagined it all.'

'It doesn't matter if it's given you some comfort.'

'Like the social worker, Sophie thinks I should just get on with my life.'

'Perhaps you should.'
'I'll never give up.'

Chapter 24

Private Detective

While searching the pockets of an old jacket, before putting it into the Oxfam bag, I found a business card for 'Natural Parents Network' with the name of a counsellor, Janice Walker, printed on it.

I thought for a moment, and then where I got it from came back to me ...

It was on my second visit to St Catherine's House with Lily. We'd stayed with Derick's Uncle Herbert and Aunty Iris in their spacious Victorian three-storey terrace in Slough. The ground floor had a huge patio window that looked out on a beautifully kept garden, the tiny green shoots of next spring's bulbs forcing themselves up through the frozen soil. We wondered why they lived in the basement. Lily started singing the song 'I am a mole and I live in a hole', and I joined in.

'Hush!' I said, putting my finger to my lips. 'They'll hear us.' We laughed until our stomachs ached.

We slept in a room on the top floor heated with a tiny gas fire, which Iris switched off every time we left the room. It was November and freezing; I huddled up to Lily in the double bed, wearing Iris's old dressing gown, but I was still cold. 'What's it like to have an adopted sister?' I asked Lily.

She sat up in bed and stared at me. 'I never think of you as being adopted, I never have. You're my sister.' She snuggled back under the sheets and hugged me. 'Not my adopted sister.'

You've always made me feel special, I thought. *I'm still your Christmas present.*

In spite of their frugality, Iris was kind and accompanied Lily and I to St Catherine's House. On the bus journey into town, I was optimistic, convincing myself we'd find some previously missed clue, but the search was fruitless. The dark panelled walls closed in on me and I sat sobbing in a corner: Lily did her best to provide comfort. *Where are you, Carole?* I asked myself, as a kind-faced, fair-haired woman approached.

'My name's Janice,' she said, empathy radiating from her eyes. 'I deal mainly with mothers trying to find children, but is there anything I can do for you?'

Why isn't Carole looking for me?

Lily explained the difficulty in my search.

'I'm thinking of getting a private detective,' I managed to say through the tears.

'I know of a few detectives,' Janice said. 'If you give me a ring, I'll let you have some numbers and good luck.' With this she handed me her card …

I put the Oxfam bag to one side. *Is it worth calling Janice after nearly ten years? Is it fate or coincidence finding her card?* Brushing aside the heavy sinking feeling that nothing would come of it except disappointment, I gave her a ring.

She was sat in front of her computer using a CD-ROM that covered the electoral roll for all of the country. 'Give me Carole's name and where she came from and I'll look it up for you.' I gave her what meagre details I had: I could hear her tapping away at the keyboard. 'Yes, a very difficult one,' she said. 'Sorry. There's not a clue.'

'I'm thinking of trying a private detective and that's why I'm calling you.' I told her how I'd found her card. 'I thought, anyone you recommend would be reliable, if they're still working as detectives after all this time.'

'You'd be surprised what they can do nowadays. I have three names. One of them lives in Tunbridge Wells and he's definitely still working.'

'That's a coincidence. Carole lived there for a while.' *Is this an omen?*

'I think that he's an ex-policeman and they have access to National Insurance records and all kinds of other information.'

'Oh! I've tried the DHSS and they don't give out information in adoption cases.'

'Not to us, they don't, but these detectives have a way round it. I don't know how but I know they do. But don't spend too much. Put a limit on what they can spend.'

'I'll have to, I'm afraid.' *Will he succeed where we've failed?* 'What got you into helping mothers search for their children, if you don't mind me asking?'

'Not at all,' Janice said. 'I had a son thirty-two years ago and had to give him up for adoption. I got pregnant when I was fifteen, seduced by a married man, friend of the family. The old story. I babysat for him and his wife. On the way home, he'd stop the car in a quiet spot. At the start he'd give me a kiss on the cheek and stroke my hair, and tell me how beautiful I was. I was young and flattered. I knew it was wrong but it was exciting and he was very handsome. One thing led to another and the rest is history. I had to give up my son. The bastard took advantage of me and got away with it. His wife forgave him and they lived happily ever after as far as I know.'

'I appreciate your frankness, Janice, and I'm *so* sorry.'

'Don't be sorry, it ended happily. I found my boy eight years ago. He's like part of the family now. I get on with his adoptive parents and he visits me regularly. My other two sons and my daughter treat him like a brother, which he is. It's all turned out wonderfully.'

'That's great.' I was genuinely pleased for her, but envious. I wished all adopted people could be reunited happily with their birth parents, but most of all me: where was my happy ending? We exchanged emails and I told her I'd keep her updated.

I contacted the detective from Tunbridge Wells, who assured me that he'd find Carole or find out what had happened to her. Impressed with his confidence, I forwarded copies of all the relevant documentation and correspondence, together with his initial charge of £200. He contacted me three weeks later saying he had a strong lead, but it would cost another £150 to apply for documents. Thrilled that he was on to something, I sent the money immediately. He sent me one email stressing the difficulty he was having because she didn't stay in one place for long, and I never heard from him again. I was frustrated and angry.

***

In one of our phone calls, I told Thomas about the detective. 'Unscrupulous devil,' he said. 'Bet you'll not get caught like that again.'

'No, I won't. Wasting all that cash just before Christmas. I'm ringing because I want to send Margaret a Christmas card. Can you get me her address in Wales?'

'I haven't got it,' Thomas said, 'but our Judith has it. I'll ask her.'

'Who will you say wants it?' *Is he going to tell her about me?*

'I'll have to tell her, won't I.'

'You mean you'll tell her everything? She might want to meet me.'

'Yes, I'll have to, if you want the address.'

I could hear the door opening downstairs. It was Derick. I'd been on the phone for nearly an hour so I made my excuses and hung up. Energised, I relayed the conversation.

'What's brought this change of heart?' Derick asked. 'Is it the Millennium?'

'New beginnings and all that!' I laughed, thrilled. 'He also said he'd ring me back with the address. He even asked me what was the best time to ring and he wrote down my number again. He's never rang me, ever. Maybe he wants a closer relationship now that Dorothy's died?'

'Sounds promising, but don't get your hopes up too high. Perhaps the old beggar's feeling guilty – wants to put things right before *he* kicks it.'

'He sounded as though he meant it. Imagine meeting my sisters – what a Christmas present that would be!'

I waited weeks but he never called me back: I rang him.

'... I've got Margaret's address for you. It was in the phone book all the bloody time.'

'Thanks,' I said, flatly. *He hasn't told Judith about me. No need to, the address had been in the phone book. Five days before Christmas. Some hope of me getting a card to Margaret now.* 'Maybe Margaret will remember something about Carrie, now she's had time to think about it. I'm sure she was in a state of shock when I first visited her, as you probably were when Derick called on you.'

'Yes, I was,' he said. 'You know Margaret's younger than me and might not remember much. It's a great pity you never met my mother before she died. She'd have even took you in if you'd wanted her to.'

I thought of myself in Wellington boots wading through shit to feed the pigs – milking the cows – driving a tractor down narrow country lanes – living in a farmhouse with people who looked like me – a different me – a different life.

'She'd have done it just to spite me,' he said. 'You see, I was the devil incarnate after Carrie. She never forgave me, none of them did. Nothing was ever the same between us. She got on well with Carrie, really liked her. She'd have had all the answers for you. She'd have welcomed you into the family.'

Unlike you. You don't want to know me – you don't want me as part of your family. You have no idea how that makes me feel.

'If I'd gone off to Cheshire as a teenager, my mother would have been broken hearted. But I *do* wish I'd met your mother. She sounds like a good woman.' *Even though she didn't help Carole keep me.* Deep regret rose from the pit of my stomach.

'Finding you was so easy.'

'I wasn't a wanderer, like Carrie.'

'That's one of the reasons she's been difficult to find, so the detective said.'

'He just wanted your money.'

To stop the longing for that missing part of me, I had to be active. I wrote a letter to Margaret and posted it with the

Christmas card, hoping she hadn't forgotten me after three years of silence. I never got a reply.

Chapter 25
Meditation

Kath, my colleague and friend, put her foot down in her battered old Metro; it shuddered, groaned and jerked to life, kicking off our four-hour journey to Hereford and the Vipassana Meditation Centre. Dressed in T-shirts, denim shorts and sandals, we wound the windows down and sang along with Leonard Cohen, crooning 'Hallelujah' from the cassette player.

Kath, dark-haired and slim, had done the course before and encouraged me to join her in the college summer holidays. The idea of spending ten days without speaking appealed to me but Kath was very chatty and I wondered how she'd coped.

'Has anything happened lately?' Kath asked, as we drove along the A6.

'What do you mean?' *Oh no! People have noticed.*

'A few colleagues have asked if there's anything wrong. Just out of concern for you.'

No use lying. I opened my mouth to tell her; I burst into tears.

'Hey, don't get upset. I'll stop as soon as I can.'

Sat in the nearest lay-by, Kath offered me a tissue, unscrewed a bottle of water and put her hand on my shoulder. 'What's all this about?'

I took a deep breath and sighed. 'In May – the 16th to be exact – I'll never forget that date – we got a phone call from Derick's sister Ann who lives in Phoenix.'

'Oh! Has she found your mother? She's not dead, is she?'

'No. She's not found my mother dead or alive.' I looked down, twiddled with my seat belt and mumbled, 'She rang to tell us that

Shaun had been arrested on serious drug charges.' I glanced up, dreading her reaction.

'Oh no!' She frowned deeply. 'No wonder you've been distracted at work.'

'He's being held at Madison Street jail, run by the most notorious Sheriff Joe Arpaio, who revels in his reputation of being America's toughest sheriff.'

'I can't imagine how awful it must be for you. He was doing so well, wasn't he?'

'Yes. He used some of the money he made stockbroking to run massive rave parties. We knew about the raves … but he didn't tell us that he was selling ecstasy.'

Kath's forehead wrinkled. 'We'll start a campaign to get him released. He's been very foolish but Shaun's not a bad person. Everyone knows that.'

'Hang on before you start campaigning. We don't know exactly what he's done or how bad things are. His alleged crimes were spread across the front pages of the *Phoenix New Times*, the city rag. When I go into our newsagents, I scan the headlines, terrified they'll be about Shaun. I've imagined people daubing "drug dealers" on the walls of our house. I thought I'd lose my job.'

'That would never happen.'

'I freaked out in an ESOL class the other week. I ran around shouting at the students, "You all know, don't you?" I had to be taken home. I think you were off that day. The doctor put me on tablets. I'm still in shock. I haven't even told Lily. I've made Derick and Karen promise not to speak of it to anyone.'

'Bet they're both traumatised.'

'Yes, they are. Shaun's started to write a blog that I type up for him and Derick puts on the Internet. It's the first prison blog. It makes me feel close to him, although he writes some scary stuff. It had all been about finding my mother previously, but this has overtaken everything now.' *There, I've told someone.* Tension fell from my body like a snake, shedding its skin.

We drove on in silence. The winding country lanes gradually

became narrower, the hedges thicker, and the trees overhead more lush and shady. I was immediately calmed by the silence and peace of the isolated venue, green and tranquil, with small wooden cabins nestling in the trees.

***

A gong reverberated through the darkness, waking us at 4 a.m.: lights went out at 9.30 p.m. Wearing soft, comfortable clothing, we sat for ten hours per day in the large candlelit meditation hall, listening to the audio tapes of Mr Goenka's strong, charismatic voice, chanting and pointing us in the direction of salvation.

Why have I come here? Is it to confront the demons of my past – abandonment, rejection – or to be able to cope with the demons of my present – the dangers facing my son?

Each day, my anxiety levels lessened and a spaced-out feeling overtook me, heightening every sensation. I stared at the poppies, purple and red, that grew three feet high in the garden. Bursting from bud to full bloom, the petals slowly faded and fell, revealing the fattening seed pod, mirroring the cycle of life: birth, death and regrowth.

As I got deeper into the meditation process, the anxiety of my childhood resurfaced. Unable to silence my tears, I cried softly in the meditation hall.

There was an hour each day when students could talk to the tutor. After hours of silence, there was always a queue. 'Don't repress anything,' he told me. 'Cry as much as you like.' Sitting in the lotus position on a raised platform at the end of the darkened hall, a soft light from the shaded windows rested on his face; kind eyes looked down on me seated below. I told him about Shaun and the path of destruction he'd taken.

'Your children are separate from you.' The lines of understanding deepened in his face. 'You do not own your children. You must not look to them to find fulfilment in yourself.'

'I was ambitious for my children. I wanted them to go to

university and be successful. Did I push them too far, pandering to my own ego, trying to prove that adopted or not, I was as good as anyone else? Was I a bad parent? Is this all my fault? That's how I feel.'

'Do not blame yourself or others. Forgive yourself, forgive him. Do not regret past mistakes or worry about his future. The past is gone and you can never change it. No one knows what will happen in the future. Most important is to do whatever you can for him in the present. Put your energy into helping him now. Everything else is irrelevant.'

What a wonderful message. If only I could live by it.

Later in the week, I visited the tutor again and told him about my search for Carole.

'You must acknowledge what happened in your childhood and accept how it shaped your life, but do not dwell on it.' He looked at me with gentle eyes. 'Forgive your parents – your biological parents and your adopted parents – especially your mother. Don't start thinking why didn't they do this or that. It's passed. Deal with what's happening now … just observe it and let it go … let these thoughts go … live in the present.'

'But I want to find Carole so much, or at least find out what happened to her.'

'Continue to look for her, but do not let it overtake your life. If you become attached to these thoughts and you do not find her, you'll be disappointed and unhappy.'

'That's how it makes me feel.'

'Think of finding her as a bonus to your life, but accept the fact that it might not happen. You will not find contentment if you cling to this longing for the past. Concentrate on helping your son now. He needs you now.'

I knew he was right. On the last day of meditation, I mentally said goodbye to Carole and Thomas, and my mother – loving them – forgiving them – freeing myself from the drama of those years. I willed myself to let them go.

I didn't lose my job: everyone at college was wonderfully

supportive. With the love and kindness of Derick, Karen, my family and friends, I got through the devastating consequences of Shaun's six years of incarceration. He was released and came to live at home in 2007, the same year I turned sixty and Karen got married to Andrew at St Bede's. Shaun was institutionalised but his confidence gradually returned and after a year he moved to the South of England. He continued to write and started giving talks to children in schools about the dangers of drugs. I was proud of the way he'd rehabilitated himself.

Chapter 26
Conceived in Love

No longer preoccupied with helping my son, thoughts of finding Carole returned, triggered by a word, an overheard conversation, a TV show or a newspaper article.

I dug out the old files and agonised about starting to search again. I rang Thomas, my body stiff with tension, until he picked up. I didn't tell him about Shaun: he wouldn't have understood. We chatted about our families and the awful weather we'd been having. Abruptly, he turned the conversation to Carrie. 'You were conceived in love.'

My God! I gripped the phone tightly, my heart pumping blood to my brain. I was unable to find the right words.

'You weren't an accident. She wanted a baby, and I did, too … that night,' Thomas said, softly.

If he'd told me earlier that they'd carelessly brought me into the world and then abandoned me, I'd have been furious. But now, knowing they loved each other so intensely, if only for one night, somehow made sense of my existence.

'It means a lot to me … knowing that you loved each other … that I was conceived in love.' My legs became weak and I sat on the next-to-bottom stair in the hall.

'I knew what to do to prevent a pregnancy,' he said, 'but I let my guard down that night. I loved her so much. She was all I wanted.' His voice was slow and distant, as though he was remembering, imagining them together. 'I can still see her now, teasing me with those eyes. I've never seen eyes that blue. We were attached to each other as if we'd never be parted.'

'But you did part!' I had a strange feeling in the pit of my belly.

'Aye, we did. My mother and her sister Barbara had it all planned ... the wedding ... but I couldn't go through with it.'

'You've never mentioned Barbara before.'

'That's where you got your name.' His voice perked up. 'Carrie called you after my Aunt Barbara. They were very close to each other.'

'What was she like?'

'She was a nice enough woman.'

'If they were so close, why didn't Barbara – or your mother, for that matter – support Carrie so she could keep me? Why did everyone abandon us?'

'I don't know.' The sadness crept back into his voice. 'My mother threw me out, remember, so I don't know what happened after I left. It was a terrible time for us all.'

Especially Carrie. He sounded so melancholic, I couldn't talk about it anymore. I asked him about the farm.

'A calf was born, but it ran off when it saw me and we couldn't find it. We searched everywhere.'

'It'll die if it doesn't get fed, won't it?'

'Yes, but we saw the mother today and she was lying down chewing the cud as though nothing was wrong with her. So, she must have found the calf and fed it. Otherwise, she'd be mooing and running round getting distressed looking for it.'

'A bit like me looking for Carrie,' I said.

We parted with laughter – sad, ironic laughter.

***

For days after, I went to college, cooked dinner and did the housework in a daze. The words *conceived in love* kept recurring, stimulating daydreams about their relationship – when he first saw her – how they fell in love – when it all went wrong ...

He noticed her stepping from the truck – tall, blonde, striking blue eyes. Even in the drab Land Army uniform she stood out; her self-assurance scared and attracted him. His eyes wandered over the rest of the group, who were chatting and giggling as they collected their belongings from the back of the truck ...

The dance band was in full swing when he arrived, and he was feeling merry after a few pints at the Bull and Dog with his mate, Arthur. He scanned the room, hoping to catch sight of the tall blonde with the magnetic eyes. St John's Hall was big, and packed with couples jitterbugging, some in uniform, others in civvies. When the music stopped and the dance floor cleared, he saw her sitting near the stage with her pals, out of uniform, in a blue floral dress, with a sweetheart neckline, her fair hair caught up in a matching blue slide. He had to have her ...

... They wandered across the flat, open fields of the Fens to her grandmother's house, a tiny dot on the distant horizon. The sun burned their faces, sweat stained their clothes. They stopped for a drink. Hidden by tall reeds swaying in the oppressive warmth of the breeze, they made love; the noise of the stream and the buzz of insects ceased. Only they existed ...

... The days were golden, working the fields with the farm hands, helping the men load the sheaves onto a horse-drawn cart, which delivered them to the corner of a field where Carrie and her Army pals helped build them into stacks. Watching as she forked the heavy sheaves onto the stacker, he thought how strong she was and he ached to touch her. Like him, she loved the land – was at one with it. He'd marry her and they'd have their own farm. But why hadn't he asked her? When they made love, he had no doubts. Because they'd been intimate, he knew he should marry her – it was the right thing to do – but something held him back ...

... *Towards the end of September, the harvest complete, work slackened off. It was Saturday evening and they'd finished early. The air held onto its daytime warmth, as though afraid to let go. They met in the village near the church hall, but they didn't dance that night. They strolled down a familiar country lane towards their favourite place, a sheltered wood. He took off his jacket for her to lie down on. This night it was different. He felt different, and when she looked up at him, he knew she felt the same. Her past, her history – none of it mattered. He wanted her. She wanted him. Kissing her tanned forehead, her eyelids, her lips, he told her that he loved her. As he undid the buttons of her blouse and kissed her breasts, he promised he'd be with her forever ...*

... *That night transcended all that had happened before. They were a part of nature, melded together with the smell of the dampening grass, the dark earth and the rustle of woodland creatures in the undergrowth. After, they lay gazing up through branches silhouetted against the diminishing autumn light. The leaves were still green, but a faint tinge of decay was spreading inwards, curling their edges, despoiling their splendour ...*

... *When her period didn't happen, she was distraught. The morning chill was everywhere, as she found him alone in an outhouse. When she told him, he thought back to that warm night in the woodland. Now, faced with the reality of what they'd done, he wasn't so sure. Carrie, sensing his reluctance, started to cry. He held her close and told her it would all be fine and that he'd marry her, but his thoughts were all over the place ...*

... *She was alone in the farmhouse when he told her of his decision three days before the wedding his mother and aunt had planned. It was January and it had been snowing all week. She was sat by the fire, peeling vegetables for the evening meal, in the large draughty kitchen of the farmhouse, thinking that at last she belonged. His mother, father and siblings were working the frozen fields, tending the stock. She knew his attitude towards her had changed, but she wouldn't accept it. Their lives were changing and would change still further with the birth of their baby. Now he was telling her that he couldn't marry her, that he wasn't ready for marriage ...*

... His father seemed pleased, his mother openly furious, casting him out, unable to forgive. Relief stronger than guilt, he left her ...

... On the day she should have married Thomas, Carrie sat in her room, wondering what she should do. Watching the door, hoping he'd call to tell her it had all been a mistake, that he loved her and the unborn child she could feel kicking inside her ...

... Forced from the farmhouse, her room in the shelter was dark and bare, a spider's web of frost covering the inside of a small high window. She'd always been independent. Now she needed charity from the cold, patronising nuns whose furtive glances told her she was a bad woman ...

... Placing her few belongings in the wooden chest, she was overcome with despair. She didn't want to give her baby away. Placing her hands on the noticeable swell of her stomach, she felt the warmth and movement of her child. 'You're the only thing in the world that really belongs to me,' she whispered, 'and they want me to give you away. I won't do it. Somehow, I'll keep you. Don't you fret, my darling, I'll not give you away' ...

... When she wasn't scrubbing floors, her time was spent in prayer, asking forgiveness for her sin. Every Sunday they were made to parade their shame through

the streets on their way to church. She was grateful for a bed but desperately unhappy, and relieved when a month later the Mother Superior told her that they had found her a position with Dr and Mrs Cranshaw, who had agreed to take her as a 'companion help' until her confinement ...

... The Cranshaws were kind, generous people, who accepted Carrie into their home without making her feel that it was charity. They had two children, a boy aged ten and a girl aged twelve, who Carrie grew to love. She helped care for the children, and she cooked and cleaned the house. While the doctor worked long hours in his surgery, Carrie kept Mrs Cranshaw company with her lively chatter ...

... By the end of April, Carrie had grown large with the child and Mrs Cranshaw looked after her, insisting that she get sufficient rest. The doctor checked that she was healthy and that the pregnancy was progressing normally. But the Cranshaws did their upmost to convince Carrie that the best thing for her and the baby was to give it up for adoption. She valued their opinion, agreeing with them when they talked about how difficult it would be for her to bring up a child on her own with no family support, but every inch of her being longed to keep the child ...

... At three o'clock on the morning of 2 June, Carrie's waters broke. Mrs Cranshaw took her to the Jericho Hospital, the Public Assistance Infirmary, on Old Rochdale Road in Bury, which was part of Bury Union Workhouse. Being both strong and healthy, she had a straightforward birth, but lying alone during the later stages of labour, she called out Thomas's name. Cursing him for the pain, but longing for him to return to her and the child that was forcing itself out of her womb. At 9 a.m. she gave birth to a healthy baby girl ...

> *... Five days later, Dr Cranshaw arrived at the hospital. Carrie had just finished breastfeeding Barbara and the nurse had taken her to the nursery. 'I've got a place for Barbara at St Vincent's Nursery Home at Facit,' Dr Cranshaw told her. 'It's near Rochdale. It's a very good place. They'll look after Barbara and arrange an adoption. It's a Catholic home, so there's no need to worry on that count.'*
>
> *'But, but ... do you have to take her so soon?'*
>
> *'Yes, I'm taking her today. It's better sooner than later. The longer she's with you, the harder it will be to part with her.'*
>
> *'Can I say goodbye to her?'*
>
> *'It's better if I just take her,' he said, not wanting to witness an emotional scene.*
>
> *Sensing his thoughts, she said, 'I won't make a fuss. But please let me kiss her goodbye.'*
>
> *She didn't make a fuss – defeated – helpless – as she kissed Barbara's cheek and touched the softness of her skin. 'Goodbye, my darling, goodbye' ...*

'Their story is like a Catherine Cookson novel,' I said to Derick.

'It is,' Derick agreed with a smile. 'Illicit sex romps in the hay, country girl gets pregnant by farmer's son, then he abandons her. It's got the lot.'

'Except a happy ending ... Catherine Cookson always has a happy ending.'

'There might be one yet.'

Chapter 27
Thomas

The last three times I'd rung Thomas, I'd got no answer. Concerned, I left a message on his answering machine. When no one called back, I wrote a letter to his house for whoever might read it, asking if Thomas was ill.

'Make that coffee strong.' I yawned, covering my mouth. 'I'm so groggy, I didn't sleep well last night.'

'Worrying?' Rita placed the hot mug of coffee in front of me and sat down opposite. I held the cup, warming my hands.

'I was thinking about my father.'

'Jim or the other one?' she asked with a smile.

'The other one.' I rolled my eyes. 'I think he might be ill or something. He's not answered his phone for a couple of weeks, and no one's responded to the messages I've left. He's always been so fit. But he was just a voice at the end of the phone. That's all he's ever wanted. Our relationship wasn't important to him.'

'I'm sure he's enjoyed talking to you.' She gave me an overly concerned look and touched my arm. 'They should have let you know if he's in hospital.'

'They may not know anything about me.'

'The old beggar should have told them by now.'

'He won't.' I paused and sipped my coffee. 'He doesn't want me in his life.'

'Maybe he'll change his mind one day.'

The phone rang. 'It's Derick,' Rita said, handing me the phone.

'Are you OK?' Derick asked, in a strange voice.

'Yes. We're just having coffee before we go to Debenhams on a shopping spree. What's up?'

'I hate to tell you this over the phone …' He sounded upset.

'What's wrong?' My belly muscles stiffened. 'The kids are OK? Nothing's happened, has it?'

'Yes, they're fine, it's not them.'

'Good.' I experienced a second's relief. 'What is it, then?' I asked impatiently.

'It's Thomas. His daughter Judith just rang in reply to the message you left on his answering machine.'

'Is he ill?' My heartbeat quickened.

Derick took a deep breath. 'He died on 11th January this year.'

'Oh no! *He's* left me now.' My voice croaked and tears stung my eyes. 'He was my only link to the past, to Carole.'

'What's happened?' Rita mouthed, handing me a tissue.

I covered the speaker with my hand and told her.

'Oh no!' Rita hugged my shoulders.

Suppressing the tears, I asked Derick how Thomas had died.

'He wasn't ill. He was out collecting the milk money and died at the wheel of his car, driving very slowly, saying goodbye to a customer. He just dropped dead.'

'That's awful.' Curiosity about my sister dried up my tears. 'What did she sound like?'

'She was friendly enough. We joked about it being a good way to go, if you have to go, that is. No pain. Here one minute, gone the next.'

'At least he didn't suffer.'

'No. I said you'd ring her when you got home. Are you going to be OK? Do you want me to come up and get you?'

'No. It's just a shock. Rita will look after me. See you later. Love you, bye.'

I told Rita how Thomas had died and she made another coffee.

'I didn't really think anyone would let me know, but I feel robbed. I'll never again hear him ramble on about politics and problems with fences, ditches, cows and neighbours. But the worst thing is … I'll never again be able to talk to him about Carole. He was the only person alive who knew her. He was a difficult old beggar but I'll miss speaking to him. It was all I had … those phone calls. I feel such a sense of loss.'

'For what might have been, I suppose.'

I sipped my coffee. *Why wasn't I at his funeral? I was his daughter, too.* I imagined his elderly relatives – my relatives – all dressed in black, gathered round his grave and at the funeral breakfast. *Why didn't he want to be my father? Why didn't he love me?*

'I wonder if he's left you anything?'

'I doubt it. He didn't see me as part of his family. It's not the money … but it would have meant so much to me … if he … if he …' Tears blocked the words. '… If he'd acknowledged me as his daughter in some way. If he'd left me some small token.' I cried.

'Get it out of your system.'

'Occasionally, during my conversations with Thomas, I'd felt a moment of closeness, especially in our last phone call. He'd felt it, too, I could tell. But he never thought of me as his child, or he'd have given me more than the crumbs of attention I'd been so grateful for.'

'Try to look on the bright side,' Rita said with a smile, 'there's nothing to stop you contacting your sisters now.' Rita's words halted the flow of negativity. *What would they be like?*

***

'I can't get through to Judith.' I slammed the phone down. 'I've tried four times this week. Perhaps she doesn't want to speak to me.'

'Take it easy. Of course she does. She was very friendly when I spoke to her.' Derick put his arms around me. 'She's probably got a lot on. Try again.'

He's right. I'm the older sister. Take charge. I took a deep breath, lifted the receiver and dialled. She answered. My stomach tensed, afraid she'd hang up when she heard it was me. 'I've been trying to ring you for a few weeks now.'

'Sorry. I've been busy since Father died, running the business. How are you?'

I relaxed and we made small talk. She sounded like Thomas but a lively, jolly version. Although she had a lot to say, she listened. I brimmed with curiosity.

'Did you have any idea that I existed?'

'Sort of. I found a photo at Father's house of you and Karen. At first I thought he'd had an affair and that Karen was his love child.'

'Oh!' *Secrets and lies.*

'I plucked up the courage to ask Mother but she said you were distant relatives.'

'Did you believe that?' *How that generation lied to themselves as well as everyone else.*

'Yes and no. I thought it was strange him having a photo and us not knowing you, but I put it out of my mind.'

Too painful for her to delve further. 'He told me he'd left the photo in the drawer. It was as though he wanted you to find it.'

'He was a dark horse never telling us.' Her tone was resentful. 'After he died, I went through his possessions and found a letter you'd written to him, and realised that you were his child and Karen was his grandchild.'

'I bet that was a shock?'

'Yes, it was. I still haven't got over it. What with the death of Father and then finding out about you, it's been a lot to take in.'

'Did you tell Diane?'

'Yes, but she's in a worse state than me about it. She'd no idea at all.'

'I'm sorry about that.' I felt genuine sympathy for them both. 'It must have been awful him dying so suddenly. Derick told me what happened.'

'Yes, fortunately he was driving very slowly.'

'How was the funeral?' I asked, jealousy creeping in.

'It was a grand funeral, just as he would have wanted it. The hearse was pulled along on a horse-drawn carriage and he was buried in the family grave. All of his remaining brothers and sisters attended. He liked to be the centre of attention. We gave him a good send-off.'

'It sounds like quite a spectacle.' *I should have been there. I should have met them all. But the attention would have been on me, not him. He'd never have forgiven me for that.*

'There has to be an inquest,' she said. 'Because of the suddenness of his death.'

'Yet they let you bury him?'

'They had to remove parts of his internal organs before we could bury him. It was very upsetting. We won't know the results of the Inquest for a few months.'

She told me about her eight children, and her life and upbringing with Thomas.

'He was very strict, and chased all our boyfriends away.' She laughed. 'He threatened to thump them when they came up to the house. We had to sneak out and meet them down the road.'

Bloody old hypocrite. 'He said he'd been strict.' A churning started in my belly. 'And that he couldn't face telling you he had an illegitimate child.'

'In a way, we feel betrayed, me and Diane. They should have told us about you.'

'Yes, but I don't think your mother would have done anything behind his back.'

'No. He ruled the roost, and he was quite hard with my mother, and expected her to carry on working with him no matter how she felt. When she died, I took over from her cooking and looking after him. I've worked with him in the milk business since I was twelve.'

'Isn't that child labour?'

'Yes, it is.' We both laughed.

She asked about my parents and upbringing, and listened attentively.

Should I tell her about the planned wedding? Is she ready for it? I enjoyed acknowledging that but for a twist of fate, I'd have been his legitimate daughter not her, and telling her gave me a weird sense of satisfaction.

'Oh, really! That shines a different light on it. Why didn't it go ahead then?' she asked, her voice shaky.

'He called it off three days before.'

'How awful for your mother.' She gasped, then fell silent.

'Look on the positive side, you and Diane would never have been born, if they'd stayed together.'

'No.' She gave a weak laugh. 'Strange how things turn out.'

'My fate was in the balance. She could have kept me anyway.'

She was silent again. 'It would have been difficult for her to keep you in those days.'

'His mother, your grandmother, threw him out and didn't speak to him for years after.'

'Oh! I knew they didn't get on. Now I know why.'

'Carole went to live at the farm and your grandmother and Aunty Barbara – who I was named after – arranged the wedding.'

'Good heavens! We had no idea that all this went on in our family.'

She sounded distressed: I reassured her. 'I'm not bitter. It's all in the past. None of us are to blame. We were innocent children.'

'The sins of the father,' she said, and we laughed, a gentle, ironic laugh.

'Would you like to meet up?' I asked, clenching my stomach. *Please say yes.*

'Yes, I'd love to meet you.'

'Great.' Sigh of relief. 'Will Diane come?'

'I'll ask her but if she's not ready, I'll come by myself. I'll ring you next week to make arrangements. Bridgemere Garden Centre is very nice near Nantwich.'

Each day, my emotions changed: expectant, hopeful, and fearful that I'd remain a voice at the end of a phone, like I was with their father, and that I'd mean no more to them than I had to him. The same fear of rejection that had always lived inside me became a voice telling me it wasn't worth it, that they'd resent the intrusion of a stranger into their lives. She didn't ring me back.

'Try her again,' Derick said, two weeks later.

'I don't know if she wants me to. She seemed so eager to meet me, I can't understand why she's changed her mind.'

'She's in a state of shock. Try her again. You've nothing to lose.'
Only my mind! 'OK, I'll try again.' I lifted the phone.

She sounded entirely different, distant and sad. 'I'm sorry I've not got back to you. I've spoken to Diane.'

'Oh good. Is she coming?' I asked, as cheerfully as I could.

'Diane's still very upset and too shocked to deal with it right now, and to be truthful we both need more time to get our heads round what Father did. It's because they didn't tell us that hurts.'

My spirits plummeted. I wanted to scream down the phone but I tried to sound understanding. 'I've known about you two for twenty years. You've only just found out about me. I understand how shocked you must feel.' *No! I don't understand. Why aren't you as anxious to meet me as I am to meet you?*

'It's just too difficult at the moment.'

'You do still want to meet me, don't you ... when you and Diane get your heads round it?' *Do I sound as desperate as I feel?*

'Oh, yes. I'll get back to you as soon as I can.'

I paced up and down the living room feeling cheated, ready to cry. 'After years of waiting, I have the chance of meeting my sisters, and they don't want to know me.'

'They'll come round eventually,' Derick said. 'They might be suspicious of your motives, thinking you're after money.'

'I suppose I could be lying, even though he had my photo and my letter in his drawer. Until they see their father's name on my adoption papers, it's a possibility.'

I wrote a letter to Judith hoping I'd reassure her. She never replied.

***

'Someone calling himself Uncle Frank rang about an hour ago,' Derick said. 'I told him you'd be back from shopping soon.'

'Oh! That's a surprise.' I took off my raincoat and draped it over the radiator. 'April showers in March, I'm drenched!'

'Well, he said he was Judith's Uncle Frank from Wales. Didn't you write to him a while ago?'

'Yes, don't you remember? Margaret and Robert sold up in Cheshire and went to live in Wales near him. Judith gave me his address in our first phone call, when she was friendly, and I wrote to him briefly telling him the story.'

'Wonder what he wants?'

'Maybe he wants to meet me?' I said, with optimism. 'I'll ring him back when I dry out.'

'Hello, this is Fletchers,' a well-spoken female voice answered my call.

I explained who I was and she shouted Frank to the phone. He was friendly and I relaxed. We talked about his brothers and sisters past and present, and I asked him about Carrie.

'Oh, yes. I was only thirteen at the time, but I remember her. You couldn't forget Carrie. She was a lively girl. Everyone liked her. There were so many of us on the farm but she got on well with us all. She'd muck in with all the jobs, and she helped Thomas with the milk deliveries.'

'Did you know about me?' My heart thumped.

'Yes, I did, but I was too young to remember all the circumstances. I doubt if it was even talked about much in front of us younger children. I know Mother wasn't very happy with our Thomas. He disappeared after that but I didn't know she'd thrown him out. It wasn't very nice of him leaving Carrie like that. But he was always a bit of a wild card, our Thomas.'

'Don't suppose you've heard from her since?'

'No. I've never thought about it for years. It was a surprise getting your letter.'

His chatter gave me the confidence to ask for more. 'Do you think I could visit you and see Margaret and Robert?' I held my breath.

There was a long pause. 'Not just now. Margaret said it's all in the past and she'd rather forget about it.' His voice changed and I could tell he wanted to get off the phone. 'But I hope you find her, your mother, Carrie.'

I wished them all well and said goodbye. He'd rung out of politeness, not to have any future contact. They didn't want the past dragged up again. I meant nothing to them except an embarrassing reminder of their brother's mistake. I wanted to cry but I couldn't. I was angry inside and resentful. *Why am I bothering with them? They don't want me as part of their family and they're not bringing me any closer to Carole.*

***

Typing up lesson plans at the computer in our back backroom, I paused to check my emails. *My goodness! What's this?* There was no secrecy between Derick and me but we rarely looked at each other's emails. Why I'd opened his in-box by mistake is probably one of those inexplicable coincidences. I would normally have clicked out straight away but I couldn't resist looking. It was from Karen. My heart thumped as I read, 'Subject: Judith & Diane'. Karen was asking Derick if it was all right to send the attached letter to my sisters. Derick replied saying it was fine. I had to know what it said. Full of guilt, I opened the attachment.

April 2009

Dear Judith & Diane

This is Karen, Barbara's daughter, and I hope you can take the time and have the kindness to read this letter.

I meant to write a letter to Thomas years ago but I never got around to it, and it is too late now.

I hope that this letter finds you in good health. I know you must have been experiencing a lot of mixed emotions on your father's passing.

I guess you need time before you can process what has happened and it may take some time before you feel ready to be able to meet my mum.

I would just like to tell you what I meant to tell Thomas all those years ago.

My mother is the kindest, most loving person that you could ever meet. She was fortunate to be adopted into a warm and loving family and although her brothers and parents have died now, she has a great relationship with her older sister Lily, who has kind of mothered her over the years as there is a seven-year age gap.

It was a terrible shock to my mum as a twelve-year-old child to find out that she had been adopted. She may have already told you in a letter that my nan told her that she was not wanted and had been abandoned. This feeling of rejection caused many problems for my mother but she managed to get over it and meet my dad and have her own family.

... I met Thomas just the once. I wasn't that interested in meeting him because I was very angry that he had abandoned my mum and that he continued to treat her poorly by not recognising her to the rest of the family. However, he seemed a very likeable man on that day.

However, all that is in the past. I just wanted to say that it would be an awful shame now for you to not try and get to know my mum, your sister. Life is short and everyone makes mistakes. My mum did not do anything wrong in all this. She was an innocent child and she grew up into a loving and kind person.

I just find it so terribly unfair that she has had to deal with so much rejection all her life and now it seems as though you do not wish to know her either.

Maybe it is too painful for you and you do not want to dredge up the past?

But perhaps a meeting would heal some wounds and answer some questions?

I would just like my mother to have the chance to get to know some of her blood family before it is too late.

I do think that it would be very much your loss if you don't because you would be missing out on the chance to meet a wonderful person, who also happens to be your older sister.

I send this with the best wishes and do not mean any harm to you or your family. I am just asking for some understanding of what my mum has gone through – but I understand if the time is not right or it is too early for you to process. I have not told my mum I am sending this.

Tears rolled down my face onto the keyboard. *I'm so lucky to have a daughter who feels my pain so deeply. Will her words touch them?*

Chapter 28

Diane & Judith

'Post's early today. Looks like a card for you. Car tax for me.' Derick handed me a pale blue envelope.

I turned it over; the sender's address was written on the back. 'It's from a Diane someone in Cheshire. Oh! Of Course! It's from my sister Diane.' *It must be a reply to Karen's letter, but I can't tell Derick that I've read her email.*

'Fantastic! Get it open.'

My hands trembled as I ripped open the envelope. I read it aloud to Derick.

May 2009

… Sorry it took so long to write but Judith and I have had a lot of things to sort out.

… It has come as quite a shock to find out Dad had another daughter. He never said a thing, but he never showed his emotions easily. I am so sorry you cannot find your mother. My daughter Louise and I have been doing a family tree, which we find very interesting. I have sent you some information from Dad's tree. Will send some pictures and information when I get it all together. Dad wrote a poetry book when he was young so will give you a copy.

… I am glad you had lovely adopted parents and your family looks lovely.

> *... I met up with Dad's brothers and sisters at his funeral. Some I have not seen since I was a child. It was lovely to see them again. Dad's younger sisters don't remember much about your adoption. Things were kept quiet in those days. They said they thought we must have known ... I am happy to meet up and help you with any history ...*

I bubbled with excitement. 'She's actually going to see me and here's the family tree.' I held up a typed sheet of paper and read the names, 'May Chandley, Thomas's mother, died in 1985. That was the year before I started to search.' My stomach ached with regret. *Why did I wait so long?* I buried my head in my hands but I was too frustrated to cry.

'It's no use beating yourself up about that, now,' Derick said, firmly. 'You're going to meet your sisters, try and focus on that.'

I looked up at him. 'You're right! I'm going to look forward, not back,' I said with determination. 'I'll ring Diane now.' I rang numerous times; when we finally spoke, I thanked her for the card and family tree.

'It's the least I could do.' Diane sounded quieter and more guarded than Judith. I had to fill in the gaps. When I talked about Thomas's relationship with Carole, she fell silent. *She's still in shock. Tread carefully.* She told me about her three children and six grandchildren, and ended the conversation saying that we would meet up but she seemed to prevaricate when I tried to set a date.

***

'I haven't heard a word from my sisters,' I complained to Derick. 'It was June when I spoke to Diane, that's four months ago. How long do they need? I'm not going to bother anymore.'

'They should be delighted to have a sister like you.' Derick shuffled through the post. 'There's something for you here.' He placed a blue envelope on the kitchen unit.

'Looks like another card from Diane. Just when I'd given up. Will you finish this?' I offered him the wooden spoon I was using to stir the porridge; I slit the envelope open with a sharp knife.

'It *is* from Diane!' I shouted, light-headed. 'She wants to visit with her husband, Paul. She's going to bring Thomas's poetry book and some photos of the family. She's had her grandchildren for the summer. That's why she's not written sooner.'

'Thank God for that.' Derick sighed and dished out the porridge.

I didn't phone her straight away. I had to get my head round her wanting to meet up all over again. When I did call her, she sounded pleased to hear from me, but our conversation was short and to the point. We arranged for them to come over at 2 p.m. on Sunday 27 September, which was in two weeks' time.

I cleaned the house, frantically dusting and polishing until everywhere shone. The powerful smell of newly opened air fresheners filled the rooms. *What should I wear?* I changed into a smart black top and pants, with a deep pink cardigan.

They were late. My mood swung up and down from relief to disappointment like a fairground rollercoaster, and I wandered around the house rearranging ornaments and furniture. *If they don't come, I'll forget them all and never contact them ever again. But if they do come, how should I behave? Will I cry? Will Diane cry? Oh goodness!* I tried breathing exercises but I couldn't concentrate.

'They're here!' Derick shouted into the kitchen, where I stood nervously re- arranging the plates of sandwiches and cakes I'd made earlier. *Oh no! This is it!*

I walked out into the street to meet them, eagerly scanning the car windows. There were two people in the front.

Diane got out of the car, looked across at me and smiled. 'Hello.' I moved cautiously towards her and we hugged a long, lingering hug. We cried.

'Thanks for coming. It means a lot to me,' I whispered.

'It's lovely to meet you at last,' she said through her tears, still hugging.

The crying faded and we looked at each other, scrutinising each other's features. I could see no immediate resemblance. She had auburn hair, grey eyes and a pretty round face with cheeks that dimpled when she smiled. I liked her immediately. *It's going to be OK.* Paul, her husband, handsome with black, slicked-back hair, looked on with an expression that said he understood everything. Derick hugged Diane and I hugged Paul. They followed us into the house and I sat next to Diane on the sofa.

'I'm naturally very dark,' I said, running my fingers through my newly dyed blonde hair. 'The hairdressers at college are responsible for this.'

'I'm more like Mum. I've got her red hair,' Diane said. 'You look more like Judith and the Fletchers; they're dark-haired and olive-skinned. *You* look more like Judith than *I* do. No one has ever thought we were sisters.'

'I'm looking forward to meeting her.'

'I've brought these for you.' She removed the contents of a large brown envelope and handed me a studio portrait of Thomas's family. They were all dressed smartly; the mother and father sat proudly in the centre of their twelve children. The youngest child looked about four; the oldest two were in Army uniform.

'What a handsome family.' I examined each face. 'Thomas and this brother here remind me of Shaun. Don't you think so, Derick?' He moved to sit beside me on the sofa.

'And this one looks just like you when you were a child.' Derick pointed to one of the younger children.

'Yes, that's Robert,' Diane said.

'I met him when Thomas took me to the house in Bunbury. Can I have a copy of this?'

'I've copied everything for you. They're yours,' she said.

'Thank you. It means a lot to me.'

Diane talked about her father's strictness, his temper and how he ruled the house. I'd had a lucky escape, I reminded myself.

'He chased me off down the road when I came courting Diane,' Paul said, and we all laughed.

She handed me a set of small photographs of Thomas posing in the horse-drawn carts they'd used for the milk round over the years. 'He loved having his photo taken,' she said.

'He was a real ham,' Paul said. 'Had to be the centre of attention.'

'Yes, you can tell that.' I noted his unselfconscious pose and natural smile as I sifted through photos of country scenes: Thomas walking the horses; Thomas as a young lad swinging from trees. *Such a different life, so removed from mine.*

'And these are his poems.' She handed me a coloured copy of the poetry book he'd written. 'He was very proud of them. He had them published.'

Titled *Early Spring and Other Poems*, a path leading through tall trees into a distant light decorated the cover. The price was one-shilling net.

'He didn't seem the type to write poetry,' I said, realising how little I knew him.

'No, he didn't,' she said. 'He was a dark horse, my dad.'

I fingered the book. 'Thank you for this, Diane.'

'You're very welcome.' Her face became serious. 'He wrote a poem about a girl with blue eyes. It's in there ... I think he might have written it about your mother.'

'Why do you think that?' I asked, startled.

'My mother had brown eyes.'

Oh! Wow! I wanted to immediately find that poem and scrutinise it, but I didn't dare, and I scanned through the pages, the poems a blur. I closed the book. 'I'll read them properly later,' I said. 'Let's have some tea.'

Seated in the dining room, Diane looked out through the large patio windows. 'Your garden's lovely.'

'Barbara's the one with green fingers,' Derick said.

'I love the autumn colours. The japonica goes a deeper red and stays that colour all through winter.'

Diane looked at the table, laid out with my best china. 'You've gone to a lot of trouble.'

'I'm just so glad you both came.'

Paul was from a farming family, and he told us of his love of horses and how much he and Diane had in common. 'It's great that you two have met up after all this time.' His smile showed genuine pleasure and gradually I relaxed.

'We're having the land and the cattle, and Judith's having the house,' Diane said.

I didn't expect anything, but the feeling of being unimportant – not his real daughter – tormented me again and my stomach tensed.

'Would you like to see my adoption documents.' We moved back into the living room. Part of me was anxious to prove that I hadn't made any of it up.

'Yes,' she said, but there was sadness in her eyes. She examined the adoption certificates carefully, slowly reading the evidence of her father's betrayal. She paused over the note with his signature at the bottom, relinquishing all legal obligation towards me. She looked up at me, grey-faced, eyes red-rimmed, unable to speak. I showed her Carole's letters, and weeping she confessed, 'The main reason I was reluctant to meet you was because I felt guilty. I couldn't deal with it.'

'Why should *you* feel guilty?' I asked.

'Because Dad didn't marry your mother, and the way he left her pregnant with you.'

'Oh! Please don't feel like that.' I was touched by her empathy. 'It's not your fault. I don't blame you.' I hugged her closely.

'Come on, you two, cheer up!' Derick said. 'Old Thomas will be laughing his head off up there.'

'Shaking his fist, more like,' Paul said, and we all laughed.

We arranged to meet up again the following month when Karen was visiting. As soon as their car pulled away, I rushed into the house and scanned through the poetry book until I found it, 'Could I Ever Forget You':

Could I ever forget
Those two blue eyes of yours.
That smile that was only yours,
Could I forget you?

My life has been such misery,
Since you said good-bye to me:
If I could only live the past,
And enjoy the memories we knew.

For life is so short, so people say,
But those happy times seem far away.
For you were so gay with your many charms.
Who would have thought your best did most harm?

The poems were published in 1952, five years after my birth. He wrote with such sorrow, such longing: the last two lines struck me. I squeezed my eyes tightly shut. *It must be Carole.* I read it again. I felt both his loss and mine deeper than I thought possible. I wondered if Carole ever forgave him.

A month later, Diane and Paul visited again. Karen was home, and keen to meet her new aunt, uncle and cousin Louise, who was around the same age as her. They arrived loaded down with albums. I looked through Thomas and Dorothy's wedding album enthralled and saddened. The photographs were larger versions of the tiny photo Margaret had given me. They made a handsome couple, Thomas in top hat and tails and Dorothy in satin and silk. An expensive wedding for its time. My anger and jealousy had faded and I was thankful to have the opportunity of looking into the past. I stared at the faces of the guests. The relatives and friends I never got to know – some dead – some living. Smiling, I kept the conversation bright to hide my sadness. Having Karen and Derick there helped.

***

'It's another card, from Judith this time,' I said.

'They like their cards, those sisters of yours,' Derick said. 'What's wrong with a phone call?'

'They're old-fashioned country folk.' I smiled at Derick. 'She wants to meet me at a garden centre near Nantwich.'

I arrived early. To ease my mind, I wandered through the aisles admiring the coloured blooms and potted shrubs. The dank smell of the recently watered foliage mingled with the whiff of fresh brewed coffee drifting in from the café. *What will she be like? Different from Diane, I guess. Will she look like me?* I stood near the entrance, pretending to look at a stand holding handmade greetings cards, glancing every few seconds at the revolving door until she appeared. Without introductions, I knew it was her. Casually dressed, with dark hair, and slightly taller than me, she looked like Thomas – much more than I did.

'There's no doubting who you belong to,' I said. We bear-hugged and a tear slipped down my face. She was crying, too. We quickly wiped away the tears and made small talk about the journey and the weather until we found a seat in the café in a quiet spot away from eavesdroppers. The food smelled good, but I was too nervous to eat. We ordered coffee and sat opposite each other in a booth, looking timidly at each other's faces.

'We have the same greeny-brown eyes,' I said. 'Mine have gone greener as I've got older, if that's possible.' I smiled.

'Yes,' she said, smiling back. 'I've got my dad's eyes and colouring.'

'I must be a mixture of both Thomas and Carole. I've got photos of her.'

'Have you?' she said, surprised. 'I'd like to see them. Where did you get them from?'

'Let's order some food and I'll tell you the story.' I felt a bond with Judith and I started to relax.

She ordered steak pie and I ordered vegetable lasagne. Her

interest in my adopted parents and Carole's plight touched me. When she looked sad, I tried to make a joke of things. We ordered coffee and blueberry cheesecake, and talked about her family while we indulged.

Three hours passed quickly. We hugged – a long, meaningful hug – and agreed to meet again the following month. Although we'd connected in a special way, there were too many missing years for us to feel like real sisters. *Will we ever be able to replace those missing years?*

***

'I've got an idea that could help you find Carole or someone who knows her,' Karen said down the phone.

'Oh! Brilliant!' My stomach leapt and I gripped the phone tighter. 'What is it?'

'What I'd like to do is write an article about you meeting your sisters, and pitch it to the most popular women's magazines or even one of the Dailies – you know, the kind of human-interest story frequently featured. Try to get the widest circulation possible.'

'That's a brilliant idea. Someone somewhere must know her. She might read it herself.' My head spun with thoughts of similar stories I'd read. *How would she react if she read it?* The fear of her not wanting to know me momentarily stifled my excitement.

'What angle will you take?'

'Well, I'll have to give the backstory about Carole and Thomas's meeting and separation. The media like a happy ending, so there'd have to be photographs of you with your sisters. Do you think they'd do it?'

'I don't know. It's all a bit soon after Thomas dying but I'll ask them, though. Would we have to give Thomas's name? They might be a bit touchy about their father's past being written about in such a way.'

'You mean telling the truth about him?' she said scornfully.

'I suppose they may want to protect his memory.'

'Even though he's lied to them all their lives.'

'He's still their father.'

'It would be better if we could mention his name, but it's not entirely necessary.'

'They both seem very concerned that I've never found Carole. Perhaps they'll be glad to have the opportunity to help me.'

'I'd interview Diane and Judith, ask them how they felt about you coming into their lives.' Karen sounded enthusiastic. 'I'd want to ask Lily how she felt having an adopted sister. Then I'd interview you about being adopted and meeting your new sisters.'

'That's very clever. I can see it now.' *What a good journalist she is, and what a wonderful daughter.*

'Do you think they'll agree?'

'I hope so.'

I emailed Diane and asked her if she'd be involved in Karen's article, mentioning there would have to be a photograph of the sisters. She replied saying she didn't see why not. *That was easy*, I thought.

Weeks later, I emailed again but she never replied. The next time I saw Judith, I asked her if she would be involved.

'Has Diane agreed?' she asked, at our monthly meeting in the garden centre.

'Initially she agreed, but I've not heard from her since.'

'I'll think about it.'

I emailed Diane three more times before she replied:

> *... I am not too keen as I don't want to do anything that would have upset my mum and dad. I know they are both dead but I know they were very private people. I am happy to have found you. I think you are lovely and my family and friends know I have a sister. You could ask for information yourself in the national papers if you think it might help. I do hope you can find out what happened to her.*

I wrote back saying that I understood and that most people don't like to be in the papers – we'd become hardened with all the publicity over Shaun. After assuring her that I wouldn't ask again, I pressed send on the computer, sad and disappointed. *Why do I always let them off the hook? I was the same with Thomas – behaving as though he was doing me a favour by talking to me – never demanding anything from him. Their parents are dead, why don't they help me?*

Chapter 29
Media Frenzy

Over lunch, an old friend from college, Fran, fumbled in her bag. 'I've got something for you.' She leaned over and handed me a scrap of paper. 'I was watching TV the other night and there was a programme about this lady, Cat something or other. She said she can trace anyone, or help you to trace people. She sounded really professional.'

'Cat Whiteaway,' I read, 'an unusual name. Thanks, Fran, I'll give it a go.'

A few days later, I found the note at the bottom of my bag. *Is it worth the heartache? Will anyone ever be able to find Carole?*

Cat had an impressive site. Media savvy, she'd worked on various TV and radio family history research programmes. She'd helped locate missing beneficiaries, but it was the 'Reunited' icon that interested me. Here she said she'd help you find '... whatever you'd lost apart from your hair, your car keys or your marbles.' She said that if she could find the person within fifteen minutes there'd be no charge. I knew there'd be no chance of that. Initial research would cost £150. *A small price to pay if she can help.* Clicking on 'Contact', I sent a long email detailing my search for Carole.

Months later, whilst having lunch once again with Fran, my phone rang. It was Derick. 'Remember when you contacted that woman Cat something or other? Well, you've got an email about the possibility of being on a TV show that traces people. Something about taking part in a film.'

'That's amazing! I'd forgotten all about her!'

'It's not a done deal. You have to write to the producer, but they sound interested.'

Relating what he'd said to Fran, excitement bubbled between us.

On my arrival home, I dropped my bags in the hall, ran upstairs to my computer and went straight to my in-box, and there it was:

10th March 2010

> *... I thought you might be interested to know that I've been asked to film a programme in the next few weeks for BBC 1 in which a team of trackers will trace people. It might be possible to include your research request but this would obviously require you to take part in the filming ...*
>
> *If this is something you might like to consider or you would just like to talk to the production company about the programme please contact Dave Reed, the assistant producer ...*

I was eager, thinking of all the people a TV programme could reach. Even if she was dead, they might find some of my relatives. I had to try, and so wrote the requested email to Dave Reed. Two weeks passed. Cat had said they were starting filming in a couple of weeks so I figured they must have already chosen their people. I felt let down and desperate. I decided to send another email pleading my case. Cat replied:

26th March 2010

> *I'm right in the middle of filming the BBC 1 TV programme and also recording a radio series for BBC Radio Wales so I am travelling all over the country every day and just about catching my breath at the weekends. Remind me again after Easter and I will give you some advice.*

Major disappointment. *Why not my story? Was no one interested in a challenge? Did they all want easy pickings?* I seethed with frustration, but my passion had been rekindled.

I decided to revisit the NORCAP website to see if they'd made any advances. I clicked on 'Appeals and Requests' and found information about another film company, Wall to Wall, who were looking for people to take part in a documentary about tracing people called *Find My Family*. I filled in the application form detailing my story and sent it off. *Surely one of these companies will take the bait.*

I rang a lady at NORCAP who said they would carry out a search for me at a cost of £375, which would go up to £500 in April. The search would last for twelve months and if they couldn't find the missing person, they'd give me some of my money back. I explained what I had already done, and she doubted whether they could do any better.

Months later, I got a reply from Wall to Wall saying they had been overwhelmed with applications and sorry but they couldn't help. I rang Karen.

'They'd want to film a tearful reunion,' she said. 'That's what people watch those programmes for, the emotional outpourings. Shame your sisters wouldn't do the article. It's a fascinating story.'

When I put down the phone I cried. It was hopeless. I railed against the media. They didn't want to help anyone: they just wanted the story that would make the most sensational viewing. In desperation, I sent copies of Carole's letters to the film company, thinking that anyone who read the distress she suffered at our parting would surely want to help me find her. I never received a reply.

***

'I've got an email from Diane telling me about a programme called *Trackers*,' I told Derick. 'It looks like another help-you-search programme and I can't get excited about it, but look at this. It's really interesting.'

'What is it?' Derick looked over my shoulder.

'The site was started by a woman called Patricia Basquill, who was an unmarried mother forced to give her daughter up for adoption in the 1960s. She was put in an unmarried mothers' home and assigned a Moral Welfare Worker, which reminded me of Carole and Miss Housden, her Moral Welfare Worker.'

'It's surprising that they were still doing this in the 1960s,' Derick said.

'Yes, that's twenty years after my birth and nothing had changed. So much for the liberated Sixties. Patricia's *moral* person told her that she had no legal rights, no entitlement to state benefits or housing and couldn't afford to keep her baby, so she had to give her up.'

'Well, that was the case then, wasn't it?'

'Actually, no, it wasn't. Listen, it gets worse. Patricia did research and found out that the government in 1948 gave unmarried mothers the right to the same state benefits as young widowed mothers, with additional entitlements and rent-and-rate-free housing.'

'Wow! So, these social workers never let the girls know. They're the bastards.'

'Exactly. She says the law was ignored by figures of authority who neglected to inform the pregnant women of their rights and coerced them into giving up their babies. This went on until the 1970s. Patricia calls it an adoption conspiracy of Holocaust proportions.'

'That would have been too late for Carole, wouldn't it?'

'Yes. It wasn't in place when I was born in 1947 but even if it had been, chances are Carole would never have been told about it.'

'What a legacy of misery.'

'Patricia fought with the authorities for five months but was forced to have her baby adopted. It's heartbreaking. She writes of the unbearable pain of losing her daughter and how forty years later she still has nightmares hearing her daughter's screams mingling with her own as they were pulled apart.' Momentarily, I thought of Dr Cranshaw taking me from Carole's arms, but I shrugged away the sadness. 'She says that millions of mothers worldwide had their usually firstborn babies wrongfully removed simply because they weren't married and/or did not have the funds to protect their civil, legal and human rights.'

'It was a scandal.'

'Are you sure you're OK to go on with this?'

'Yes, I'm all wound up with it. It's compelling.' I couldn't stop reading.

I smiled at Derick. 'She found her daughter and they were reunited. But there's more. Patricia points out that adoption is never in the best interests of a baby that is loved and cared for by its own mother, nor is it in the best interests of a mother who had not abused, abandoned or neglected her baby.'

'She sounds very angry and frustrated,' Derick said.

'She says that if her baby had been non-white, unhealthy or handicapped, making her unadoptable, she would have been able to keep her. Everyone wanted healthy white babies, and these so-called moral people made sure there was a good supply.'

'Shocking what went on. Is that it?'

'No, hang on. Look here. There's a survey at the bottom.' I clicked on 'Survey 100'. 'It claims to be the most comprehensive survey ever conducted of unmarried mothers in the UK during 1950 to 1975. Ninety-eight point nine per cent of mothers who were questioned said that they did not want to give up their babies and were pressured or forced to do so.'

'Unbelievable!'

'What amazes me is that no one knew about the changes in the law, but I suppose there was no Internet then and not many people had tellies in the Fifties. There was nothing on the Trackers International site about a television programme.'

Derick looked at me. 'Don't be upsetting yourself.'

'Thanks. I'm OK. There's a Manchester number that I'm going to ring.' He went back downstairs and I thought of the thousands of women who would have kept their babies if they'd known there was help available. Tears ran down my cheeks. I wiped them away and picked up the phone.

Patricia's husband answered. Sadly, she'd died a few years earlier. I offered my condolences, and told him how deeply moved I was by her story and how I would love to have spoken to her. Briefly, I related my unsuccessful search for Carole. He said the 'Trackers' they were involved with was different from the TV programme.

Disappointed, but thankful that I'd accidentally accessed their site, I realised Carole was far from alone in her suffering.

Ping! Another email came in from Diane telling me the site was Missing-You,

not Trackers, and wishing me luck with the search.

I visited the Missing-You site. It looked very professional. You could leave a message but you had to register first. Derick had already registered me on there along with on numerous other sites, posting messages on them years ago. I realised that if Carole or anyone associated with her was looking at these sites, they would have found me. *Did she make the conscious decision never to contact me again?* I was overcome with the utter hopelessness of my situation. *Is it all just a waste of time?*

Chapter 30

Birth

'Now that I've given birth, I can't think of anything worse than having your baby taken away from you.' Karen was breastfeeding Yasmin, sat on the sofa in the living room. She'd given birth to Yasmin Sophia, a robust eight-pounder, on 1 July 2010, five days previously.

'Yes, we were parted at the same age Yasmin is now.' I stared at them, imagining Carole's pain, and the longing to find the part of me that was missing resurfaced. *Will I ever experience one moment's intimacy with the woman who gave me life?*

'I bet she had to breastfeed you until you were snatched away. No one's snatching you away, darling.' Karen kissed her daughter's mop of dark curly hair. Forcing the sad thought away, I focused on how lucky I was to have my family.

A different kind of birth occurred a month later: on 5 August, Shaun's memoir *Hard Time* was published. While he'd been incarcerated, Shaun had started to write a blog to expose the awful conditions in the prison. Knowing the cathartic value of writing, I encouraged him to write short stories about prison life. I entered one of them into a competition run by the Koestler Trust, Arts for Offenders, and he won first prize – which was a mentor (a published author) to work with him for a year. His mentor, Sally Hinchcliffe, met with him every month and helped him to improve and structure his writing. He found a literary agent and a publisher, and family and friends travelled to London to celebrate his book launch. I was proud of Shaun and how he'd made something positive out of a negative situation.

With a new baby and Shaun's literary success, there was everything to look forward to, and I was determined that the old sadness should not overshadow my life.

***

'Everything's fine. Your BMI, your weight, diet and lifestyle are all spot on,' Nurse Mitchell said, after a routine Well Woman check-up at my doctor's surgery.

'That's good to know,' I said, as cheerfully as I could, but inside I felt flat.

'You need to get a blood test at the local hospital but I'm sure that'll be fine. Take a seat and we'll go through this checklist about previous medication and then you're done.'

When she asked about antidepressants, I started to cry, my tears gradually becoming more violent. I hadn't expected my outburst and neither had she from the expression on her face.

'What's all this about?' she asked, sympathetically, handing me a tissue.

I told her about my new granddaughter and Shaun's success. 'Everything's good now, but I get days when I feel terrible all the time, and I'm tired of pretending that everything's all right, putting on a happy smile when inside I'm dying.'

'How long have you felt like this?'

'For months. Maybe a year or more, but it's gradually getting worse,' I said in between sobs. 'You can see I've been treated for depression before and I've tried to put the various therapies into practice, but when I feel like this, nothing seems to work. I just can't get the dark thoughts out of my head.'

'Even though the trauma with Shaun is over, you're drained of energy and that's what's causing you to feel low. Six years is a long time to live with worry and stress, and this could be a delayed reaction. You're most likely suffering from Post-Traumatic Stress.'

'Yes, you're probably right.' I didn't tell her I'd been visualising myself jumping off the Widnes-Runcorn Bridge: I didn't want to be sectioned, but she guessed the seriousness of how I was feeling.

'You'll have to see a doctor, and today,' she said, lifting the phone.

After some difficulty, she got me an appointment with Dr Kay, a kind and understanding woman, who said that I'd have to go back on antidepressants. I agreed: I couldn't go on feeling that way. *Was it Shaun or was it all the disappointments I'd faced in my search for Carole?* My thoughts were jumbled.

Lack of sleep was part of it. I'd lie awake for hours ruminating. I'd never been a good sleeper, so I read in bed. As an early Christmas present, Derick bought me a Kindle and downloaded the new Jeanette Winterson book *Why Be Happy When You Could Be Normal?* Her ability to relate so succinctly the feelings of being adopted astounded me. *That's just how I feel.* Her powerful prose expressed the violent emotions she felt towards the world she'd found herself in. If I'd been locked out, left on the doorstep, shut in the coal cupboard as Jeanette was, I wouldn't have survived. Shy and introverted as a child, my violence turned inward, causing depression.

Jeanette's courage and achievements against difficulties inspired me to continue writing my story and to have faith in myself. *It's all I have left in my search for Carole, but I need a conclusion.*

***

'The post's arrived!' Derick shouts. 'There's one for you. Handwritten with an Australian postmark.'

I tear frantically at the envelope. 'It's from a Barbara Martin.' I look up, grinning so hard it hurts. 'You won't believe this! She's my half-sister – Carole is her mother, too!'

'Fantastic!' Derick's grin is wider than mine. 'Is Carole still alive?'

'Yes! 'She wants to see me. Oh my goodness!'

'We're off to Australia!' Derick picks me up and swings me around the room till my head feels dizzy.

'Stop it! Let me read the rest.' He puts me down. 'Her father died last year and Carole never told him about me – that's why she didn't contact me sooner. She's ill now and her dearest wish is to see me before she dies.'

Derick's face is a distant blare. I hear him shouting, 'Let's get booking!'

I laugh hysterically and he picks me up again and swings me higher this time. Weightless, I float through the air, overjoyed. 'Put me down now!' I thump his shoulders. 'I can't read while I'm flying!' I land on the ground. 'Barbara's married, has two boys and they have a sheep farm. Mother is longing to see me. It's signed your loving sister Barbara.'

She's still alive – she wants to see me – it can't be true – this must be a dream.

Derick takes my hand and we do the polka around the room, our feet barely touching the floor. 'Carole! Carole!' we shout over and over, laughing loudly.

'She called her daughter after me!' I scream, as our dance grows more frenzied.

Derick swings me up off my feet and I fly out of his arms – soaring through the air, through fluffy white clouds edged in golden sunlight, my heart bursting with joy. *After all those years of searching, of waiting and hoping, I'm finally going to meet her.*

I'm on the plane travelling to Australia, aching to hold her – to hug her – to kiss her – and to tell her that I love her.

I'm off the plane – Barbara, my sister is pushing Carole in a wheelchair along the runway away from the plane – it's windy – the sky's grey – not like I'd imagined Australia to be – where is the sun? – I try to run after them – my legs are heavy, pulling me down as though I'm stuck in treacle – I struggle and break free – waving my hands wildly in the air shouting, 'Carole! It's me! Your baby!' – I run and run, but the strong wind pushes me back – until I'm there – pushing Barbara aside – grabbing the handles of the wheelchair. I turn it around – it's empty …

… A sudden jolt. I opened my eyes. Shock. Fear. *I'm not in*

Australia. I'm at Euston Station. I looked down at my hands tightly clutching a teddy bear. 'Are you all right?' the woman sat opposite me on the train asked. 'You've been making some strange noises and doing all kinds with that bear. I think you've had a dream.'

'Yes, yes, thanks, I'm OK. Sorry if I disturbed you,' I said, averting my eyes. I grabbed my case from the rack, relieved to get off the train. I saw Karen at the end of the platform, smiling and waving. Yasmin struggled to get free of her buggy. 'Nana! Nana!' she shouted, her little legs running towards me. Her arms clasped tightly around my neck, she smothered me with kisses. *The love of a child – the best antidote.*

Chapter 31
Constable Country

Sat in an Italian restaurant, celebrating my sixty-fourth birthday, and enjoying a bottle of Rioja, I asked Derick if he'd like to go to East Bergholt. 'I'm getting old and time is slipping away.'

'You're not old, and you're as beautiful as ever.'

'You old smoothie.' We smiled at each other.

Derick took hold of my hand across the table. 'But you do need some resolution about Carole, especially when you're having crazy dreams about Australia and flying around the room.' We laughed.

'Seriously.' My gaze fell to the table and I fiddled with my napkin. 'Every time I have a birthday, I think of Carole. I've read about mothers who've had their babies adopted. They always say that they think of them every day but that the day they gave birth to their missing child is the hardest to bear. Is Carole somewhere thinking about me today?' I felt a lump in my throat. Not wanting to get upset in the restaurant, I took a large gulp of wine and forced a smile.

Derick smiled back and squeezed my hand. 'Let's go in October. It'll be beautiful there in autumn. It's Constable country, where he painted his most famous paintings.

'Let's just think of it as a holiday,' I said, feeling more positive. 'If we find some clues, great, but I'm not going to be upset if we don't.'

'It sounds probable that it was the area Thomas visited with Carole,' Derick said. 'The Fens and a church with the bell tower on the floor, and the Brooklands estate. It's all too much of a coincidence.'

'I'd just like to walk in her footsteps, as they say. Perhaps that's the closest I'll ever get to her.'

'Don't despair.' Derick took both my hands. 'We'll find her one day.'

'Sure we will,' I said, with false conviction.

'Let's drink to a wonderful holiday.' He lifted his glass. 'And to finding Carole, wherever she's hiding.'

Light-headed and suddenly optimistic, I raised my glass. 'To finding Carole.'

My life was good. My depression had abated and I was off the antidepressants. I'd visit Karen every few weeks, amazed at Yasmin's progress, overwhelmed with love. Shaun's hard work was paying off. He was getting more talks at schools and his book was selling well in the UK.

I'd settled into retirement with Derick: we joined a gym, where we swam and did yoga every week. We hiked at weekends, and took frequent holidays. But a part of me was still missing.

***

'I wonder if you were conceived on that visit to her grandmother?'

'Who knows.' We were driving down the M6. I lay back, closed my eyes and imagined what it would be like to find Carole and how she'd react to meeting me.

'Wake up. We're off the motorway. The countryside's beautiful here.'

'I wasn't asleep. Just daydreaming,' I said, sitting up. 'Oh! The flatlands make the sky look massive.'

A stunning cloud formation met the horizon and draped itself against the blueness of the sky. Tall trees and shrubbery edged the ploughed fields, breaking the skyline like silhouettes haloed in golden light. I watched mesmerised until we reached the bed and breakfast, it's honey-coloured stone bathed in a soft rosy glow.

'It's beautiful.'

'We've made good time.' Derick pulled up outside. 'It's only four o'clock.'

The landlady, Penny, plump and middle-aged, welcomed us and over tea and homemade scones I gave her a synopsis of why we were there. She took a business-like interest, and assured us we were in the right place. 'I have a positive feeling about you and I'm not often wrong.' She stared intently. 'You're going to find something down here, I'm sure of it.'

'Let's hope you're right.' Irrationally clinging to her words, the hope of finding some clue rose.

'It's famous, you know. It's the only church in the area with no steeple and with the bells in a cage on the ground.'

'Let's go and find it, then,' Derick said.

We explored the tiny village as the sun was setting. The church, St Mary the Virgin, perpendicular in style, with no steeple, was magnificent against the orange and gold setting sun.

'And there's the bell cage.' Derick pointed to a square wooden building. We peeped inside to observe the massive bells, which were kept upright by the wooden structure.

'This must be the church they visited.' Ghosts of Carole and Thomas hovered in the fading light – along the path – beneath stained glass windows – besides ancient gravestones – walking together – laughing – holding hands – stealing a kiss. *Please let this be the place, please, please.*

The door was open: we stepped inside. There was the pungency of overripe fruit laid in baskets, mingled with the smell of ancient brick. 'Must be from the Harvest Festival,' I said.

Derick picked up a leaflet. 'The oldest parts date from 1350 to 1550.'

'What does it say about the bell tower?'

'It was begun in 1525,' Derick read aloud, 'at the expense of Cardinal Wolsey, whose death in 1530 stopped the work through lack of funds.' He looked up. 'So, the steeple was never built and the bells were kept in the wooden cage. It's the original wood. The bells are still rung by hand, and that's why they're upright, as they would be too heavy to ring otherwise.'

'Fascinating.' I picked up a copy of the East Bergholt parish magazine, and slotted 75p into a wooden moneybox. 'Look at this. It's an event at the Women's Institute, *Finding Out About History Using Local Newspapers*. Somebody there might know something. It's at 7.30 tonight in Constable Hall. Should we go?'

'Of course. Who knows, Carole might be one of them.'

'That would be something.'

There were no street lights in the village and Derick drove carefully through the darkness, joking about blue-rinsed ladies and attending a WI meeting. The hall was empty apart from a young woman who approached us, smiling brightly, and asked if we were there for the Argentine tango class.

'That sounds like more fun,' Derick said.

I elbowed him, thinking he was probably right. 'No. We're looking for the WI meeting.'

She smiled, gave us a quizzical look and directed us to a room at the back of the hall.

'Do you mind if we join you?' I asked the lady in charge. 'We're on holiday and want to know something about the area.'

'No, not at all. Do take a seat.'

We sat down, acknowledging the curious smiles and glances. The historian, middle-aged and eccentric, used a slideshow of clips from various local newspapers and magazines, some dating as far back as the 18th century, depicting quirky stories and photographs of events in the area. They were amusing, shocking or sad, but had no relevance to my search for Carole, and when questioned, he knew nothing of the Dalton family.

Disappointed, we stood to leave when a lady named Irene introduced herself and asked us to stay for tea. We accepted her invitation and she directed us to a large table in the middle of the room. With nothing to lose, I told them my story. They were fascinated and I heard the name Dalton being passed around the room.

'There is a lady named Dalton living here, in East Bergholt, a widow,' Irene said.

'How old is she?' I asked. *It could be her. Please let it be her.*

'She must be in her eighties,' someone said. 'But she's not a Dalton, she married a Dalton.'

'Of course,' I said. 'And if Carole married, she won't be a Dalton. But she'd be around the same age as Carole, and it's a small place, so she'd know who else was living here.'

Irene invited us to a coffee morning at 10 a.m. the next day. 'Mrs Dalton always attends,' she said, smiling reassuringly.

Visions of Carole interrupted my sleep – her turning up at the church – meeting her – speaking to her – discovering the life she'd led without me. In spite of my insomnia, I woke alert and expectant, chatting excitedly to Derick over breakfast.

In a room at the back of the church, in the dappled light of stained glass, groups of middle-aged people sat chatting at rustic, wrought iron tables, the smell of coffee and pastries sweetening the air. Irene's welcoming smile put us at ease. We ordered coffee and she introduced us to Mrs Dalton, who looked at us thoughtfully. 'Sorry, dear, there were no other Daltons in East Bergholt at that time except us, and there were no Caroles or Carries in the family. The population was very small then. It still is. I would have known her. Everyone knows everyone here. My husband, who was the Dalton, was from Hadleigh.' *Another disappointment.* She introduced us to her son, a tall, stocky gentleman standing close by, eavesdropping on our conversation. 'Eric knows all the local history. Perhaps he can help you.'

Preening from his mother's acknowledgement, Eric gave us his full attention and I told him that my mother may have attended school at the convent in the 1930s.

'It's been a commune since 1974,' he said with authority. 'Originally, they were a gang of hippies, but now they're older and have become professors and such like. The Old Hall was bought by nuns in the mid-19th century, but it's not been a school since 1876, when it became a closed order. So, your mother couldn't have gone to school here.'

'I felt so sure that was the one.'

'No, afraid not, but there's a convent school at Ipswich, which is still a school. That'll be the most likely place she went to if she lived round here. If there was no school in their village, children had to walk to the nearest town.'

I imagined Carole, a poor village girl, walking through the green fields to school.

'Thanks for clearing that up.'

We finished the dregs of our coffee and I gave Irene my contact details.

'Let's try Ipswich,' Derick said.

The convent school in Ipswich was no longer there. A new school had been built on the site, but the original convent house remained. In a small private room, we spoke to an eighty-nine-year-old nun, Sister Thomas Moore. Alert and articulate, she told us of her life as an eighteen-year-old noviciate, and later a teacher.

'The convent school, St Mary's, was an expensive fee-paying school, but in the elementary school, St Joseph's, they had small groups of children from broken homes resident in the dormitory and paid for by the parish. They were from poor families or were orphans.'

'Orphans,' I repeated. *This must be where she went.*

'Yes. Some were weekly boarders and a few went home at weekends. I can't recall a Carole Dalton, but that doesn't mean she's wasn't here.'

'That would figure,' Derick said. 'She was brought up by her grandmother, possibly in poverty, and she said she was educated by nuns.'

'There's a records office in Ipswich,' Sister Thomas said. 'The school attendance records are kept there. I've done some research there myself. If she lived in the area, you'll find a record of her there.'

That sounds positive. 'Well done, using the Internet at eighty-nine years old!' I said before we left, and exchanged email addresses.

Driving through the congested streets of Ipswich, I longed to return to the peace of the village, but I was desperate to find some clue.

The records office was situated in a magnificent old red-brick school building. The gentleman on the desk was helpful. He showed us a free search site and checked the records for births, deaths and marriages, all of which proved negative.

'Looks like she fell out of the sky,' he said.

'That's how it appears,' I said.

The original attendance register for the convent school was available, long columns of names written in black ink. My eyes darted from name to name but there was no Carole Dalton recorded in the book. *I said I wouldn't get disappointed but I am.*

The records office was warm and claustrophobic. 'My head's totally cabbaged now,' I said. We left and called for a coffee before driving to Brooklands. The houses looked too modern to have been built in Carole's time, except for a single row of older houses at the beginning of the estate, with unusual dormer windows. Spying an elderly couple at a bus stop, Derick asked them if there were any Daltons in the area. 'No. I'm eighty and I've not heard of any Dalton family living on the estate or round here, but there's some Daltons in Hadleigh.'

Derick asked him about the row of old houses.

'They're the new village houses, and were built in 1890 to house the workers from a nearby factory. Sorry I can't be of further help. You might have more luck in Hadleigh.'

The next day, we took a picnic and walked along the River Stour to Deadham, relaxing in the sunshine, pondering on the mystery of Carole.

'It's not over yet,' Derick said, as we approached Deadham, another beautiful village with an historic past. While we looked round the church, the verger approached us and asked where we were from. I told him my story.

'That's a coincidence,' he said. 'I'm of Dalton descent. On my mother's side.'

'Oh really?' *He's going to be my brother!* 'Her name wasn't Carole, was it?'

'Sorry, no – Margery. I think that there was a Carolyn

somewhere in the family's past, maybe some distant aunt, but I'm not sure. Most of them are dead now. There aren't any Daltons living in Deadham. They were from Hadleigh. There was a family who lived in George Street.'

We must get to Hadleigh.

'Sounds like the houses are teeming with Daltons in Hadleigh!' Derick said. 'We'll have to call in the morning.'

'If only.' I allowed myself the pleasure of imagining her opening the door and welcoming in the child she'd given away.

Early the following morning, we drove to Hadleigh, an old market town, the main street lined with 17th-century houses. We found George Street and stood admiring the architecture. Derick approached an elderly couple walking past, and asked if they knew of anyone called Dalton living in the area. *We're going to get arrested for harassing people.*

'There's a Mrs Dalton who lives on the corner.' The gentleman smiled and pointed to a house at the end of the road. 'She lives on her own. She's quite elderly and she's lived round here for years and knows everyone.'

'Do you know her first name?' I asked, excited, expectant.

'Cathy, Cathy Dalton. She'll help you, if she takes to you.'

'Cathy! Carrie! They're so similar. This really could be her.' My heart thumped as we hurried along, holding hands.

I hesitated outside her door. Derick knocked. It wasn't cold but I shivered and Derick hugged my shoulders. Minutes passed before she slowly opened the heavy door. An old woman, brown and wrinkled, eyed us suspiciously.

'Sorry to have interrupted you.' I couldn't stop the hammering in my chest. 'Are you Mrs Dalton?'

'Yes, I am. What do you want?' She scowled.

'We're looking for someone called Carole or Carrie Dalton, and we thought you might know her.'

'Why do you want to find her?' *Is it her? She looks too old.*

Her face softened, when I told her my story.

'No. Sorry, my dear, there's no Caroles or Carries in our family.

There was a Carolyn but she died a long time ago, in her nineties, she was. The young ones moved away from here long ago, and the old ones, they're all dead now. Only me to go. But I do hope you find her.'

'Thanks.' *Same old story ...*

We strolled back to the car in silence. *It's hopeless. I'll never find her.*

The following day, in bright autumn sunshine, we did the Constable tour, enjoying the incredible scenery around Flatford Mill, which had inspired the artist nearly 200 years earlier. 'It probably hasn't changed much since the 1920s/1930s or whenever Carole was here, if she was ever here,' I said.

'No. Just a few more houses,' Derick said.

'Did she grow up here wandering these fields?'

'Are you OK with all this?'

'Who could be sad in sunshine and scenery like this.'

Derick gave me a lingering look. 'The verger in Deadham got me thinking, when he said Carolyn not Carole. She might have made the name up to cover her tracks. She may not even be Carole Dalton.'

'She's led us a merry dance for the past twenty years if she did. There's so much mystery about it.'

'Why didn't she put the name of her grandmother on the report?'

'She didn't want to be found, I suppose.'

On the way back from Essex, we stopped in London to pick up our granddaughter, Yasmin. We were taking care of her for a week while Karen and Andrew went to a wedding in India. Seeing Yasmin lifted my spirits, and made me think positively about the future.

***

I finished writing the first draft of my search for Carole in February 2012. I'd been writing it on and off for fifteen years but I still didn't have the ending I hoped for. Sitting at my computer, wondering how I could end it without finding her, the phone rang.

'Is that Mrs Attwood?' a frail voice asked.

'Yes. Who is it?'

'It's Sister Thomas Moore. I've got some good news for you.'

'Oh!' I said, my thoughts switching back to our meeting in Ipswich. *She's found Carole!* 'Lovely to hear from you. What is it?'

'I met a lady who knew your mother from St Joseph's.'

Oh goodness! 'Just hold on, Sister …' I grabbed a notepad, covered the mouthpiece on the phone and quickly told Derick who it was.

His eyes widened. 'Brilliant!'

'Sorry to keep you,' I said. 'It's so kind of you to remember me. Where did you meet this woman?'

'We had a Mass at a Mrs Clayton's house. She isn't able to get out, and this other lady – the one who knew your mother – was there helping out. She told me she went to St Joseph's and I suddenly thought of you, so I asked her if she knew Carole Dalton. Her response was immediate. She said that she was friendly with her.'

I couldn't believe what I was hearing. I scribbled down everything she said. The woman's name was Janet Hay and she lived in a cottage near the convent house.

'Was she an orphan?'

'No. Janet's parents wanted her to go to a Catholic school but they lived too far away, so she boarded in the week. That's how she knew your mother.'

'When did you speak to Janet?'

'It was before Christmas, but I lost the piece of paper with the address on. It turned up the other day, so I thought I'd ring you.'

What if it'd been lost forever? It's fate. It's going to lead me to her!

'Thank you so much. It's wonderful to know she was actually there, and that someone is still alive who knew her. Were they friends?'

'Yes, she said she knew her well, and I think she might still be in touch with her.

She'll tell you all about it.'

She might still know her; have her address! I couldn't control my heartbeat or the heat rising up to my face. I wanted to end the conversation immediately and ring Janet, but I forced myself to chatter as long as I could, and promised to ring her if I found anything.

'I'm sure He guided you to me for a purpose,' Sister Thomas said, 'and now He's guiding you to her. God bless you both.' I made a note to send her a thank you card and a donation.

'I've got to wait a few minutes to calm myself down before I call Janet,' I said to Derick immediately after speaking to Sister Thomas. 'Look, I'm shaking.'

Derick hugged me. 'Sounds like we're getting close.'

I breathed deeply, picked up the phone and spoke as calmly as I could, explaining my meeting with Sister Thomas Moore. Janet remembered going to Mrs Clayton's and I asked her about Carole and St Joseph's.

'Yes, I was at St Joseph's,' she said. 'What was your mother's name again? I'm a little hard of hearing.'

'Carole! Carole Dalton! Sometimes known as Carrie!' I shouted. 'You said you knew her?'

'Carole … the name rings a bell.'

'Carole Dalton.'

'I'm getting very forgetful now, my dear. I'm sorry. I'm just trying to think.'

'You told Sister Thomas that you were friends.' I tried to keep the frustration from my voice, and clung to the hope that she was having a temporary loss of memory.

'Carole or Carrie Dalton?' I repeated, willing her to remember.

'The name does sound familiar. Oh, yes, I remember. It was Carole Felton. I remember Carole very well. She was a boarder like me, but I don't see her now.'

It could still be Carole. She could have the names confused. With my free hand, I squeezed the tendons at the back of my neck. 'How old are you, if you don't mind me asking?'

'Seventy-nine.'

All hope collapsed. 'Carole would be eighty-six now. You wouldn't have been there at the same time.'

'I was there with Carole Felton, in the same class. I'm sure of that.'

'Yes, but that's not the person I'm looking for.' Aware of the anger in my voice, I apologised.

'I'm sorry, my dear. I do hope you find your mother, I really do.'

'Yes. So do I. Thanks for talking to me.'

'I used to think that I'd just pick up the phone one day and it would be Carole or someone who knew her at the other end.' I said to Derick. 'But that's the first time anyone's *ever* rung me with information … wrong information.'

'You've got another chapter for your book.'

'But no happy ending.'

'Not yet!'

Chapter 32

Ariel Bruce

Fran and I were staying at a spa in Bath. We'd explored the Roman ruins and we'd swum in the mineral-rich pools. After dinner, we sank into huge comfy chairs and sipped herbal tea: lavender and Jasmin candles scented the air.

Fran touched her bright red hair – worn long in her college days, now closely cropped. 'You've had some disasters in your family lately,' she said, with compassion. 'First Shaun's troubles, and now your gorgeous granddaughter's got leukaemia. How is Yasmin?'

'She's such a brave little girl, and she chuckles easily in spite of the painful treatment. Her hair's curly, like her mum's, and the worst thing is seeing her lovely dark curls fall out in handfuls, but the treatment is on track and doing the job, so we've got to be optimistic.'

'And how's the baby, Isaac?'

'His birth brought such joy to our lives and relieved the stress we were all suffering. He's a darling. He just smiles all the time, as if he knows he has to be good.'

'So, the search for your mother is on hold again?'

'Yes. Yasmin's all I can think about now.'

'Do you think it's been worth it – the search, I mean? All the ups and downs.'

I looked her straight in the eye, surprised at her question. 'Oh yes! Definitely.'

Fran knew the struggle I was having. She'd been a true friend and supported me through the years of Shaun's incarceration.

When I was at my lowest, she was there, a shoulder to cry on. To cheer me up, she took me for holidays to her house in the South of France.

'I have to think of the positives,' I said. 'If I hadn't started the search, I'd never have met Thomas, so I wouldn't have known the truth about their relationship ... or the truth as he saw it. I wouldn't have known that Carole was lively and sociable, and had lovely blue eyes, or that they were almost married and that they loved each other passionately, if only for a brief time.'

'So, no regrets then?'

I sighed. 'Only that I've not been able to find her ...' Sadness sank to the pit of my stomach. 'To hell with herbal tea!' I said, raising my head and forcing a smile. 'Let's have some wine.'

Fran grinned. 'Great idea.'

I waved the waitress over and ordered a bottle of Sauvignon Blanc.

'What's with all the deep questions?' I asked.

Fran frowned. 'My friend's son, Simon, was adopted. He found his mother, who had him when she was only fifteen.'

'That's good news, isn't it?'

'Not so good. His mother is married to a domineering man who won't let them meet up. He's not Simon's father. Simon doesn't know who his father is. So, I think it's caused him more distress.'

'That's awful. He has a right to meet his mother.' I wondered again what sort of reception I'd get if I did ever find Carole.

'Do you think it's affected your relationship with your family?' Fran asked, her face intense. 'I think that's what my cousin's afraid of.'

'*You* know my adopted family loved me – they *are* my family. I forgave my mother for not telling me the truth a long time ago, and we got along fine ever after. Derick probably suffered most being the closest to me, sharing my disappointment and putting up with my sadness at each dead end. Without his support, I couldn't have carried on. I don't think it affected Shaun and Karen that much; they both had college to occupy them and I kept my frustration from them. I try to live in the present and I consciously stop myself longing for the past, but it's not easy.'

'I think I'd have given up long ago.' Fran shook her head. 'What's kept you going?'

'Re-reading Carole's letters. That's enough.'

'Yes. I cried when you showed them to me.'

'If I'm truthful, I'd give anything to find her or to know what happened to her, but I doubt very much if I ever will, now. I've left it too late. It's too exhausting and I need all my energy to help with Yasmin. I go down there every month.'

Fran nodded.

'Here you are, ladies!' The smiling waitress placed the stainless-steel ice bucket on the carved oak coffee table together with two chilled wine glasses. 'Enjoy!'

***

Perhaps it was Fran's questioning that stirred me. *Should I have one last go at finding Carole?* Sat at my computer in the back bedroom – now my office – I stared at the photographs of my grandchildren hung on the wall – Zivi, Yasmin and Isaac. *Would she want to know them? Be as proud of them as I am?* Carole would now be eighty-seven. She could still be alive somewhere, but time was running out. I'd started the search in 1987 when I was forty. Glancing at the cute cat calendar hanging on the wall, I was reminded that it was 2013. I'd been searching for twenty-six years!

It was warm in the room and I opened the window, cheered by the chirping of blackbirds fluttering in and out of the ivy that clung to the fence at the back of the garden. I stared into the cloudless blueness of the sky above the rooftops and made a decision.

I typed 'adoption tracing birth parents' into the search box and the name 'Ariel Bruce' popped up in the results. I clicked on her website. A dark, attractive, efficient-looking lady appeared, an independent social worker who, for the past twenty years, had specialised in tracing people affected by adoption. I remembered my dealings with the previous detective who had taken my money and done nothing, and so I hesitated. *She'll be different. Go for it.* I typed my details and an outline of what I'd done so far into the boxes on the enquiry form. Clicking on 'Submit', I momentarily felt elated, then fearful that she'd turn me down or say it was an impossible task.

I heard Derick, home for lunch, open the front door and put his briefcase down in the hall. I hurried downstairs and I told him that I was going to give my search for Carole one last go. 'I've contacted Ariel Bruce.'

'Ariel who?' he asked.

'Ariel Bruce!'

'Calm down. You sound excited and your cheeks are glowing.'

I touched my cheeks. They were hot. 'I *am* excited. She's a private detective and she's supposed to be the best.'

'Haven't we been down that path before?'

'Yes, but she's legit. The programme *Long Lost Family* used her in the last two series to trace and make contact with lost relatives all over the world. I know she'll be expensive, but if she can't find her, I'll give up.'

'You sound determined.'

'I am.'

The phone rang. Derick picked it up. 'It's Ariel Bruce,' he said, handing me the phone. *That was quick!* I was taken off guard. *What am I going to say?*

After I thanked her for the quick response, she asked me a number of questions about the circumstances of my adoption and how much research I'd done myself.

'It may take six months to two years, but I'm 85 to 90 per cent certain that I can find her or find out what happened to her.' She sounded confident.

'Really? That's brilliant!' *Is this going to be it? Ariel is going to find her.*

'For a start, you say she spelled her name "Carole". That spelling was made popular in the Thirties and Forties by film stars like Carole Landis – in the original film *One Million B.C.* – and Carole Lombard, who was one of the highest-paid stars in Hollywood.'

'Oh really!'

'Girls born in the 1920s were usually christened "Carol" or possibly "Carolyn". So, there's a strong possibility she changed the spelling of her name.'

'We did search for Carolyn, Carol and Carole when we went to St Catherine's House, but there was nothing from the area we were looking at.'

'She may have changed her name completely.'

Impressed by her immediate observation, the excitement I'd felt so many times in the past rose up, increasing my heart rate. She said it would cost between £1,000 and £2,000 depending on whether she was successful. I had some savings: I told her to go ahead.

'It's done,' I told Derick, when I put the phone down. 'My last shot.' I gathered all the documents and correspondence I'd accumulated over the years, ready to send copies to her.

'Are you sure you want to go through all the emotional turmoil again?' He looked concerned. 'She's expensive and you have to be realistic – she might not find her.'

'I accept that. I've tried to convince myself that it's not worth the heartache and that I'll never find her, but I've got to give it one last try.'

'Let's go for it, then. Give me the documents. I'll photocopy them for you.'

***

A November fog misted the bedroom windows. The phone rang. Derick picked it up and his eyes locked on mine through the dressing table mirror, where I sat combing my hair. 'It's Ariel.' He handed me the phone, which he'd put on speaker. I froze, aware that she must have some news.

I took a deep breath. 'Hello, Ariel. How are you?'

'Very well, thank you, Barbara, and you?'

'I'm fine.' *She's found something!*

'Good. Is your husband still there?' Her voice was grave.

I shivered. *It's not good news.* 'Yes. He's sat on the bed beside me.'

'Good …'

'She's dead, isn't she?' I interrupted.

'I'm sorry. Yes, she is.'

All hope vanished. I looked at Derick's face, creased with sadness. My shoulders sagged and my body became a heavy weight, dragging me down into a well of grief. Derick took hold of my free hand. I couldn't speak. I couldn't cry. A million regrets filled the silence. Ariel waited.

'When did she die?' I struggled to ask.

'2006.'

'Oh God! She was alive seven years ago. I could have met her. That door's closed to me forever now.' Even though I'd known from the start that Carole could be dead, I was desolate hearing the words and I hated myself for not contacting Ariel sooner.

'Where did she die?'

'In the Peak District.'

'So close! *Alive seven years ago – living in the Peaks. What a fool I've been!* 'Why couldn't I find her before she died?'

'You did everything you could.'

But it wasn't enough. 'Did she marry?'

'Yes, in 1959. She married an Irish doctor, William Macnaghten.'

'Thank goodness!' I sighed. 'She didn't spend her life pining for Thomas and me.'

'In my experience, the mothers rarely parted with their children willingly, and they never forget the children that were taken from them.'

'She must have met William and decided to start a new life. I wonder if she told him about me.'

'If she wanted to put it all behind her, probably not.'

'She'd tried so hard to maintain contact, leave a trail, after my mother stopped her visiting. She must have decided on a clean break.'

'Many of them do. It's the only way they can cope.'

'She probably had a more comfortable life with William than she would have had working on a farm ... And children?'

'She had three girls.'

Three more sisters. The thought cheered me and I smiled to myself. *Caring for them would have stopped her longing for the past.* 'I'll meet them one day,' I said, firmly.

'I'm sure you will.'

'How did you find her?'

'We sent for hundreds of birth certificates. She did change the spelling of her name. On her birth certificate her name is spelt "Carolyn". She was born in Worthing.'

'Not the Fens, where her grandmother was supposed to have lived.'

'She *was* illegitimate as suggested on the report. That's how we narrowed it down. We looked at the birth certificates with father unknown. You would never have found her. She lived with William, her husband, and gave birth to their eldest daughter before they got married, which was quite unusual at the time. She took his name, Macnaghten, probably for appearances, and got married as Carolyn Macnaghten. At one time she started using the name Deborah.'

'We'd never have found her,' Derick whispered, squeezing my hand.

'She certainly had a thing about names.' *Who were you, Carolyn?*

'Perhaps it had something to do with her harsh upbringing and the sadness of her early life – creating a different persona, maybe.'

'You couldn't blame her for that. What a strong person she must have been to survive and reinvent herself.'

'Yes, indeed.'

'What about the girls? Do you know where they're living?'

'I've made contact with the elder daughter, Caitlin.'

'That's an unusual name.'

'Irish for Kathleen.'

'Had she told them about me?' *Will they resemble me?*

'No, she hadn't. So, it was quite a shock, but Caitlin has been helpful. I sent the photographs of Carolyn to her for identification, and she said she'd seen early photographs of her mother and confirmed it was her.'

'It's strange to think of her as Carolyn. Do the other daughters know?'

'Not yet. But Caitlin is going to tell them.'

'What are their names?'

'Una is the middle one and Cloe is the youngest.'

'Pretty names.' My head whirled with all the new information: I broke down.

'Why didn't I contact you earlier?' I cried uncontrollably down the phone.

'This is hard for you, I know,' Ariel said. 'Cry it all out. I'll still be here.'

Derick hugged me and gradually the tears quietened to a gentle sob.

'Look, this is a lot for you to take in,' Ariel said. 'I'll send you a report and copies of the certificates, but now you must look after yourself. Be very careful this weekend to rest. You've been looking for her for so long, it's a shock to finally find out, especially when you said you'd almost given up hope. Will you send me a couple of photos of you and your family, so I can forward them to Caitlin.'

'Yes, of course, and thank you, Ariel,' I managed to say. *Caitlin must be interested if she wants to see photographs.*

I put the phone down and cried in Derick's arms, until I could cry no more. I shivered uncontrollably. Derick wrapped a soft woollen throw around my shoulders and left me sitting with blurred images of Carolyn's life filling my mind. I'd thought of her as a poor, sad girl abandoned by her lover, which she was, but she was also a strong woman who created a new life for herself. *I'll never know you, Carolyn: that book is now closed to me forever.*

'Your sisters will tell you all about her life and what she was like,' Derick said, handing me a cup of tea.

'Yes.' I smiled. *But it'll never be enough.*

Not wanting to worry Shaun and Karen, I was as upbeat as possible when I phoned them later in the day. They both expressed concern and joked about having six aunts. I called Lily and told her that I had three more sisters. 'No one can replace you,' I said. 'If I had to choose a sister, it'd be you.'

'That's three more Christmas cards to buy!' she said. We laughed.

'Yes, I've six sisters now.'

That night, I lay awake tormenting myself with imaginary reunions. I would have been twelve when she got married in 1959. It was the year I found out from the psychiatrist that I was adopted. Would she have wanted a troubled teenager knocking on her door, disrupting her new family?

I dozed and saw Carolyn, her face blurred, sitting on a bench in our garden. She held an enormous sunflower and, leaning forward, she offered it to me. I grasped it with both hands. As I held the flower, its petals fell one by one, gently floating to the ground, and I was left holding the black centre, soft and moist in my hand. It grew bigger and I saw her face in its darkness. 'Say goodbye to Aunty Carole,' my mother's voice whispered. The centre slowly fell apart, distorting Carolyn's face like an image in the hall of mirrors. I woke abruptly. *She's dead.*

The next day, I woke with a tense sensation in the back of my neck. My temples pulsated, as though a rubber band was being tightened and released around my forehead. *She's dead, she's dead, she's dead.* I reached for a paracetamol from my bedside cabinet and washed it down with a glass of water. My stomach hollow, my mood flat, I lay awake, immobilised with the realisation that it was over.

The headache eased. I heard Derick moving about downstairs

and I forced myself out of bed. Completing the simplest household task was an effort. As the day progressed, my depression worsened. By the evening, I was unable to communicate a single word to Derick. We watched TV in silence, my mind elsewhere, oblivious to the images flickering on the screen, until it was time for bed.

***

'Look at that sunshine!' Derick drew back the curtains. 'It's a lovely Sunday morning and perfect for a hike. Cool and crisp! It'll be invigorating up Moel Famau today.'

'I haven't got the energy.' I rolled over and buried my head in the pillow.

'Yes, you have.' He rolled back the sheets and coaxed me out of bed.

He's right. Hiking always clears my head.

As I made my way up the hill, the cool air touched my cheeks; refreshing my thoughts and putting my loss into perspective.

Warm after the exertion of the climb, we ate our sandwiches sat on a rock overlooking the glorious landscape below, and talked about meeting my sisters. I looked out to Snowdonia on the far horizon, majestic and snow-capped. 'I wonder how much she told my sisters about her past life?'

'You're going to find out,' Derick said.

'If they agree to see me. You know how long it took Diane and Judith to come to terms with it.'

'They came through in the end. You'll meet them.'

***

'There's an email from Ariel!' I shouted. Excitement. Trepidation. I opened it up.

'Hang on.' I heard Derick climbing the stairs.

'It has two attachments, Carolyn's birth certificate and her death certificate.' I clicked on the documents and printed them off. Derick lifted them from the printer and handed them to me. I looked at her birth certificate. 'Her name *was* Carolyn and she was born on 8 July 1925.'

'*Why* did she change the spelling of her name and hide her date of birth?'

'Perhaps she didn't want anyone to see her birth certificate because she was illegitimate herself.'

'Could be. Her mother's name was Ida Dalton and she was a general domestic servant. Maybe her employer got her pregnant?'

'Men in power taking advantage. Very *Upstairs, Downstairs*.'

'I wonder if Ida told Carolyn who *her* father was. So many questions I'll never get to ask.'

'Who knows what we might find out from your sisters.'

Forever the optimist. I continued reading. 'They lived in Worthing, which is in West Sussex, quite a distance from East Bergholt and Ipswich where Thomas said they visited Carolyn's grandmother.'

Breathing deeply, I mentally prepared myself before looking at the record of her death. 'The name on the certificate is "Carolyn Deborah Macnaghten". She died of heart disease, aged eighty, on 11 October 2006 in Royal Derby Hospital in Derby.'

'She moved from the South then up to Derbyshire?'

'Yes.' The close proximity of the location and the recent date of her death filled me with regret. 'I can't bear to think that she'll never know how long and hard I tried to find her; we tried to find her. Was she disappointed that I never knocked on her door?'

'She won't ever have stopped loving you.'

Derick went downstairs and I lay on the bed, closed my eyes and saw Carolyn delighted that I'd found her, hugging me as though she'd never let me go. 'It broke my heart to leave you,' a voice whispered, 'and I never stopped loving you.' I blinked my eyes. *She's dead.*

I went back to the computer room to read the email again. Ariel said she was sending copies of the letters Carolyn had written at the time of my adoption to Caitlin. *Would she cry at the agony our mother had suffered when she was forced to give me up?*

The following day, Karen sent me an email:

> *... I think you need to be more gentle on yourself. You keep saying 'I must look on the bright side and be positive' which we all must try and do in all circumstances. However, I think you also need to recognise that you have just lost your mother – even though you have not seen her since you were very small. You will be feeling real grief among all the other emotions and you need to allow yourself to grieve and feel sad. It is perfectly natural for you to feel shock, anger and sadness, and it's important to let all these emotions out. Don't put more pressure on yourself and feel that you must be all jolly and happy about it. There will be grief for her death and grief as it is the end of your dream of meeting her ...*
>
> *... It will be wonderful to meet Caitlin and find out more about Carolyn, and there are so many wonderful things that will come out of this. So much to find out and what a relief to know she had a happy life surrounded by children ...*

Reading her thoughtful words helped me to understand the emotions I'd been experiencing: I was grieving and continued to grieve.

As Ariel had requested, I wrote a letter to Caitlin enclosing photographs of the family and sent it via Ariel as I didn't have Caitlin's address. I told Caitlin that I wanted so much to know about Carolyn, what she was like and the life she lived.

Months passed with no reply. I no longer cried. To protect myself from further rejection, I convinced myself that being acknowledged by my half-sisters wasn't important to me. Deep inside, I knew that wasn't true.

We had a traditional family Christmas followed by a holiday in Tenerife. Thoughts of my other family were firmly repressed. I felt positive about my life. In early March 2014, I received an email from Ariel asking me if I'd heard from Caitlin. I replied:

> … *Caitlin hasn't responded to my letter. I do understand that it will take time for them, but I feel that a little push might be needed. I wonder if you could ring her on my behalf. Even if they don't want to get involved with me, I would like to visit Carolyn's grave – if there is one – and say goodbye to her …*

The old emotions lingered on: sadness she was dead – rejection by my sister's silence – anger with myself. *Why don't you just let it go?*

A few days later, Ariel replied saying she had put a note in her diary to contact Caitlin again.

'Why can't she just give you Caitlin's address?' Derick asked.

'I'm not allowed to contact them directly; it's to protect families from harassment by relatives they don't want to get involved with.'

'That's crazy! Now we know her name, I can trace her for you.'

'No. If they don't want to know me, I'm not forcing myself on them.'

'They don't know what they're missing.'

Ariel wrote saying that she didn't get anywhere with Caitlin but she didn't want to give up and after a fair warning would try again. I knew I should put them out of my head, but I wanted to know more about the mother I'd lost and only they could tell me.

Chapter 33

Cloe

Twelve months had passed without a word from my new sisters. It was October and Derick and I were going on a ten-day meditation retreat to the Peak District in two weeks' time.

'I was just looking on Google Earth for the location of the centre,' Derick said. 'I want to check whereabouts your sister Cloe lives in the Peak District.'

I got the file from the shelf and took out Carolyn's death certificate. Cloe was named as the informant and her full address was given.

'This is incredible!' Derick turned to me with eyebrows raised. 'Her house is a five-minute drive from the centre at Thornhill. I bet you can see it from over the fields. All this time you've been going to the centre, not knowing you were so close.'

'No!' I said, deep regret resurfacing.

'When the course is over, we'll call on her,' he said, as though it was a done deal.

'I'm not sure about that.' *Would she want me to?* I imagined Cloe telling me that I had no rights to call on her and shutting the door in my face.

'I'll call,' Derick said. 'You can stay in the car while I suss them out.'

'I'm not sure,' I repeated, excited and afraid.

As the week progressed, I changed my mind. If I actually turned up on her doorstep and convinced her that all I wanted was to know about our mother, then surely she'd understand. 'If she's the sort of person who would shut the door in my face, she's not worth knowing and I'll forget about her, forget about them all,' I said, trying to convince myself. 'Let's do it.'

***

'We've got here early.' Derick pulled into a car park in Castleton. The sun shone through a canopy of surrounding trees. 'It's a beautiful area.'

'We don't have to go into the centre till five o'clock. Should we call on Cloe before we register? Then, if she doesn't want to know me, I'll have ten days to recover?'

The fear of rejection grew as we approached the big old farmhouse, ivy clinging to the grey stone walls, window frames in need of a paint. I breathed deeply to slow the thumping in my chest.

We walked through a wrought iron gate, and I followed Derick along an unkempt path. He knocked on the large oak door. Dogs barked frantically and threw their bodies at the windows.

'Glad they're on that side of the wall.' I shuddered. 'They're only small but they look fierce.' We walked round the side of the house and saw extensive vegetable gardens, and horses in a distant field. 'They must grow veg and sell it.'

I saw some movement in the house. 'No! It's one of the dogs jumping on the kitchen table. There's no one in,' I said, disappointed and relieved.

We called at a neighbouring farm and the farmer's wife confirmed that Cloe lived there, and we asked her to tell Cloe that we'd call again at the end of the course.

'Who should I say called?'

'Just say it's a distant relative, if you would, please.'

Ten days later, when the course ended, we called at the house again in the afternoon. The calmness I'd achieved on the course dissolved into dread. *What lies behind that door?* The house was empty. Relief. A friendly farmer unloading his cart nearby told us that Cloe had a small grocery shop in the town, and was in and out all day. This time, I told him my name so she'd know who I was.

'I sometimes see Bob, her husband, in the pub. I'll tell him,' he said, red-faced and grinning.

'He's bound to remember,' Derick said afterwards. 'There can't be much happening around these parts. Cloe's going to meet her sister, whether she likes it or not.'

'Let's hope she likes it!' I said, forcing myself to be positive. 'If we call around six o'clock, someone should be in.'

Driving from our bed and breakfast, we got lost on the winding country lanes and it was dark by the time we got to the farmhouse. With no street lighting, the isolated building, silhouetted against the moonlit sky, was like a setting from every horror film I'd ever seen. I shivered and zipped up my jacket against the November cold. 'It doesn't feel right calling so late.'

'It's only eight o'clock. There's a light on. Someone's in. You knock,' he said.

I shivered again, this time with fear. No reply. We both knocked louder for longer. No reply. Derick walked round the side of the house. 'There's a young woman in there ironing.'

'It must be her.' I carried on knocking at the front. No reply. I followed Derick round the side of the house. In the distance, there was nothing but blackness. I saw her through the window. 'She looks tall and well built. Shine the torch so she can see me,' I said, not thinking that my torchlit face might scare her. I tapped on the window and she looked up, stared straight at me but continued to iron as though I was invisible. *She's purposely ignoring me.* 'Her hair's long and blonde, looks dyed, but she's not that young.' My voice became shaky and I wanted to cry. 'It must be Cloe. She knows who I am and she looked right through me. We've left enough messages. She doesn't want to know me. Let's go.' I turned away, rejected, ready to give up.

'No!' Derick grabbed my arm. 'We don't know what she's been told and we're not giving up now! Shout through the letterbox. Tell her who you are. She might respond to your voice.'

'She might call the police!'

'It's a risk we'll have to take.'

In desperation, I did what he said. On bended knees, I lifted the letterbox and spoke loudly but as calmly as I could. 'Cloe, I'm Barbara. I'm your sister. I just want to talk to you.' No response. I raised my voice and continued to plead. Minutes passed with no response. *It's hopeless.* I heard her footsteps as she came to the door and my hopes lifted, but she kept it closed.

'What are you people doing here? Go away!' Her shouts were muffled through the door. 'I don't answer the door to strangers at night.'

'We're sorry to shock you,' I said, still crouching at the letterbox. 'Didn't your neighbour tell you I was coming? It's Barbara.'

'Nobody's told me anything. I don't know you.'

'But didn't Caitlin tell you? Didn't she show you the letters I got from your mother?'

'No, she didn't. What letters? I don't speak to either of my sisters.'

'I'm sorry to hear that.'

'Don't be. I'm not.'

I wonder why they don't speak. 'I'm your sister, now.'

'That's rubbish! Go away! If you don't go, I'll call the police.'

Oh no! I stared frantically at Derick.

'No!' he mouthed, shaking his head. 'She won't call the police. Keep talking!'

'Please don't call the police,' I begged. 'I really am your sister. Your mother had a baby before she got married. I'm that baby. I thought you knew about me. Why should I lie? It's true.'

Silence, then the rattle of her unbolting the door.

As she struggled, Derick took my hand and helped me to my feet. She held the heavy door slightly ajar, peering through the gap. 'I don't believe you,' she said. 'Where's the proof? Have you got documentation to prove this?'

'Yes, we can show you photos of your mother. They're in the car.' Opening the door wider, her eyes darted from one to the other, resting on my face. *Please believe me.* 'I'm your sister.' I started to cry, but stopped myself. 'I'm telling the truth. I *am* your sister.'

The frown lines in her brow softened, revealing an attractive oval face. *She looks a bit like me. At last, she's starting to believe me!*

'You might as well come in,' she said. We followed her into a traditional country kitchen, scented with pine cones. An open fire blazed, in a massive cast iron grate, the flames creating shadows on the bare whitewashed walls. The dogs barked fiercely from the adjoining room. 'Be quiet!' she shouted. 'Don't worry, they're locked in. They'll settle down.'

Staring at me again, a look of resignation crossed her face. We lost eye contact and she lowered her head and stared into the flames. 'She was a dark horse, my mother.'

She knows I'm her sister. I sighed. 'This is all new to you, isn't it?' I said. 'You've not seen the letters?'

'No. I told you, I don't speak to my sisters. A family feud, you really don't want to know what about.'

'OK, but you've got *me* now. I'm your real sister.' Without thinking, I grabbed her shoulders and hugged her, and kissed her on the cheek. She hugged and kissed me back.

'Yes, I know. There's something about your manner that reminds me of her. Things are starting to make sense now ... the gaps in Mother's life. She never spoke much about her early life. Now I know why.' She looked at me, smiled and raised her eyebrows. 'You.'

'Yes.' I smiled. 'I just want to know what she was like.'

'There she is.' Cloe turned her head and pointed to the floor.

I looked down, expecting to see a photograph of our mother propped against the wall. Instead, I saw a large plastic jar.

Oh no! I don't believe this.

'Can I hold her?' I asked, releasing the tears locked in my eyes.

'She liked to sit in the kitchen, near the fire. That's why I keep her in here.' She lifted the ashes from the floor and placed them in my arms. I hugged the jar, tears streaming down my face, cradling it like a baby, rocking the remains of my mother to and fro. *Well, Mother, I never imagined that my twenty-six-year search for you would end with me holding your ashes.*

When my eyes met Derick's, the bizarreness of the situation struck us both. Laughing and crying at the same time, I continued to embrace what was left of my mother. Cloe looked bemused. What better proof could she have that I was her sister. Reluctantly, I put my mother back in her resting place. My head throbbed and I was too emotional to speak. Derick took charge and we arranged to meet the following day at her house.

Derick feared that on reflection Cloe might change her mind and he warned me not to expect too much. The B&B was cosy, the bed soft and warm, but I shivered uncontrollably. Derick held me tight.

'What's wrong with me? It's not cold in here.'

'You're in shock. It's been quite a day! You'll calm down.'

My sleep was fitful and I woke every few hours, remembering Cloe with that suspicious look on her face – Cloe acknowledging her mother's secret life – me holding my mother's ashes, feeling close to her in a way I'd never imagined.

The following morning, I nervously sipped my tea, unable to eat a thing. Cloe rang and told me that she was in a state of shock and hadn't slept. 'I'll leave the veg shop closed for the day,' she said. 'You can come and meet my husband and family later in the afternoon.'

Relieved that she hadn't changed her mind, I looked out on a grey sky heavy with rain. The man who owned the B&B, touched by my story, let us stay in our room till lunchtime so we didn't have to trudge round Castleton in the cold and wet.

As we approached Cloe's house, excitement shot through my body. It had stopped raining and the door opened before we got out of the car. *You know you're welcome. Stay calm.* Bob, Cloe's husband, ruddy-complexioned, wearing a checked shirt with sleeves rolled up, was busy mopping the porch with bleach. 'Should I take my shoes off?' Derick glanced down at his feet.

'Hell no! You get more muck on your feet when you come in here.' They laughed.

Dark-haired, tall and muscular, Bob's natural wit and friendly manner made me relax. We shook hands and he seated us in the living room on chairs opposite each other, where we warmed our hands at a fire that crackled in the grate. 'I'm tickled pink with you. Can't believe old Carolyn had a child out of wedlock.' He grinned and looked me up and down. 'You look just like her. Very elegant, she was.'

'Thank you,' I said, pleased that I resembled her.

'But she was a stickler,' he said. 'She gave me and Cloe a real hard time because Cloe was pregnant when we got married. I'd love to rub her nose in it now, if she was still alive.'

I gave him a weak smile. I couldn't imagine the girl who had written those letters being that moralistic.

'I have to leave to sort out 200 sheep that are being delivered to the farm this afternoon.' He grabbed a well-worn waxed jacket and a flat cap from the back door. 'They graze on my land for six months, to fatten 'em up, but it won't take long. I'll be back in a tick. Cloe, your sister's here!' he shouted upstairs.

'OK. We're fine.' *This is the life I nearly had.*

Cloe, pale-faced, walked carefully down the stairs, her arms full of photograph albums. *I'm going to see photos of my mother! I'm going to get to know her through Cloe!*

When I told Cloe about my family and the events in our mother's life that led up to my adoption, she accepted the information without emotion.

'Come and sit with me while you look at these.' She smiled, patted the cushion and lifted the first album.

The photographs were old and annoyingly Carolyn had her head down or partly hidden behind her children on most of the ones taken while she was young, so it was hard to see a resemblance to myself.

'She hated having her photo taken,' Cloe said. 'She always hid behind someone.'

That doesn't fit in with the description of her being outgoing.

'The opposite of my father, Thomas. He loved being photographed, so my other two sisters told me.' I told Cloe about my relationship with them.

She showed me a studio photograph of the three sisters, but only Cloe bore any resemblance to me. 'We have the same smile,' I said. I was afraid to ask about the row with the sisters.

'Yes.' She smiled back. 'My sisters are more like our father. I can see a strong resemblance to Mother in you. That's why I believed your story, and why I didn't call the police.'

'I wouldn't have blamed you if you had, sneaking up on you in the dark. I can't believe we did it.'

'Well, I'm glad you did.' We all laughed.

'This is Father.' Cloe pointed to a photograph of William looking proudly at the camera. Carolyn knelt near him, hiding her face behind the two older girls on the vast lawn of a grand old house, surrounded by bushes and trees, a small golden-brown dog standing in front of them. *A different sort of life than she'd have had with Thomas.*

'What sort of a life did you have?' I asked.

'My father was twenty-one years older than my mother. He was a doctor, a consultant in cardiology, from an upper-class family, originally from Ireland.' She pointed to a photograph of two genteel-looking ladies. 'They're his sisters. They were very posh. Mother had to fit in with them.'

'How did she do it?'

'She had a lot about her, my mother. She could hold her own with anyone.'

'What was he like, your father?'

'He was the nicest, kindest man you could meet.' Her face softened as she showed me his portrait, a serious-looking man with circular glasses, his hair combed flatly across his head. 'That was taken in a studio.'

'I always thought she'd marry a farmer.'

'When my father retired, they bought a farm, not far from here. Next time you come down, we'll show it to you.'

'He must have bought it for her.'

'He died when I was four, so they were only married for fifteen years when she became a widow.'

'Oh! How awful for her – for you all.' *Her life continued to be difficult.* 'Did she never remarry?'

'No. She brought us three girls up on her own, and she was very strict.' Cloe looked directly at me. 'If she told us to be in at a certain time, we had to be in or we were in trouble. She wouldn't have any messing about.'

'My other two sisters said Thomas was strict. If they'd stayed together, I dread to think of their combined parenting skills.'

'She wasn't averse to giving us a smack if we were naughty.'

Florrie and Jim never physically punished me.

Cloe looked guilty and quickly added, 'But it must have been hard for her on her own.'

'Very hard,' I said.

'This is her in her later years on holiday.'

I stared at the photograph of a middle-aged lady, her hair perfectly styled and tinted, dressed immaculately, sitting next to her friend. *You're nothing like I'd ever imagined.*

'She's very smartly dressed.'

'She always took a pride in herself.'

Bob burst into the living room. 'The sheep are all sorted. Should we have some tea?'

When he'd served the tea, in mugs, with freshly baked scones, he sat next to Cloe. 'What a dark horse the old girl was.' He continued to grin and stare at me as though I wasn't real, his face getting redder with the fire and the tea. 'Who'd have thought she'd had a past!'

I felt uncomfortable but it was impossible to take offence with such a friendly person. 'Delicious scones,' I said, hoping to take the attention away from myself.

'Cloe made them.' Bob smiled at his wife. 'She's a great cook.'

'What did she like to do, our mother?' I asked.

'She was very cultured,' Bob answered in a serious way. 'She liked opera and the theatre. She got involved in everything round here. She had to be mother and father to Cloe and her sisters. She'd been left on her own so she made a life for herself and was well respected in the town.'

'She did a lot with the church and helped raise money for a new roof,' Cloe said. 'We were all involved. There's a photo of us here with the vicar.' She flipped through the album to find it.

'She was a Catholic, wasn't she?' I said, confused when I saw the vicar. 'She wanted me to be brought up in a Catholic family.'

'When she married my father, she changed to C of E.'

'Always reinventing herself,' I said.

'Yes, she was known as "Deborah" and "Jane" at various times by different people,' Cloe said, raising her eyebrows.

'She must have been quite a character.'

'She was a strong woman,' Bob said. 'A member of the Tory Party and prominent at meetings and functions, and she campaigned at election time. Everyone knew her round here.'

I looked at Derick, reading his thoughts *Oh no! Not a Tory!*

'She sounds like a pillar of society. It makes me wonder how she would have reacted if I'd turned up when your father was alive, if she'd never told him, or even after he died. She was so respectable.'

'She'd have turned you away,' Cloe said firmly.

'Oh!' I was stunned by her certainty.

Cloe must have noticed. 'But she would have come round eventually and accepted you.'

'She struggled to give me up,' I said, determined to make the point that her mother did love me as well as her. 'I'll send you copies of everything, including the letters she wrote at the time of my adoption. They'll make you cry. She was all alone. Her mother had died and she had no family. She had no one to support her.'

'What?' Cloe put her head to one side and screwed up her face, frowning deeply. 'Who told you that?'

'It's written in the social worker's report.'

'Well, it's most certainly not true! Her mother, our grandmother, Ida, only died in 1990. Look, there's a photo of her brothers and sisters here.' She pointed to a picture showing a row of four men standing behind five smartly dressed seated women. Carolyn sat at the end of the row in a dark woollen dress decorated with a double row of pearls, smiling broadly at the camera. 'Two of her brothers had already died, and here's our grandmother.'

I stared at the image of my grandmother, a tough-looking lady, who bore no resemblance to Carolyn. 'But it says on the report that she was brought up by her grandmother.' I stared at Derick. He shrugged his shoulders.

'See for yourself. She had a family.'

'But she didn't tell the social worker about them.' I felt bewildered and didn't know what to say.

'We never had much to do with them. But I remember her taking me once to see them when I was little.'

'Do you think they would have known about me?'

'She probably never told them.'

Who were you, Carolyn? Unanswered questions floated in and out of my mind like shadows in an empty house.

'Look at these,' Cloe said, distracting me from my thoughts. She pointed to photos of our mother in her later years with Cloe and Bob's two children – Mark and Lisa. 'Our mother looks like a real grandmother there, very homely,' I said.

'She loved the children.'

A young, dark-haired girl appeared round the door, perky and bright-eyed, wearing a sweater with the Three Peaks emblazoned on it. 'This is our daughter Lisa,' Bob said. We shook hands.

'You must be shocked, me turning up like this?' I said.

'Well, yes, it's a bit of a surprise, but it's great.' She grinned widely. 'It's cool Grandma having a past. Makes her more interesting.'

'Lisa's just started work with the Mountain Rescue,' Cloe said.

'That's brilliant,' I said. 'Our hobby is walking up mountains – done most of the big ones in Snowdonia, the Lakes and Ben Nevis. You might get to rescue us sometime.'

'I hope you're more careful,' she said.

'We've had some close calls,' Derick said. 'Will tell you sometime.'

As we chatted, a fair-haired young man and woman came

through the door. 'Mark, this is your new Aunty Barbara,' Bob said, grinning. 'She's your grandma's love child.' Mark hadn't been forewarned and was so shocked he could hardly speak. He stared from me to his parents, with wide eyes. When he recovered, he introduced me to his Scottish wife, Kelly.

'They got married there three weeks ago,' Bob said. 'We had a big family wedding. Mark works with me on the farm.'

We'd talked non-stop for four hours, interrupted only by sandwiches and tea. 'We'll have to leave,' I said. 'It's a three-hour drive and it's getting dark.'

'We'll show you all the places where they lived with your mother when you come back to see us,' Bob said. 'You can retrace her steps.'

'And I'll cook you a meal, something special,' Cloe said.

We hugged and kissed and promised to return soon. 'Still can't get over you.' Bob chuckled and shook his head as they stood at the gate waving goodbye. *I'm lucky. They're so warm and friendly.*

Driving off, I looked at the house and imagined Carolyn – not her ashes – sitting in the kitchen surrounded by grandchildren. A happy image I'd always have, a contrast to the lonely figure I'd imagined.

'How are you?' Derick asked.

'I can't believe what's just happened. Thanks for pushing me into it. I never imagined such a warm reception. I can imagine Carolyn bustling around the town, constantly busy.'

'Like you, always doing something.'

'I'd thought of her as a bit of a rebel, breaking the rules of society, but then she conformed ... to survive, I suppose.'

'Her life wasn't easy. Thomas left her. We presume she found happiness with William and then he died. You have to admire her courage, reinventing herself and making a new life. What a story she could tell.'

'It's strange her lying about having no family. All I can think is she never told them about me. She gave birth to me up north. They lived in the south, so why should she tell them.'

'It might have been different if Thomas had done the decent thing and married her.'

'Then Cloe and her sisters would never have existed.'

'Strange how things turn out.'

'Thomas said she never talked about her family.'

'Just remember, she wasn't lying in those letters. She loved you and didn't want to give you up. Don't forget that.'

'What did you think about Cloe saying that if I'd have tried to contact our mother, she'd have turned me away? She had a grand lifestyle with William and she'd become this pillar of respectability after his death. Perhaps it's as well I never found her.'

'I don't believe that for one minute,' Derick said. 'Cloe's not read those letters.'

'She was an intriguing character, wasn't she?'

'I wish I'd met her,' Derick said. He'd travelled this journey with me. It was his loss as well. 'She'd have made a formidable mother-in-law,' he said.

'We'll never know now,' I said, the grief resurfacing.

'Don't get sad now. Think about all the new information you have.'

'Yes. It's like I've suddenly been given access to a room I've never been allowed to look in before. But what I'd really like to know is what happened to her after Thomas jilted her and before she met William. The evidence is she went to Tunbridge Wells. Where would she have met a wealthy doctor, and how did their relationship begin? If she'd been working on fruit farms in Kent, it's a big jump up the social ladder. How did she do it?'

'All you know is that she sounds like an incredible woman. Maybe Caitlin, being the eldest, could throw some light on it.'

'If she'll agree to meet me. What about this family feud?'

'All families have arguments.'

'It's sad, but I don't want to get involved in any of that. I have enough to deal with.'

'Maybe you turning up out of the blue will unite them.'

'That really would be something.'

I rang Karen as we drove along winding country lanes, the sky quickly darkening. She had a different perspective on the story. 'We know that Carolyn's mother, Ida, had her before she got married, so maybe Carolyn wasn't lying about being brought up by her grandmother, as that frequently happened with illegitimate children in those days. Then Ida probably went on to get married and have the other eleven children. Maybe Carolyn wasn't brought up with them and that would explain why she didn't tell them. She probably wasn't close to them if she lived with her grandmother. That's why she lied to the social workers so no one would ever contact them and tell them about you.'

'Of course. Yes, that makes sense.' *What a clever daughter I have.*

Chapter 34

Sisters

'I'm going to contact Caitlin one last time,' I said to Karen, on a visit to her house in London.

She looked up from her computer, where she was working from home, and smiled.

'Good. I think you should. They probably know about your visit to Cloe last month and are wondering what she told you.'

'Well, if they agree to meet me in daylight, they won't get me knocking on their doors in the dead of night scaring the life out of them.'

'No! I can't believe you did that.' We laughed.

'I've written a short letter telling her that I've met Cloe, in case she doesn't know, and asking if her and Una would like to meet me before I go back up north next Wednesday. I doubt if she'll reply, after all this time.'

'She might do. It's worth trying.'

'Can I write a letter on that nice blue paper, Nana?' Yasmin asked.

'I want to write a letter as well,' Isaac said. 'To Father Christmas.'

'Yes, but I'm going to post my letter now. Do you want to come with me?'

'Yeah!'

'Yeah!'

'It's cold out there. Make sure they're well wrapped up,' Karen said.

'Who's Catlin?' Yasmin asked, as we walked to the post office.

'She's my new sister,' I said.

'Where did you get her from?'

'I found her.'

'Where did you find her?' Isaac asked.

'In the sister shop.' They both chuckled.

The following day, I was teaching the children how to draw cats, brightly coloured markers and paper scattered across the table, when my mobile rang.

'It's Caitlin!' I shouted to Karen, my heartbeat quickening. 'Can you get the kids?'

I could hear Yasmin shouting, 'Nana, can I speak to your new sister?' as Karen led them from the room.

'Be quiet, Nana's on the phone.'

'I'm sorry it's taken me so long to get back to you,' Caitlin said. 'Una's daughter was very ill when you contacted me last October and we were all too preoccupied with that to get involved with anything else.'

I'm just anything else. 'I'm sorry to hear that,' I said. 'I hope she's better now.'

'Yes, thankfully, she's much better now. I did write to you in the summer and because you didn't reply I thought you'd lost interest.' *I wouldn't lose interest after twenty-six years.*

'I never received your letter.'

'That's strange.'

'Yes, it is.' *She never sent a letter.*

'Are you coming down again before Christmas?'

'That would be difficult. I'd rather meet up now, while I'm here, if you can arrange it.' She said she'd try.

'It's unusual for letters to go astray but it does happen,' Karen said, when I put the phone down.

'They both live within a twenty-mile radius of the city centre. I'll ask them to meet me at Euston Station on Wednesday if they can make it, and I'll get a later train home.'

After many phone calls and deliberations – Caitlin seemed reluctant to come on her own and Una was having difficulty getting off work – I arranged to meet them both at the station at 4 p.m. outside of Boots the Chemist. I'd sent a photograph of myself so they'd recognise me.

I arrived early, fear and excitement simmering inside me, but I felt strangely in control. *I'm an old hand at meeting new sisters! What will they be like?*

Two middle-aged women emerged from the dense crowd and I knew straight away it was them. They smiled shyly as they approached me, holding onto each other as if they were glued together. Grey-haired, tall and slim, they both wore glasses. *These are my sisters.* We hugged each other hastily. No tears. They seemed embarrassed and unsure of what to say. I took charge and made conversation about the cost of left luggage and where we should eat.

'Let's get out of the station, away from the crowds,' I said. 'There must be some proper restaurants near here.' I pushed through the throng, my sisters shadowing close behind.

We walked the nearby streets, scanning for restaurants, talking politely about nothing. It seemed like an agonisingly long time before we spotted an Italian restaurant on the corner of an otherwise bare red-brick row of buildings. I stared through the glass doors, hopeful. It was empty except for a couple sat on the opposite side of the room. *Relief!*

'This is perfect,' I said. Warm air, dense with the smell of Italian cuisine, welcomed us as we walked through the door. I parked my suitcase under a nearby window and we sank into comfortable brown leather armchairs in the reception area.

'Do you like wine?' *Please like wine.*

'Most certainly!' Una said.

'Oh yes!' Caitlin waved to the waiter. 'Red or white?'

'Either,' I said. *Thank heavens for that.*

They both laughed a lot and seemed like fun as we chattered. The waiter showed us to our table and poured the wine.

'Here's to new-found sisters!' I said, raising my glass.

'To new sisters!' We smiled as we chinked our glasses.

I took a large gulp. So did they. On an empty stomach, the alcohol quickly took effect and I began to relax. The small talk dried up and I looked at them properly for the first time, wondering who'd begin the real conversation. It was Caitlin.

'How do you feel about all this?' She looked into my eyes.

'It's exciting meeting you both, but it's a bit overwhelming. Are you two as nervous as me?'

'Not now the wine's hit the spot.' Una raised her glass and smiled.

'Tell us all about your early life and adoption,' Caitlin said.

'Let's order first.' I attracted the waiter's attention with a wave. 'It's going to take some time.'

We all chose the same dish, vegetable pasta with pesto sauce. As we ate, they listened to my story, expressing sadness and surprise at the details of our mother's secret past.

'I adopted both of my children, a boy and girl,' Una said. 'I brought them up knowing that they were adopted and they've been fine.'

'Being truthful is so important,' I said. 'I wouldn't have had so many problems with being adopted if my mother had brought me up knowing the truth, but that was how it was with her generation, secrets and lies. 'Tell me all about Carolyn, now,' I said. 'I want to know everything. What sort of person she was and what kind of mother she was?'

They gave each other knowing looks, as if to say *Where should we begin?* 'Waiter, another bottle of wine please!' Caitlin shouted. 'And the dessert menu.'

They confirmed much of what Cloe had said, that she was a strong woman, a strict disciplinarian and a lively character. After we demolished our food, Caitlin took some photographs from her handbag, one of Carolyn standing next to a man with a moustache.

'Who's that?' I asked.

'It's her boyfriend, Frank.' Caitlin grinned at Una.

'Oh! I'm glad she found someone else after your father died.'

'There were a few boyfriends,' Una said, grinning back at Caitlin.

'Yes, she was very sociable.' They both burst into giggles.

She was a healthy young woman and she liked men. So what? 'She was on her own for a long time,' I said. 'Why not?'

'Mother was never on her own.'

I joined in their laughter, but my stomach churned with regret. 'I wish I'd have met her. She sounds like such a character.'

'She certainly was,' Una said. 'When we were growing up, I think I was about twelve or thirteen, Mum started fostering children.'

'Oh!' I said, surprised and deeply moved. 'What sex and how old were they?'

'Mostly girls, and quite a bit younger than us,' Caitlin said.

'Was she compensating for leaving me?' I asked. They both agreed that must have been her motive.

We chatted until 7 p.m., at which point I had to catch the last train home. They walked me to the station; we kissed and hugged goodbye, and promised to keep in touch. Sat on the train, I was thankful that I'd taken the chance and contacted Caitlin. My sisters were fun: I really liked them.

A fortnight later, I received a letter from Caitlin. After our meeting, she'd thought long and hard about the argument with Cloe, and she'd written to her in reconciliation. It worked. They talked on the phone for hours and patched up whatever had caused them to fall out. I was delighted that my contacting them had been a catalyst that healed their wounds. There was no reason now why we couldn't all meet up.

***

It was July, and we sat having pre-lunch drinks in a European restaurant on the Southbank, waiting for my sisters and their husbands to arrive.

'You had two mums who really loved you,' Karen said. 'That's the way you want to look at it.'

'Yes, two strong women,' Derick said. 'Florrie and Carole.'

'My nan wasn't one to be reckoned with,' Shaun said. 'But she was always kind to us kids.'

'She loved kids.' Lily turned to me. 'That's why she got you.'

I held back the tears. We were in the south visiting Karen to celebrate Yasmin's fifth and Isaac's third birthdays. Yasmin's treatment had successfully come to an end and she glowed with health. There was everything to be happy about.

The gin and tonic I'd quickly downed calmed my nerves. *I hope my sisters get on.* The weather was perfect and we sat outside beneath a veranda, street music playing in the distance. The smell of garlic and fresh herbs filled the air, and a gentle breeze travelled up from the Thames, cooling my heated emotions. 'Here they are!' Karen stood and waved.

I introduced my three sisters, Caitlin, Una and Cloe to Lily, who hugged them warmly and told them how pleased she was to meet them at last.

'More drinks!' Derick waved to the waiter.

Karen looked over her shoulder. 'There's a surprise on its way.'

'What?' *I can't take any more. Hope it's a cake or a bottle of champagne.*

'Any minute now!' Karen got up from the table and walked towards the door, where I could see her talking to two women. As they got closer, I recognised Diane and Judith, my two other sisters.

'It's all Karen's doing,' Derick said. 'She asked them to come down. They're staying in a hotel near here. Making a weekend of it. Seeing the sites of London.'

Amidst loud voices and self-conscious laughter, they all got to know one another. Eyes bright with amusement twinkled in the soft light. I wanted to cry, but with happiness. *My six sisters all together. How lucky am I?*

Derick must have read my thoughts. 'This calls for champagne, two bottles, please, waiter.'

Over dinner, we talked about our families, our jobs, holidays, the theatre and what music we liked. After dinner, we settled on Carolyn.

'Do you think she would have told your father about me?' I asked my maternal sisters.

'She might have,' Caitlin said. 'He was very much in love with her and very protective towards her. Remember, she was a lot younger than him. He'd have probably forgiven her anything.'

'Would you have welcomed a new sister ...' I scanned my sisters' faces. '... If I'd turned up all those years ago?'

'Of course,' Cloe said. 'Someone else to argue with.' Caitlin and Una laughed and nodded in agreement.

After dinner, satisfied with food and drink, everyone settled down in the warm evening air, the northerners and southerners chatting as though they'd known each other all their lives.

Una leaned forward, and resting her arms on the table, she coughed loudly, tapped her glass and waited for everyone to be quiet. 'I think you should know this ...' She looked intensely at me.

The noise stopped and everyone stared at Una.

'OK!' I looked at her in surprise. *My God! What's she going to tell me?*

Una cleared her throat again. 'A few days before she died, Mother seemed troubled about something. She couldn't settle and she looked disturbed.' Una paused, as if to judge my reaction. 'Mother's face became animated and she tried to speak, but she couldn't get the words out and she sank back into the pillow defeated. I asked her if there was something troubling her and she became more agitated. I was getting concerned. Perhaps it was something important that the family needed to be aware of. I sat by her bed, held her hand and pleaded with her, "Whatever it is, get it off your chest, Mother."

'"It seems so long ago ... a lifetime," she said. "It'll make no difference now ... wherever she is."

'"Wherever *who* is?" I asked her. Mother's eyes clouded.

'"If only you knew," she whispered, and fell asleep.'

I touched Una's hand, struck by the significance of her words. 'Thank you for telling me that.' She didn't have to tell me and I was grateful for her honesty. *Was this just consolation or was I in our mother's thoughts right up to the end?*

'It can only be you that she was talking about,' Caitlin said with a smile.

'It *has* to be you, Mum,' Shaun said.

'Of course it was.' Derick squeezed my hand.

'She never forgot you.' Karen had tears in her eyes, as did Diane and Judith.

They all started speaking at once, confirming the message, then suddenly there was silence and all heads turned in my direction.

I looked down at the wine-spattered tablecloth. 'It could have been me – it possibly was me.' All the regrets I'd ever had about not finding my mother flooded my mind, then somehow dissolved in the warmth of my family. I lifted my head and smiled. 'It was me.'

'It was you,' they repeated, in jumbled unison.

Derick stood and lifted his glass. 'To Carolyn!'

We all stood and chinked our glasses. 'To Carolyn!'

'And Florrie,' I said.

'To Florrie!'

Get A Free Book:
Join Shaun Attwood's Newsletter

http://shaunattwood.com/newsletter-subscribe/

To contact Barbara, please email Gadfly Press at gadflypress@outlook.com

If you have enjoyed this book, we would appreciate you leaving a review on Amazon or Goodreads.

Gadfly Press Socials
  Website
  Facebook
  Twitter

Other Books by Gadfly Press

By Steve Wraith and Stuart Wheatman:

The Krays' Final Years:
My Time with London's Most Iconic Gangsters

By Natalie Welsh:

Escape from Venezuela's Deadliest Prison

By Shaun Attwood:

English Shaun Trilogy
Party Time
Hard Time
Prison Time

War on Drugs Series
Pablo Escobar: Beyond Narcos
American Made: Who Killed Barry Seal? Pablo Escobar or George HW Bush
The Cali Cartel: Beyond Narcos
Clinton Bush and CIA Conspiracies: From the Boys on the Tracks to Jeffrey Epstein
Who Killed Epstein? Prince Andrew or Bill Clinton

Un-Making a Murderer: The Framing of Steven Avery and Brendan Dassey
The Mafia Philosopher: Two Tonys
Life Lessons

Pablo Escobar's Story (4-book series)

Acknowledgements

Thank you to my publisher, Shaun Attwood, for having faith in me and whose help, advice and editing made this book possible. Thank you to the team at Gadfly Press, Mark Swift for editing, and Jane Dixon-Smith for cover design.

A huge thank you to my husband, Derick, who was by my side all through the search for my birth mother, encouraging me to continue on the many occasions when I was ready to give up. He gave the same support and encouragement while I was writing this book, helping with proof reading and editing; and just being there for me. Thank you to my daughter, Karen, for emotional support; encouraging me when I waivered, and for editing. Thanks to my lovely grandchildren, Zivi, Yasmin and Isaac for making me smile, and my great grandson, River. Thanks to my sister Lily and her children, Tony, Lynne, Sue, Gill and John, for love and support all my life. Thanks to my sister-in-law, Sue for her detective work and support. Thank you to all my family, long standing and newly discovered. Thanks to all my friends, particularly Joyce Harper, Rita Wilkinson and Kath Redmond for their support.

Thank you to Barbara Lloyd Jones for the many hours she spent editing, and Yvonne Taylor and Lynne Barnes for editing. Thank you to Mark Leyland's writing group, Vic Hansen, and Michael Jackson's group: Stockton Heath Writing Club, for significant feedback. Thanks to Kerry Ryan of Write like a Grrrl, and Anna South for constructive reports on my early drafts. Thank you to Ariel Bruce for her detective work.

About the Author

Barbara Attwood was born in the north of England. She is a retired English and psychology lecturer. During the search for her birth mother, she kept a log of the rollercoaster events that led her to the truth of her birth. Based on this log and memories from her childhood, and teenage years during the 60s, she wrote *Blue Plastic Cow*, a memoir, and her first book.

Printed in Great Britain
by Amazon